BEAUFIGHTERS, BOAC & ME

First edition, published in 2001 by

WOODFIELD PUBLISHING
Woodfield House, Babsham Lane, Bognor Regis
West Sussex PO21 5EL, England.

ISBN 1-873203-86-1

Beaufighters, BOAC & Me

*My flying days with the Royal Air Force
and British Overseas Airways Corporation*

SAM WRIGHT

Woodfield Publishing
~ WEST SUSSEX • ENGLAND ~

Contents

Preface

Some explanation should be given of the reasons for the writing of any fairly lengthy volume, such as this endeavour, and also how the practical means to do so came to hand.

The writing of the first, unedited draft occupied about three hundred hours, usually spent in daily sessions of about an hour. Progress was initially very slow, as I had no typing skills whatsoever and even less skill with the simple, basic Word Processor, the acquisition of which had triggered off the strongly felt urge to set down my experiences during the time I was involved in aviation.

It was a bit like the "chicken and the egg"—with handwriting of the "illegible kind", such a task would have been overwhelmingly tedious,— so did the ownership of the computer solve this problem, or did the instinct to capture those memories of so long ago, subconsciously prompt the need to get the tool (computer).

Whichever the case, it was another facet of the deep friendship which had developed with my good friend, Cy Potgeiter. Meeting in Kalamunda nine years ago, we were amazed to find, when comparing notes, that our life's paths, in post war years, had criss-crossed in so many interests and activities, such as aviation , railways, and, of course, the backdrop of South Africa, as to be positively uncanny.

Cy applied much pressure on me to have a stab at becoming "computer literate", and when he offered, at a ridiculously modest figure, a very early model of a Word Processor, —it was, of course, bribery at it's worst—I finally capitulated, a few notes changed hands, and I took home what I had previously regarded as a tool of the Devil. Thus the die was cast, and my grateful thanks go to Cy and there, lurking in the background and covered in wealth most fabulous, Mr William Gates.

Having got the mental go-ahead, and the tools to "finish the job", some, but not a lot, of thought, was given to the broad format that the recollections would take, and these were, in no particular order of importance or priority...

My "target" readers would be primarily members, and future members, of my family, but other close friends with personal knowledge of our families background and origins would be included as recipients if they indicated sufficient interest.

No attempt would be made to write at a level for the final product to warrant commercial consideration or publication.

It is said that history is written by the "winners". True, but subsequently, when all has once again settled down, a breed, now know as the "Armchair Warriors", invariably with no personal experience of the previous dust-up, set about explaining that all that was done was done wrongly, and that wartime leaders were stupid—giving rise to one of the most grossly offensive statements, that, "the British fought like Lions but were led by Donkeys". The gift of hindsight is a gift mankind could well do without, unless used to positive effect.

For the individual serviceman, engaged in the real action, the view at the time is virtually what he sees with his own eyes, and censorship, absolutely vital towards winning battles, puts a discreet blanket over the broader picture of the activities of friend and foe alike. So for most of us it was simply a matter of obeying, and with alacrity, the orders of those in command, and only after the fray, is it possible to get a wider perspective of the progress of the war.

In writing of my involvement I have tried to weave into my narrative some wider aspects that I have only later become conversant with, together with some comparisons, with today, of the amazing development of aviation since the years of war.

There has been a wealth of finely detailed literature on war time aviation including all the areas in which I had the honour of participating. In any case, to have included in the general text, technical details along with my broad narrative of personal impressions and feelings—also read 'emotions'— would have been beyond my abilities and records of reference. Appendices give reference to the relevant books contained in my modest archives.

Airmen were not permitted to maintain personal diaries during hostilities. Consequently, I have no written records of the wide variety of experiences that came my way—in any event I had control over only a few of the things, pleasant and otherwise, that occurred—and I have relied almost entirely on the technique of 'recall'. This demanded getting 'in the mood', switching off from the present and usually quite detailed aspects swam back from over the years, but sometimes, a session was fruitless, no matter how hard the attempt to 'time warp', with frustration dissipated by a walk in the garden!

Many memoirs contain what are purported to be actual conversations in the past. Such a technique give can give life and body to what may be a length of dull and uninteresting text. However, in no incident from the past, can I recall the actual words used, nor do I have the imagination to try to formulate any probable dialogue. It does seem to me to be "cheating " a touch, despite the temptation to try it on.

My major effort has been to try to capture the feelings and emotions that beset most of my friends and colleagues, in early years and during my career in aviation. We mostly avoided, beyond a certain point, voicing our innermost feelings and reactions to the events and dangers surrounding us at the time, but now, with the passage of time, and in our later years when emotions tend to rise a bit closer to the surface, I regard it a privilege to try to capture and set down just what we experienced in those exciting days of our youth. We all have "soft centres" which we coat with a shell of different style, be it a kind of brazen, rough, tough air of aggression, an air of withdrawal, etc, and this "outer face" we displayed to hide our true fears and anxieties.

A blank computer screen, like a blank piece of paper in a typewriter, offers an instinctive challenge to those afflicted with even a modest urge to write. Perhaps it's also related to the less attractive instinct to soil the virgin whiteness of the page with writings of the "graffiti kind", after all, not all our instincts are altruistic. But it does irk when the first words or sentence stubbornly refuse to shuffle mentally into an acceptable order, suitable to be "plonked " down before, like a will of the wisp, they retreat to a corner of the mind, there to lurk beyond further recall.

Attempting to slip back into the years of war has had many rewards. One overwhelming impression has been recalling what was achieved in human physical endeavour in the unbelievable production of the materials of war. Thousands of aircraft, army tanks, ships, aerodromes, guns, small arms, millions of rounds of ammunition, etc, together with the organisation to utilise the labours of millions of men and women workers. Seeing this facet of those years, now in new perspective, demands my small tribute to all those dedicated individuals and those who had the responsibility to make it all work.

And, finally...

Growing up as a small boy, in a working class environment, I encountered no major "trauma" but experienced the undemonstrative family affection that was standard practice in those days. During the whole of my service in the RAF, and during my time with British Overseas Airways, I was again most fortunate in that my personal contacts were all pleasant and friendly, with usually a strong bond of comradeship. Throughout all these times, I know I was more than fortunate in being happy and contented in all the circumstances that came my way, with friendships firmly established the continue to the present day.

Perhaps, during my sojourn through the events depicted in this book I had the kind ministrations of a "guardian angel", because the odds of surviving were certainly less than evens. So to whatever power stood me in good stead over this period, and also to all family, friends and relations that have made my life one of total enjoyment, this attempt to set down my experiences, is undertaken as a tribute and in gratitude.

Beaufighters, BOAC & Me

22 FEBRUARY 1922 — 3 SEPT 1939
GROWING UP IN SPONDON

Spondon, in the 1920s and 30s, was certainly not in the front of the rapidly changing scene in the world of aviation. There was a flying field at Derby, and an RAF aerodrome at Hucknall, 20 or so miles away in Nottinghamshire, but Derby was the home of the works of Rolls Royce, perhaps the developer of the worlds best aircraft engines. Certainly the noise from the engine test beds, seem to reverberate around the countryside, very noticeably at Spondon, but it was a comforting sound, indicative of progress, and, more importantly, jobs for us locals. To be accepted at RR as an apprentice was indeed a great accolade.

Somehow or other, our little gang, in addition to the adventures of fishing, roaming the countryside, learning to swim in the canal (despite the odd dead dog) playing at night under the gas lamps, etc, latched on to the fact that Hucknall was within our striking range on our bicycles. It was a memorable ride and the excitement of standing on the edge of the flying field and watching the Harts, Hinds. Furies or similar (we were not too sure of the precise types), on an English summer day, with the grass long, the buzz in the air which seems to be always there in such balmy days, and the noise of those aircraft engines, stirred our young blood. Perhaps the impact of those moments set the seal, albeit unconsciously, on the path I was to follow later in my life.

Joe Hickling, husband of Aunt Margaret, had served in the R.F.C. in the First World War, I was never sure as in what capacity, but to me he was a giant. He also supplied me with the magazines depicting the 'flying aces' of that era, with colourful pictures of 'dog fights' — white scarves flowing in the slipstream, goggles and, most dramatic of all, the horror of being 'shot down in flames', with the two options left to the pilot, neither very attractive. The German 'Aces' were afforded the same cult status as the Allied airman, and it was all depicted as quite gentlemanly and chivalrous, with a wave of the hand to an opponent who had the misfortune to run out of ammunition and the implied arrangement to "see you same time same place tomorrow". Von Richtofen and his notorious Squadron were also treated as heroes and many a tear was shed at the loss of such a gallant foe!

In those days, in addition to the main interest in aviation, related activities grabbed our enthusiasms. Anything mechanical was to be explored, perhaps dabbled with more appropriate. Our bicycles gave us endless pleasure, stripping them down, usually quite unnecessarily, adjusting brakes, comparing performance, and, for the lucky of us, fitting a 'three-speed', either a Sturmey-Archer or, even more adventurous, the relatively new Derailleur gears, which cunningly slipped the chain on to different sized sprockets to vary the final gear. It was quite important, when changing gear by operating the lever on the crossbar or frame, to do this with a flourish of the wrist, with a touch of the nonchalance of the 'old-timer'.

Also in the 'mechanical' area was the road racing circuit at Donnington Park (still in operation today), only a short bike ride away. The length of the track was about 3 miles and the mounting excitement as we joined the throngs of other cyclists to enter the area, down a leafy English lane on a warm summer day was hard to contain. In the pannier bag on thee back of the bike, were, of course a few sandwiches and a bottle of tea. What heroes we had. Prince Birabonge of Siam, 'Ginger' Woods etc. And the bikes! There was the International Norton, with its huge tank; the startling BMW with, unbelievably, a shaft drive to the rear wheel, instead of a chain; Aerial 'square fours'; Douglass 'horizontal twins'; water-cooled Scott squirrels, etc, etc. Also, providing great excitement, were the 'motor bikes and sidecars' with the passenger providing the balance on the corners by leaning way out of the car on the right hand bends and scrunching himself up behind the driver on the left hand bends. To see the passenger, on the right hand bend literally hanging in his sidecar by his toes, always had the crowd in a fever. The two greatly favoured points were the 'hairpin bend' and the 'long straight' where the maximum speeds were attained. It really was a hairpin and always a place of heavy jostling by the racers to pull away in first place. There were also strange three-wheeler cars called 'Morgans', two wheels at the front and one in the rear, driven by a two cylinder motor cycle engine of modest power; they looked very unwieldy on the corners. But to see 'Ginger' on his 500cc Norton at full speed on the straight, with the tang in the air of the special fuel that was used, and the throaty roar of the engine elevated us youngsters to unbelievable excitement.

In the late twenties, and into the thirties, aviators such as Amy Johnson, Alec Henshaw, Kingsford-Smith, Bert Hinkler and others, were constantly setting new records for flights to Australia, South Africa, across the Atlantic, etc. Some of them set off to fly to Australia, in those days six weeks away by sea and as remote to us as if it were on another planet, armed with nothing more than a school Atlas, and, as in the case of one brave flyer (perhaps 'foolhardy' is more appropriate) with as little as 40 hours of flying experience! In the restricted confines of our village and our lack of travel experience, such endeavours were of the 'Mighty Gods' and indeed, most of them attained something resembling this status.

It was little wonder that when war came along, most of us couldn't wait to 'have a go' in the 'Wimpeys' and Whitleys etc that were the mainstay aircraft of the RAF at the time. However, war was still a little way off, and we enjoyed our early years, making model aircraft (one then quite sophisticated for the day, was know as a 'FROG' (Flies Right Off The Ground). It did, but tended to do quite dramatic manoeuvres before hitting the ground again in an uncontrolled way! Another 'aviation' occurrence helped to dispel any lingering doubts as to where our interests lay and that was the R101 incident. It was summer 1930 and the equivalent of a launch, today, of the Space Shuttle, was the planned departure of the Airship, the R101 for a trip to India. I forget the State occasion, but it was quite important.) Many VIPs were in the party, including the Minister for Air, Lord Thompson, and Sir Sefton Brankner, an extremely robust character. There had been much 'aggro' between the financing and the building of the Government airship, the R101, and the privately sponsored R100, in which the Engineer and writer Neville Shute was a dominant character. So, in that lovely summer evening of 1930, just before evening twilight, and quite out of the blue, this beautiful airship seemed, to my young eyes, to fill the darkening sky. It was wonderful to behold, with twinkling lights from the long 'gondola' underneath that housed the passengers and the 'flight deck', and the rumble of the six engines in their pods. It was heading West and was on a circular 'flag waving' trip from it's base ay Cardington, Bedfordshire. From memory, I think it was about 1000 feet long and passengers and crew totalled sixty or so.

Strangely, my future path was to be linked with this 'goliath of the air'. In October 1930 it set of on it's important government mission to fly to Karachi, but crashed at Beavais in northern France and all but six crew were consumed by the flames. In those days, life was very different, and there was a community of spirit which has long since disappeared. The sheer horror of the crash was felt very deeply by the whole population, and none grieved as much as our little group of friends.

Subsequently, in 1940, I travelled to Cardington to attest in the RAF and saw the huge airship hangar which had briefly housed the R101. In 1946, when flying with BOAC as a Navigating Officer, I flew to Karachi where there was another such hangar somewhat poignantly still awaiting the arrival of the airship. In 1947, when flying from Croydon to Paris on the RAF daily communication Flight our track took us over Beavais in northern France. In 1980, when living in Hastings, on the English south coast, we frequently took the dogs for 'walkies' at Fairlight, with its lovely panoramic view of the English Channel, at the precise spot where the R101 crossed the coast, battling against winds of nearly 50 knots on the first leg of its journey to India, so long ago.

I used to look up in the sky and visualise the scene on board, with the crew going about their duties and the dining room, full of good cheer with the dignitaries enjoying another glass of wine, secure in the confidence of the airship to carry them safely through the night and onwards. Alas, it was not to be. The airship was handled as though it was a nautical vessel, with appropriate nautical terms, like 'port the helm', 'amidships', 'come astern' etc, and the designations of the crew reflected the Navy, with 'helmsman', 'bosun', 'coxswain' etc. I found the essence of the tragedy captured in the cry of the coxswain, when, just before impact with he ground, on that night of strong winds and heavy rain, and the hard battle to cross the English Channel against deteriorating conditions, his thoughts were for his men, in the exclamation, "We're down, lads!" This simple call reflects the fine traditions of the Royal Navy, with it's history of men at their best in camaraderie and common purpose.

In about 1932, Sir Allan Cobham's 'Air Circus' came to Derby. This was a major event, not to be missed under any circumstances — a chance to get close up to 'real' aeroplanes, and see them take-off and land, and, unbelievably, there was to be 'parachuting' as well. I do not recall if there were 'wing walkers' but a highlight was a jump by world famous Clem Sohn, known as the 'Birdman'. His speciality, as the name implied, was to 'fly like a bird' — using a specially designed canvas suit, which he could, after leaving the aircraft, spread like a bird's wings and so steer himself around the sky. At a safe altitude, he would then open his conventional parachute and perform his landing. My principal memory of the occasion was tearing across the large open area, with a horde of other excited child enthusiasts, to get as close as possible to the rapidly descending parachutists A few years later, the intrepid Clem Sohn became entangled in his bird-wing suit and plunged to his death, but all admired his quite outstanding daring and the icy cold chills that all felt as he leapt from an aircraft way up high.

About 1934, inspired by the Donnington experience, we got into motorbikes in a big way. One of the lads lived on a farm, just outside the village, and somehow or other, we had the permission of his father to use one of the fields as a primitive race track. It was, of course, as rough as old boots and was just circular, perhaps 300 yards in all. Having got the track, the next thing we needed was the bikes. Where these came from, I am unable to recall, but they were beat up old machines, totally un-roadworthy: a 1929 Raleigh that had the main flywheel outside the sump; a 200cc Velocette two-stroke; a Scott Squirrel horizontal twin cylinder and, 'top of the range', an Ariel 'square four' of massive capacity (I think it was 1000cc). None were licensed for road use — we were, in any case, too young to obtain a licence to ride them — so getting to and from the field was another problem to be overcome. This meant that we had to push them too and from the field, a considerable physical exercise for all, but particularly for me, being a somewhat 'puny' youth. Getting petrol was the easy part, we took one pint glass bottles to the local garage and, at one shilling a gallon, tuppence-worth gave us enough 'juice' for an afternoon's enjoyment. And enjoy ourselves we certainly did! The mechanical condition of the bikes left much to be desired and brakes were deficient to a most unsafe degree, but, of course, a minor spill was carried out with much bravado, and in any case, maximum speeds were modest enough. To get a bit oily, and fiddle around with the mechanics of the bikes was another rewarding aspect of the hobby, and it was regarded as part of routine to open up the cylinder head, adjust carburettors and tappets, and, my memorable exercise, to split the sump and expose the 'big end' of the 'con rod' of my 1929 Raleigh. The bike had cost me three shillings and sixpence –where I obtained this not inconsiderable sum escapes me—in those days many families were brought up on wages of two pounds a week or less.

Around this time, my other enthusiasm—which subsequently led me to aspire to join the RAF as a "WOP/AG (wireless operator/air gunner) when war was declared—was the 'wireless'. The first Broadcasting Station in England was '2LO' at Alexander Palace in north London, about 1922, and the first time I heard a broadcast was on a crystal set (a.k.a. 'cat's whisker'). It was very important not to jog the table as the 'whisker' would slip from the sensitive spot on the crystal and the signal would be lost, and it was necessary to wear a pair of earphones. Uncle Will, husband of Aunt Margaret, and quite a dignified (and wealthy) elderly gentleman, sported a very sophisticated portable radio, which had a kind of alligator skin cover. It was fearfully heavy, with it's high tension batteries and the low tension accumulator, to call it 'portable' seemed quite a misnomer! But I think what clinched my call to radio was a visit to a radio 'ham' at Mablethorpe on the east coast, where I was spending a holiday with the family. I was quite enthralled to see the equipment and to be able to talk to the world gripped my imagination. So much so that I embarked on a simple construction of a valve-type radio with a massive soldering iron, heated on the gas stove in the kitchen and, swept along with the quality of enthusiasm which waxes strongly at that age, built a wooden 'radio shack' at night school to house this. The aerial was strung to the back of the house, and—lo and behold—I was soon to hear Radio Schenectady, New York. While this fixed up the 'wireless operator' bit, I was not sure about the 'air gunner' part or if I would be aggressive enough to blast away at the 'Hun' with several .303 Browning machine guns!

This very pleasant way of life, with the freedom to explore the local countryside and a bit further afield and also the adventure of being exposed to the adult world with all (perhaps 'some' is a better term) its delights and challenges, took a change in early 1936.

It was time to leave school, which was Form Two at Spondon House Secondary School. The possibility of proceeding to more advanced education was not an option; it was time to go out and earn a living, as was the lifestyle in those times for those in my circumstances. Not much formality was involved, one day I was at school and the next day I wasn't. No particular guidance was offered and none was really expected, the transition evoked no great drama, such as is the way these days. We were expected to stand on our own feet and 'get on with it'. Looking back, I realise how sensible this approach was, as since early childhood we had been cared for in an unobtrusive way, which instilled a sense of independence and initiative and now it was our choice to do something for ourselves.

Which I did. My first foray into the workplace was to become a 'page-boy' for a doctor (wealthy) and his family, who lived in Derby. This was not a success. He had a couple of children about my age and I interpreted the job as incorporating time to take part in their play and games, to the detriment of putting a fine polish on the family silverware or keeping the several coal fires stoked up. With my family background I had had little opportunity to develop any particular 'finicky' habits, but when I was expected to wear a 'pre-used' page's trousers and tight little jacket for my more formal duties, I jibbed in no uncertain terms.

This job lasted precisely one week.

My next 'work experience' was much more invigorating. I saw an advertisement, probably in a shop window, for a 'Smart Lad'—the usual job description of the day—to collect library books which were overdue. I think the basis of the reward was that any overdue fees collected would be split fifty-fifty, but with the level of library fees in those days, I was unlikely to earn a living wage. However, it was not to be sneezed at, so I pitched up for duty, complete with my means of transport, my faithful bicycle. Most of the calls, to suburban house were mundane enough, the defaulting borrowers being run of the mill citizens, mostly elderly, but one call has lingered in my mind from the days of my innocence so long ago. Unsuspectingly, I gave my usual knock on the door and was greeted by a mature lady 'housewife' whose demeanour and gleaming eye should have sounded a strong warning sign.

At this point, and with the hindsight of many, many years, the prudent course of action would have been to abandon thoughts of library books and seek safety on my bicycle. Perhaps I was prompted by curiosity as to what went on in a 'boudoir', because that, to my inexperienced mind was where this call seemed to have brought me. However, nothing ventured nothing gained! Having had the door closed behind me, a touch of trepidation took over while a scan of the living room revealed no trace of the errant library books.

"Perhaps I've left them in the kitchen," was the next ploy, again without success. The lady then remarked that "reading in bed" was her usual practice. We went upstairs to check. By then an unknown world seemed to be stretching out it's hand to me and I suddenly thought that it was a lot more interesting than old motorcycles! No books were readily visible, however. The lady ventured that, perhaps in the course of midnight read she had dropped the books by the side of the bed, which was fairly close to the wall. We both had to sprawl out on the bed to grope beyond it in search of the missing books. At that moment I realised that I was but a 'callow schoolboy' and not quite ready for the adult world. I decided I was much safer with my old motorbike and fled. I have often wondered whether the library ever did get those missing books back into circulation!

Other than the incident above, there seemed to be little inspiration in chasing old library books and the next 'job opportunity' came in the running of a newspaper stand next to the railway station at Spondon. The wage was a munificent five shillings a week, with one penny deducted for 'insurance' — "not a lot but better than nowt", as the say in Yorkshire. The day started at 6am to cater for the intake to the British Celanese Works and then a bike ride up to the village — quite a haul — to deliver a newspaper to the Senior Executive of the works. The day finished about 6.30pm, after having taken the day's takings to Derby on the train. Graciously, time off was allowed during the day, but the same routine applied to Saturdays, and it was only the kindness of old Mr Pinchbeck (a quite Victorian character) who was the Manager at Derby that I persevered with the job beyond my present record of a week or so.

Prior to this job I had discovered the magical world of literature — any literature — which had started with a chance possession of a somewhat battered copy of *Sketches by Boz* (Charles Dickens), small in size and with tiny print, which I read in my equally small bedroom at 43 Nottingham Road by the light of a single candle. Being 'manager' of my own little bookstall also gave me access to all daily newspapers and a whole host of magazines etc, along with the time to read and digest. That bookstall set me up for a lifetime of enjoying the pleasures of reading, which, in old age has become even more pleasurable.

To get a job 'on the railway' was, at that time, a step up from most things, so I responded to the 'call to steam' and aspired to become a railwayman — well, a railwayboy really. The bottom rung in the railway ladder was 'messenger', so another career move took place, and I started at the Railway District Superintendent's Office at Derby, in the Pay-sheets Section. This job consisted of collecting large numbers of envelopes containing details of the weekly wages of the staff at all the stations on the LMS system, from the Parcels Office and carrying them in large wicker baskets, up steps and round corridors, to the office where they were 'processed'. The baskets were very heavy (and I mean heavy) and they were humped on the shoulder only with difficulty. My slender frame took quite a beating — I still have a badly distorted spine, in two directions for good measure — but it taught me a couple of useful things. Even with physique not quite up to scratch, the battle with those ruddy baskets taught me to 'press on regardless'. This probably stood me in good stead later on when I had to take the fairly stringent medical examination for RAF Air Crew. Standing there 'starkers' with three doctors looked long and critically at my pure white body (as I remember it was 'pure' in every sense, but I digress) rubbed their chins, muttered, cogitated, etc.

I was desperately anxious to fly in the RAF and I can only guess that they realised this and gave me the OK. Thanks, fellows! Perhaps they had noticed a couple of budding biceps, or something, giving a hint that maybe I could stand the rigours of being shot at at 20,000 feet. Then there was the dreaded test of 'blowing up the mercury' to be endured. This entailed having your nose clamped, a band on your arm to test blood pressure, and with a desperate intake of breath, blowing into a tube to send a column of mercury up to a certain level. This part was not overly difficult, but then the level had to be held for at least one minute. After 20 seconds or so, with everything throbbing and the thought that the task was impossible to achieve, it became an exercise more in will power than anything.

The other useful by-product of the stint as railway messenger was that I learned the names of all the railway stations on the LMS System, mostly in the order as they run down the line. Even now, on a clear night, I can chant a few of them in line order.

One of the other messengers was a lad named Frank Ainsworth, a tad more sophisticated than the rest of us. He had quite a swagger, smoked in the style of the film stars of the day, with that slow kind of inhale and then half closed eyes during the steady exhale of smoke through flared nostrils. It never failed to fascinate me, and he had regular features and what I suppose is now called 'presence'.

Across the road from our workplace was the 'Railway Club' typical of the clubs that were provided in those years for apprentices, mechanics, etc. There were about four billiard tables and provision for table tennis; it was like a magnet to all of us. Looking back, I think I benefited in two ways from the days of my 'misspent youth' in this establishment. Table tennis became my forte—the only game at which I achieved above average skill—and I joined a team in a league and travelled around the villages in competitions. Snooker also grabbed my enthusiasm and we challenged and competed with great energy. The outcome of these apparently innocuous activities left me with a good degree of manual dexterity, rapid co-ordination of hand and eye, and an ability to juggle balls with confidence. It still gives me pleasure to mess about handling and throwing articles, including tossing kitchen plates in the air, in the kitchen, to the concern of the 'good lady wife'!

However, the deadly sin of ambition struck again, and I realised I could only progress to the humble but traditional rank of railway clerk provided I could pass the essential written examinations. This led to a regular evening bicycle ride to Derby, where a retired railway telegraph operator was prepared to tutor youths such as me in mathematics and English, preparatory to sitting the exam. The fees per evening session, about an hour or so, were 2d a time. I was a willing pupil, and when the time came to take the test I was confident of success, which indeed fell my way. Life as a clerk began at Borrowash, a small station next to Spondon, where Mr Bell was stationmaster. He was a benign, white-haired, long-serving railwayman, close to pension. We shared an office and I messed about with invoices or similar, and he sat behind his screened desk and 'nodded off' for most of the day. I had to attend to the trains as they arrived, and with the porter (Oh Mr Porter!) collect the mail, help passengers get on and off, and more fun, shout the name, with the full blast of my young lungs, "Borrowash Station!". Mr Bell, placid enough in appearance, nevertheless, prompted me to develop my scant education, and this lead to night school at Derby Technical College. English was obviously number one, and as I remember, geography as well, but for some reason or other I plumped for German. Perhaps I was hedging my bets as the strength of the German forces was readily apparent by this time, and, of course, they were not very far away. I only made modest progress, but have an ear for the language, and the haunting melody and words of *Roslien auf der Heiden* which we were called on to sing in the classroom, still revives thoughts of that time.

Strangely enough, the occupation of railway clerk was regarded as a 'reserved occupation' and exempt from being called into the Armed Services. By this time I had worked at various other stations in and around Derby, one being a place called Ilkeston (known as 'Ilson' locally)—a place hardly likely to raise a flicker of interest... but it did. A most enterprising Luftwaffe pilot, after being shot down and becoming a POW, somehow escaped, and in the course of his attempt to make a real job of it, planned to get back to Germany and give it another go. He attempted to buy a railway ticket at Ilkeston, but this failed for some reason or other, and his next move was even more ambitious. Hucknall Aerodrome was close by, and daunted not one wit, he talked his way into the aerodrome, masquerading as a Polish pilot—there were many around—and persuaded an officer that he had force-landed and needed an aircraft to fly back to his base. He was actually seated in an aircraft, a Spitfire I think, when the duty officer became suspicious, approached the aircraft, of which, by this time, the escapee had started the engine. The duty officer drew his revolver and that was the end of very gallant and determined escape attempt. I must confess, I've always felt a bit sorry that POW who didn't make it!

For some reason or other, my 'wanderings' started quite early in life, with a trip to John-o-Groats, at the top end of Scotland, in about 1934, the main reason for such a long trip being that free passes were available to railway employees, and that spot was about as far as it was possible to travel. A couple of years later I travelled alone to Glasgow to see the World Table Tennis Finals, and shortly afterwards, again alone, a weeks holiday at Coombe Martin in Devonshire (visited again in 1947, with wife Carol very pregnant, and being propelled up hill by hand on the back!). Playing Table Tennis in the local league took me round and about the villages close to Derby and I played with great enthusiasm. This, together with the sheer pleasure of just cycling around, satisfied, nd enhanced my love of movement which has lasted a lifetime. When Lee Marvin sang *I was Born under a Wandering Star* in *Paint Your Wagon* I was firmly with him in spirit!

This not-unpleasant way of life continued with enjoyable summer days as I gradually broadened my work and worldly knowledge, but the ominous rumble of war-like noises began to be heard, and gradually the country began to gear itself for the inevitable course of history. Noticeable was the increased activity at Rolls Royce and this was more test running of the engines, which were to play such a big part in our eventual victory, powering the Lancaster Bombers, under Air Marshal Arthur 'Bomber' Harris.

The 3rd September 1939, a Sunday, was the day when the die was cast. On that day the world seemed to hold it's breath. In the front room at 43 Nottingham Rd, we heard the announcement by Neville Chamberlain, the Prime Minister, on our battery radio. Not long after the announcement, the sirens sang their mournful note — it was either a test or a false alarm — but soon, we knew, it would be for real and life as we knew it changed for ever.

SEPTEMBER 3RD 1939 — THE EARLY DAYS OF WAR

Since 1938, when Prime Minister Neville Chamberlain came back from Munich clutching in one hand an umbrella and in the other a piece of paper purporting to guarantee "peace in our time", Britain had greatly speeded up the manufacture of arms to repel or at least discourage the war-like ambitions of Germany. To all but the super-optimist, or those that should have known better, it was only a question of time before hostilities would commence.

Simple Air-Raid shelters started to appear and many instructions as to what to do when the expected air attacks began. Of major concern was the possibility of attack by poisonous gas and very primitive gas masks were issued, even to an untutored eye unlikely to provide much protection from the fiendish products of the German scientists, in those days painted as strange creatures dedicated to devices calculated to enslave the rest of the world to German will.

Then, remarkably, once the *blitzkrieg* had done it's deadly work, a kind of hiatus set in, and like resumed some kind of new pattern. We knew we were at war, but the term 'phoney war' seemed most appropriate. The skill and aggression of the German paratroopers, who had swept all before them, caused most of us a sharp tingle of apprehension, and to counteract their successes on the Continent, should they appear over England, a 'formidable' force was formed to repel their expected attacks. Perhaps formidable is not quite the word because the Local Defence Volunteers, as we were known, consisted of First War veterans, stiffened by immature youngsters like me.

Given an exceedingly ill-fitting uniform, several sizes too big, with an arm-band that would have gone twice, or even thrice, around where my biceps lurked, and armed with a pick-handle, which tended to swing me off balance, we were called to patrol the railway line and give the incoming Huns a taste of their own medicine! My beat, during the night hours, was From Spondon Station to Chaddesden, along the back of the 'Colour Works', quite lonely, but in those days, things to be afraid of did not encompass the present day presence of psychos who now seem to lurk around so many corners. Perhaps I practiced strutting, on patrol, in my 'aggressive mode' and with the whole of my seven-stone-and-a-bit drawn out in intimidating posture, quite a fearsome sight for any would-be invader of Mother England!

After the withdrawal of Allied Forces from Europe in early 1940 the summer developed hot and pleasant so I went to Coombe Martin in North Devon for a weeks holiday—a bit of an adventure in independence.

The Battle of Britain was fought largely over London and the southern counties of Kent, and Sussex and along the South Coast towards the West. The occasional foray was made into the Midlands but the progress of the battle, with it's daily tally of scores gripped the country. Our very existence, if not our very lives depended on the outcome. And then it was "England One, Germany Nil" and we breathed again.

Then came the enemy bombers, with the unmistakable drone of their desynchronised engines, quite eerie in tone; strangely disturbing and unnatural. This time the Midlands was regarded as a prime target, with the Rolls-Royce factory at Derby well up on the list. By then most cities had been enveloped by a ring of anti-aircraft batteries, and they pounded the night air with their variety of missiles of many sizes. An event that provided a lot of 'light entertainment' and excitement was the occasional demise of one of the barrage balloons, which were flown to prevent low level attacks. They frequently broke free of their steel cables and drifted uncontrolled, dragging the cable across power lines, resulting in a glorious firework display and lighting up the countryside. We little realised how dangerous these giants could be, or that there were a few instances of WAAF members of balloon handling squads being carried aloft to their deaths by balloons that had broken away from their moorings. These girls were doing a great job in difficult circumstances.

I was at this time working as a 'relief clerk', which meant travelling to different stations within a fair radius of Spondon. Out came the trusty old bicycle an d often a very early start had to be made to get to work for the early shift, usually between six and seven in the morning.

One run was to Ilkeston, some eight miles away, and it was a long pull up hills, but in the calm dawn of the summer, cycling through the farms, with the farm animals doing their bit of grazing and few motor vehicles, it really was most enjoyable.

Inspired by the Battle of Britain and considering the nation's somewhat gloomy prospects after all the setbacks of the early part of the war (it was all bad news at this stage, with our capital ships being sunk almost daily by the apparently irresistible might of the German Forces) I felt that something had to be done to remedy the situation, despite my being in a 'reserved' occupation. I volunteered to join the RAF. Whether Herr Hitler lost any sleep that night is a matter of conjecture. In August 1940, however, I received a reply from the railway saying that they were unable to release me to join the forces.

The tricky bit here was that if I just 'pushed off' and joined, the railways would not make up the difference between my Air Force pay and railway salary. RAF rank on entry was Aircraftsman Second Class and the pay two shillings per day. My salary at that time was quite a bit more. I received the same reply in December 1940. The same reply to my further application, in February 1941, but with the handwritten footnote, probably by a sympathetic clerk of World War One vintage who would have liked to 'have a go ... at the present time'. So with this softer reply, I took the plunge and, although technically forbidden, went to the recruiting office and joined the RAF, being 'sworn in' at Cardington Beds, on May 5th 1941 and given my new identity number—1433827. I completely forgot to apprise the railway that I was now one of the 'King's men'—ready, willing and ... well, more or less able.

The summer of 1941 passed, with Bomber Command giving it a go and the Luftwaffe mounting spasmodic raids, with the Midlands copping it on many occasions. More of my mates joined the services, the Royal Armoured Corps being the preferred option. The long awaited letter duly arrived and I reported to RAF Padgate on 31st October 1941.

PADGATE AND BLACKPOOL
OCTOBER 1941—MARCH 1942

Shorn of hair, kitted out with underwear (very prickly) and 'pre-used' boots, far from home, my morale was given a boost by a very simple gesture, typical of the spirit of the time and the inherent hospitality of 'northerners'. Released for the evening to explore and possibly sample the delights of Padgate, a dreary, industrial small town, I meandered aimlessly along the uninspiring streets with dozens of similarly displaced young recruits. A couple, probably in late middle age and of modest means, stopped me and said, in very pronounced local dialect, "Come home with us, lad, and have a bit of supper." They took me to their home, a 'two-up and two-down', where they fed me pig's trotters before I headed back to camp—a splendid act of kindness that I much appreciated at the time. It's a pity that such generosity of spirit isn't more in evidence these days.

Transfer to RAF Blackpool came a few days later, and into billets (small Bed and Breakfast establishments) with either one or two per unit or the larger places up to a dozen or so. Conditions were austere and a roster was laid down at my billet for pealing the potatoes for the evening meal. What a chore, but a compromise was reached with our elderly 'host' that if we contribute a penny per week he would peel those spuds! We were quite unworldly, but our ears pricked up when rumours went the rounds that at some billets our mates had 'fallen in the butter'. Apparently, the landlady was not averse to the odd dalliance (we were of course, as RAF aircrew, reputed to be a touch above the average in intelligence and physical endowment!) or better still, the landlady had a (the wilder rumours suggested more than one) daughter, similarly accommodating. Regrettably, I was never able to prove or disprove these claims, but the general demeanour of some of the platoon members, accompanied by a satisfied smirk, led me to believe that some of them might well be true.

We were at Blackpool to do our initial training, which consisted of 'square bashing', rifle drill, etc, together with the initial training in wireless telegraphy. The days, and it was winter and very cold, were alternated, one morning of drill and the afternoon of plugging away trying to learn the Morse Code, reversed the next day. Much marching was done around the streets of the city, and slowly we began to get the rhythm and sense of unity and purpose. It was quite a nice feeling, particularly as the uniform and boots had moulded to our odd bumps. The Drill Sergeant had not yet taken on human form, he seemed the embodiment of evil, determined to crush us into unthinking morons and it was impossible not to quake when, if not responsive immediately to his commands, his beady eye hovered over the ranks and alighted on you! Short breaks were taken at the NAAFI wagon, and of course, 'fags' were lit up.

Training in Morse code took place at the Winter Gardens. This was a huge hall and accommodated dozens of tables, each with about a dozen learners. An everlasting memory of this place is the sound of dozens of Morse oscillators whining away and literally filling the air. It was a strange metallic sound, not very easy on the nerves, and not conducive to concentration, but then, when operating in the air, the 'noises off' were even more distracting. Having got to the point when the code was known, in that the dots and dashes for each letter, build up in speed was the object of the exercise. At the end of each week a test was conducted, starting with four words per minute, increasing each week by two words, with the qualifying speed of twelve words per minute.

It was said that those musically inclined had less difficulty than those not so favourable endowed. Certainly high intellectual ability stood for little in our broad cross-section of English youth. We envied the tutors, who so effortlessly read Morse and talked at the same time, usually puffing on a pipe or even engaged on lighting the thing! Almost without exception, an almost desperate desire to qualify was there, and frowns of concentration told many a tale of forlorn hope. Failure to pass the test at the week's end meant another week at the same speed, with the dreaded stigma of being FT'd (further training). Two more weeks were allowed, and failure then meant being CT'd (ceased training) and reverting to ordinary duties. At the end of each week, a despondent group of formerly bright-eyed and keen young men who hadn't made the grade were told of their fate. The course of many lives was altered on such crossroads.

It was mid-winter and extremely cold and dark, the Lancashire coast in winter being renowned for windy weather, and a far cry from the summer months when Blackpool, with it's Tower of some 300 feet was a big attraction, as were the amusement arcades and illuminations. The 'clientele' was from the weaving mills of Lancashire and the annual week's holiday was looked forward to most eagerly after hours of uninteresting toil at the looms. There was a great spontaneity of spirit and the huge crowds that gathered on the seafront were boisterous and raring for a good time. A joke, current at the time, asked the difference between Blackpool and Morocco. The answer: in Morocco the Moors come down from the Hills...

60,000 airmen were under training at Blackpool at this time, broken down into platoons of 21 men. Going on parade just before daylight, we formed up and marched off, with men carrying a paraffin lamp at the front and rear of the 'squads'. Rifle drill in the snow, for four hours attracted little enthusiasm, but the end goal, to get airborne (and no doubt, proudly sport the aircrew brevet) resulted in a 'grin and bear it' attitude. Once a week we marched up the seafront to Derby Baths for a 'tub and a scrub'. My only recollection is of extremely cold water and a total loss of personal dignity, perhaps due to my inherent sense of modesty.

About this time an incident occurred which brought the reality of flying to all at Blackpool. A mid-air collision between a Blackburn

Botha—a twin engined bomber which proved to be highly hazardous and totally unsatisfactory—and another aircraft took place over the city, with the planes falling onto the main railway station. As I recall there was some loss of life but no-one was unduly fazed.

In February 1942 my Service Records had obviously been scrutinised more carefully, indicating my wish to fly and an academic test, mostly mathematics and the somewhat difficult medical test an examination, were successfully surmounted. The latter test involved the dreaded 'blowing up the mercury', described earlier. Many years after the war I realised that this was not only a physical test but also a test of motivation. But it still had to be done, and failure meant no flying.

I was delighted with my success and joined what was known as the 'Aircrew Squad' and we promptly put our 'white flashes' in our caps, stuck out our chests, and marched with a touch more pride. Another touch of the subtleties of service procedures was that as we marched to and from our place of drill, etc, through the streets of Blackpool, we frequently met officers of all the services and such meeting demanded an 'eyes left or right'. To enhance what is now known as 'self-esteem' (although I think we already had plenty) on the operative word of "eyes *right*" we stamped our foot as hard as possible. The sound of our hobnailed boots certainly rang out loud and clear in those streets and tended to startle the natives but we really enjoined carrying out this unusual action. It is difficult to adequately express the pride we all had in the wearing of our white flash in our cap—even as I write the feeling of intense satisfaction surges once more.

We were coming to the end of our training in drill, swinging along in fine style, even getting a bit 'cocky' and developing a few finer touches in our routines, but the drill Sergeant—Courage by name—was still a person to be feared. Then something happened that we thought impossible. He revealed that he was a real human being, capable of dialogue instead of the barked commands that had been our lot for the past few months. We had stopped for a break, in some street in the outer reaches of the city, when, to our astonishment, like the transformation of Mr Hyde to Dr Jekyll, he took on a new 'persona' and we gathered around him like excited schoolboys around a new chum. He had done his job in moulding us to service discipline and even expressed satisfaction with our abilities … and this was the man who, on occasions when we had 'boobed' in a drill movement had called us "horrible things" and on his question, "What are you?" we were obliged to yell "We're horrible things Sergeant!"

"Good on yer," Sergeant Courage, wherever you are!

Success also came in the sending and receiving of the Morse code, perhaps my earlier huffing and puffing on a simple mouth-organ had instil a modicum of 'ear musical' and adaptation to the cadences and rhythms of the code followed, as I remember, with not too much difficulty. The gay (sic) lights of the metropolis of the North were to be left behind for the rigours of a proper RAF Station and posting quickly followed to Yatesbury, in Wiltshire, this being No.2 Signals School.

NO.2 SIGNALS SCHOOL—YATESBURY, WILTSHIRE
MARCH–JUNE 1942

Yatesbury was set in the Wiltshire Downs—no flying facilities—our stay here was to speed up our ability in Morse code and give us a basic grounding it radio theory, sufficient only to handle minor malfunctions of our airborne equipment. Accommodation (with no sign of a landlady or daughter!) was about forty men to a wooden hut, with such a narrow margin between beds, that in today's parlance, our 'personal space' was well and truly violated! Each morning beds had to be made up 'biscuit' fashion and kit laid out in symmetrical and strict order. On the weekly 'domestic night' the pot-bellied stove was polished to a high shine and the whole hut gone over in scrupulous detail to remove any vestige of what the sergeant in charge, with some exaggeration, called 'filth'. But it was a happy place with a nice sense of organisation and purpose and we all settled down to cope with the next phase of our long training. I had rather enjoyed the square-bashing phase and missed the pleasure of participating in co-ordinated movements of a group.

Again, and quite fortuitously, my earlier interest in radio stood me in very good stead and I lapped up the technical part of the training with interest and speed. The instructor for this was an ex-teacher and had the flair for imparting knowledge. The qualifying examination was of modest standard, but of the group of forty or so, it was usual for all to pass out as Aircraftsman Second Class, with the two top students graded one up to AC First Class. This very small promotion gave me much pleasure and an extra sixpence a day. Subsequent progress up the ranks failed to equal the cachet of this 'small leap'.

The quantum leap in our speed in Morse code from 12 to 18 words per minute came readily, with a few extra wpm in reserve. The mental breakthrough in this art occurs quite suddenly and unexpectedly. I think we all had different breakthrough points, but, when unfamiliar with the sequence of dots an dashes, each dot or dash is heard separately, then a bit of mental juggling takes place and the letter or figure related to that sequence comes to mind and as written down. I recall the magic moment, when, after numerous hours of following this technique, I came to with a start and realised that I had just written down a whole page of letters and numbers quite subconsciously. Oh Happy Day! At a later day in the service, 28 words per minute were accurately received with little conscious effort.

The Camp was set in the rolling downs of Wiltshire, a few miles from Calne, noted for it's pork pies, and it was a glorious summer and service life was good. There was a small village somewhat closer and within striking distance for a run down to get a beer. The full details escape me, but it appeared that a road sign, or similar between the pub and the camp had been damaged in some way—early shades of the rampant vandalism of today—and a group, including me, were held to be responsible. Guilty or not, I was on a 'fizzer' and awarded a weeks 'jankers'. This entailed reporting to the guardroom every hour and between times, cleaning up in the kitchen of the Airmen's mess, a messy and unpleasant chore that put me off cooking for life!

Our instructor evinced pride as he showed us the 'Bessanou Hangar'. This was a relic from the First War, fabricated from material of some kind, and used in France to house the Camels, Spads and such. It was now used for a much more mundane purpose, the storage of materials etc, but to all of us keen young airmen, it was a savoury taste of combat on high!

At that time, we were unsure of our destiny after qualifying as 'observers'. The bomber aircraft, at that time were Wellingtons, Hampdens, Beauforts, Blenheims, with the large four-engined Stirlings, Lancasters and Halifaxes at our level in the service, only hinted at. One delightful summer day, however, we were assembled, with an air of conspiracy, in a lecture room and told we were not to divulge what was to follow. Unusually, it was a call for volunteers to re-muster as 'Radar operators' in, as I recall, an aircraft not specifically mentioned by name, but later transpired to be the nightfighter version of the Beaufighter. Group Captain 'Cats Eyes' Cunningham and his Radar Operator were later to achieve great success in this type of operation, and I think Patrick Moore, the Astronomer of many appearances on the BBC was such an operator).

My recollection is that few if any of us volunteered for this change of objective, our minds, and also hearts set on the bombing operations. The highly secret airborne electronic apparatus in the Beaufighter by which the Radio Observer detected the intruder aircraft was the result of research by the 'boffins' and many more complex systems were subsequently used in all spheres of air operations. To deflect public conjecture as to it's invention and use, the story was circulated that the crews were fed a special diet of carrots which miraculously so improved their 'night vision' to the point of being able to see in the dark. So successful was this covering story that for many years afterwards mothers fed their children carrots in the firm belief that this was so.

For those with no first-hand experience in the services, many of the traditions and procedures must appear to be with little foundation, other than perhaps, sheer perverse behaviour stemming from masculine quirks. It was customary, at all service pay parades to respond to the call of your name by marching up to the paymaster, salute and be given your pay and this took place every two weeks in the Airforce; not an overly formal procedure. However, at Yatesbury this was carried out but without the obligatory salute as at all other places. This intrigued me and it was explained that this omitted salute was at the request of a Sergeant Hannah, VC, who was an Instructor at Yatesbury. It was a long established custom in the RAF that any holder of the Victoria Cross could make one request at his station, and this if sensible and responsible, it would be implemented by the Commanding Officer.

"Who was this Sgt Hannah?" was our next question. An extremely brave young man was the answer. Early in the war he was a Wireless Operator/Air Gunner flying Wellington bombers and won the VC by putting out a fire in the aircraft with his bare hands and enabling its safe return to base. Very sadly, he developed tuberculosis and died shortly after the war ended.

The end of the Course arrived, with success reflected in the attainment of the trade qualification of Wireless Operator and a sense of common unity of purpose and cohesion that had been instilled through those seemingly interminable hours jumping smartly to the inclinations of our drill sergeant. The icing on the cake, though not evident by my now well worn-in uniform, was the self-confidence I had gained from my extra sixpence per day as an AC1, which had removed me from the lowest rung in the Service. There was a scurry back to the hut to sew on our badges, which consisted of a hand clutching a bunch of four flashes of what looked like lightning (or were they electrical sparks?).

I recall that I was not displeased with my progress in the service, but it was to be a long road ahead before I could be actively involved in attacking those who would "tweak the tail of the British Bulldog"—as Winston Churchill put it—by venturing over the territory of the Hun in the dead of night...

AIR CREW RECEPTION CENTRE
ST JOHNS WOOD, LONDON—JULY 1942

The Air Crew category for which I was training, 'observer', stemmed back to the early days of aviation, when it was first realised that not only could aeroplanes carry the pilot but also passengers. (One senior American General, having watched Wilbur or Orville do his stuff, apparently remarked to the effect that it was a very interesting invention but really just a one man device.) Realisation of the new contraption's military capability soon followed and the 'fighter pilot' became the blue-eyed boy until sophistication set in and the numerous airborne chores for effective performance demanded an additional crew member. During World War One, the Royal Flying Corps, apart from the aggressive role of combat at high altitudes—and what courage that demanded—the other very useful role was to support the ground forces in reconnaissance, spotting for the guns, ground attacks, etc. Such varied and complicated duties could not be carried out by the pilot, more than occupied in flying the aircraft, and the second crew member became known as the 'observer'.

The Army also used a large number of captive balloons for observing enemy activity, usually at heights up to nearly a thousand feet. Needles to say, such balloons were greatly exposed to enemy fire and attacks by their aircraft, and these were also manned by an officer observer. Remarkably, although a reasonable efficient parachute had been invented at these times, crews flying aircraft were not supplied with them, as the senior officers felt that it was not conducive to a "press-on regardless" spirit if airmen could willy-nilly avoid combat by taking to their chutes!

However, the poor old observer in the captive balloon, totally at the mercy of his attacker, having no defensive armament, was permitted to 'bale-out' should circumstances become too hot—which they often did—as the balloon invariably caught fire and fell to earth in a welter of flames.

The observer qualified in navigation involving map reading, dead reckoning etc) wireless operating, photography, bomb aiming, air gunnery, etc, and wore the half brevet, the letter 'O' with a half wing. This, but not the wearer, was known by several euphemisms some slightly indecent! However, with the increase in aircraft size and sophistication, these separate tasks became more onerous, and demanded an increase in the number of crew. This led to the introduction of the separate functions of navigator, wireless operator, bomb aimer (who usually had some pilot training and in an emergency could have a fair stab at getting the aircraft onto the ground), flight engineer, and air gunners designated to man the guns in the tail, mid-upper or nose turrets.

The training for pilots and navigators demanded more specific and academic knowledge, such as the theory of flight, meteorology, navigation, etc, and recruits were inducted into the RAF at the Aircrew Reception Centre in St Johns Wood, a rather 'classy' residential area of North London. I had completed my training as a Wireless Operator, and the next step in my journey to becoming an Observer (also known as 'Nav/W –navigator/wireless operator) was to start the course for navigators. The Empire Air Training Scheme had recently been introduced, with Canada, Rhodesia, South Africa possible future destinations for me. A very warm glow of anticipation threaded it's way through my slim form and resuscitated memories of my earlier and more youthful wanderings around old England.

At St John's Wood we were accommodated in a somewhat palatial hotel that had been stripped of all fittings and now comprised many large, stark rooms, each housing up to a dozen cadets. Service style beds and a small locker provided for our immediate needs, but as our stay there was just while our records and postings were sorted out, it mattered not a lot. By then 'our mob' had 'got some in' in terms of length of service and we tended to swagger a little and regarded most of the others as new boys or 'sprogs'. But we were all united on our lust for the pleasures—albeit blacked out—of the London scene and the cultural division between those of us who could wend their way casually around the city (the 'southerners') and the likes of me, basically a country yokel from what is now known as the 'Watford Gap', became very obvious.

Memories of the few days spent at 'Arsitarsi' include enjoying the reaction and wrath of the few disciplinary NCOs when the entrance hall was festooned with inflated condoms. Also a visit to the Lords Cricket Ground. Cricket, in England in the thirties was very serious and an important part of life. We cadets fell into the category of enthusiasts. In fact one of the pre-requisites for being keen to get shot at in the air by the enemy was to express a firm dedication to the 'noble art' and to use, when thought to be useful to this end, such expressions as 'the click of willow'. Having once seen Derbyshire play, I thought this sufficient qualification to bandy such terms. Horse riding was an activity also sure to guarantee selection for aircrew—most of the real 'leaders' in the Air Force were true indulgers in these, to us 'classy' activities, but the 'followers', who predominated, didn't do too bad a job, as was eventually found.

The visit to Lords was conducted in an almost religious air, and as we stood on the ground and walked through the stands I'm sure many a surreptitious tear was discreetly wiped away. The NCOs who marched us there were very conscious what a privilege we were about to experience, and we all came away feeling even more proud of our forthcoming role in the war and the white flashes in our caps stood just a little more erect and proud.

Regretfully, one of the cadets fell by the wayside and succumbed to the temptations of the 'big city'. I recall that his name was Cummings and he allowed his youthful exuberance to get out of control and murdered a prostitute in Soho. He repeated the offence within a few days but this time, he left behind his bag containing his gas mask. All service equipment had to marked with name and service number and it took but a short time to locate the said cadet. He was later executed for his crimes — an event of little or no concern in wartime Britain.

Wartime London was transformed into a siege city, with massive walls of sand bags protecting places of importance and austere conditions in every aspect of daily life. Every nationality was represented and uniforms of colour and style quite un-British were on every street. But the 'bulldog spirit' permeated through this fabric and there was an air of defiance that quite swept up the spirit. A sense of cooperation affected every personal contact, however fleeting and the cockney sense of humour, never far from the surface, literally bubbled over despite the horrors inflicted by the indiscriminate bombing of the city. To go below ground to the Underground railway stations, late at night, and see hundreds of citizens bedding down for the night on the platforms and even on the tracks (where the power had been switched off) was a quite moving sight. The obstinacy and tenacity of the ordinary people was so strong that it seemed unthinkable that the war could be lost.

Night-life continued at a level far beyond the financial resources of us 'erks' (the lowest form of life in the RAF) although we made good use of the various service clubs and enjoyed what was known as "tea and a wad". Overriding all was the sheer delight of being in uniform and taking part in the whole massive effort of working towards victory over the 'dreaded Hun'.

In the thirties, one of the best-known British comedians was George Formby, noted for his song *Leaning on a Lamppost at the Corner of the Street*. 'North country' through-and through, with an accent you could cut it with a knife, he had a brash and suggestive (in the nicest possible way) style reminiscent of the old music halls and seaside pierrot shows. At this time quite a few films were being made by the Government, with service themes and portraying snatches of service life, and it was our good fortune, out of the blue, to become 'film extras' for one such film featuring the aforementioned Mr Formby. It was only a crowd scene, shot in, I think, Regents Park, but it was a shot in the arm for us young unsophisticates, particularly those of us who hailed from "Formby Country".

This fascinating interlude in London was a short respite from the usual form of service life, but my next posting was nigh. This was to the West of England to learn why aeroplanes fly, what keeps them in the air and allied subjects.

NO.4 INITIAL TRAINING WING — PAIGNTON, DEVONSHIRE — JULY–OCTOBER 1942

The train journey down to Paignton was typical of travel in wartime Britain. A seat was very difficult to grab and it was then 'standing room only' in the corridor, all in a huddle, with virtually no room to even sit on a small suitcase. However, my luck was in and I managed to stretch myself on one of the luggage racks in a compartment. This was a simple frame with rope strings and having little meat on my bones, the benefit of my enterprising move was of dubious benefit. I bore the pattern of the mesh for some time afterwards!

Our billet was one of the very grand hotels at this very salubrious and genteel holiday resort for wealthy and more discerning English people. Needless to say, the hotel had been stripped of all fineries and, like in London, our accommodation was stark in the extreme. But the views from my room across a broad expanse of what had been tender lawn, to the sea of Torbay pleased me. Paignton, with neighbouring Torquay, was known as the 'English Riviera' and the climate tended to be warm and mild, with Palm Trees growing and giving it an almost un-English feel.

Our stay here could not have been timed better, because it was mid-summer, the weather and the sea temperature very bearable. An added bonus was that it was a Mecca for those fortunate enough to be able to take holidays, with the advantage that it was away from the London and eastern areas where the likelihood of being bombed was greater. Our now rudely healthy cadets were not slow to notice that a considerable number of the holidaymakers were young and (mostly) attractive ladies. Even the less attractive ones got plenty of attention, and a favourite quip of the day, by some of the less discerning cadets was "She's my type... she's a woman!" It's hardly true to say no young lady was safe, but perhaps a 'fate worse than death' was never too far away for the less sophisticated!

The course proved to be very interesting and had an immediate connection with actual flying, but with the extra-curricular activities and lots of very energetic physical training, the afternoon sessions saw many nodding heads in the classroom. We were able to swim and frolic on the beautiful sands of the bay and there was even an occasional surge of surf (though not recognised as such in those days). Most of us had learned to swim in far less congenial situations—for me in the local canal at Spondon where the odd dead dog was to be found—and our physical well-being and morale took a great boost. When we marched through the town, with our aircrew cadet white flashes freshly laundered and that rhythmic marching cadence going very nicely, we felt on top of the world. My old bones quiver a bit at the memory!

I was hardly up to the physical standards demanded for aircrew, being very much underweight, and I had to put extra effort into most activities. I convinced myself that it was 'all in the mind' (and it really was) and one day I had a chance to show my mettle when a fairly long cross-country run had been laid on. Paignton was on the coast, but going inland meant climbing up towards the moors and this was an ascent of several hundred feet. We were, at this time, very competitive, and the need to win was very strongly part of our attitude. The field of runners straggled out over a long distance, with much huffing and puffing, the hills being steep enough to cause quite a bit of distress and the need to engage a 'lower gear'. The distance was probably three or four miles and a brisk pace was being maintained, but my long legs and not an ounce of surplus fat definitely gave me an edge and to my surprise I found myself in the bunch of 'frontrunners' on the downhill stretch back into Paignton. The pace quickened, not only because of the more favourable slope but also because suddenly we all wanted to win. A popular expression current then was "bugger this for a game soldiers", which I think I must have uttered to myself as, a bit like Roger Bannister when he broke the "four-minute mile", I gave it everything I had left in my almost-exhausted reservoir of power. Only semi-aware of the finishing line, with our NCOs ready to greet us, I passed the post in third place. One of the great pleasures of service life, with its camaraderie, mateship, call it what you will, is the feeling of wholehearted acceptance into one's particular group. The reward for my efforts on this occasion was just such an acceptance and a consequent slight upward movement in the established 'pecking order'.

Most of my life I have been aware of a strong empathy with Jewish people, and even in strange and unusual circumstances, have found a great bond of understanding with strangers who are Jews. We seem to hit it off, and though I have not probed into my 'roots' in any depth, I'm sure there lurks, somewhere over the generations, a Semitic 'dark and handsome stranger of the night' (and the best of luck to him!) Anyway, on the course at Paignton was one Leslie Gee, and yes, his surname was indicative of his faith. There were very few Jewish airmen in the RAF relative to the general population, and the reasons were many, the main one being that the Pogrom of Jews taking place on the continent made it unfair that as well as facing the hazards of operational flying there was the added certainty of subsequent ill-treatment in the event of surviving being shot down.

I particularly recall Les for several reasons. We became strong friends—in some ways I think I kind of 'adopted' him. One was the reluctance of most of the other trainees to respond in a friendly way to his overtures of friendship, which surprised me and was a new experience of life. Anyway, we went as a group to the lovely beach of Paignton to swim—the weather and water was super. There was a lot of larking about and horseplay and suddenly the cry went up that Gee couldn't swim, swiftly followed by "Lets throw him in!" Poor Les totally panicked and took off up the beach at a high rate of knots, hotly pursued by most of the other swimmers. Somehow, it seemed me to go far beyond natural exuberance and took on a quite sinister aspect, definitely not 'fair play' and indicative of the inherent human tendency to make race distinctions. I think I can safely say we were all pretty average young men, devoid of any indoctrination in such distinctions so it was not a pretty sight and I recall it even today with a tingle of dismay at the quirks of human behaviour.

I used the word 'adopted' above, relative to Gee, and a very touching incident followed when, on a few days leave in London, I visited Gee and his family in North London. His Father was small and slight, I think he was a tailor, and he had a sister, Sadie. They comprised an ordinary working-class (like me) family of modest means and hard working. Father Gee was inordinately proud of Les, more so than usual because Les was an Aircrew Cadet and wore the esteemed white flash in his cap. We got on famously and Mr Gee later carefully engineered a quiet moment alone with me. He became very emotional and confidential in his concern for the safety of Les in his future aircrew duties. He was torn between his pride in his son's willingness to fly and the high possibility of his receipt, one day, of the telegram that all parents dreaded. He literally threw himself on my mercy and begged me to look after Les as far as I was able. I was greatly moved.

Thus, as well as adopting Les, I became his 'minder' too. Sometime during the course, Les was obliged to go to 'sick-bay' for some minor ailment and this was situated on the seafront. I visited him on a Sunday morning, after Church Parade (obligatory) and we were chatting, with me sitting on his bed. At this time, it had become the practice of the Luftwaffe to make 'lightning' raids on the south coast, at tree-top height and using ME 109s or FW 190s, simply flying along the coast and 'taking a squirt' at anything they fancied. It so happened that while we were chatting there was a sudden crackle of cannon or machine gun fire and the roar of aircraft engines.

Without thought other than the subconscious instinct to honour my promise to old Mr Gee to 'look after' Les, I leaned over him in a gesture of protection and with no immediate thought of danger. It was a totally spontaneous movement, but I realised subsequently the power of bonding which happens to young men in the situation of service life. Many tales have been told of sacrifice to save a mate, but I'm sure most such actions stemmed from of the unity of spirit which occurs so readily in the services.

Many of the hardened drinkers met their match at Paignton. Devonshire is noted for 'scrumpy', strong locally-brewed cider concocted from apples. Perhaps there is a secret recipe; it is certainly powerful stuff... A group of us visited a pub at a place, strangely enough called Beer, just outside Paignton and judged their scrumpy to be totally innocuous. This was a gross mistake. The consequences were almost immediate and dreadful and next day's lectures a sheer agony of bodily control. Full recovery took several days; a lesson was well and truly learnt!

This phase of training passed very pleasantly, being in itself interesting, with a beautiful English summer and plenty of extra-curricular activities to boot. We also moved one step up the Air Force ladder, being promoted to Leading Aircraftman. We were tanned, fit, well into service life and well on our way along the thorny path to qualify as aircrew. But there was still along way to go and we awaited our next posting with interest and eagerness. This was to Cranwell to 'get airborne' — the first time for almost all of us — to qualify as 'Wireless Operators (Air)'.

NO.1 SIGNALS SCHOOL — CRANWELL, LINCOLNSHIRE
OCT — DEC 1942

Cranwell, the spiritual home of the RAF, was at this time extended into many and varied activities, but we were to spend time in the classroom, polishing our speed in Morse code and also to experience, for the first time, the pleasures of being airborne. The place hummed with activity and for most of us, to see aircraft coming and going, with all the associated noise was very exciting. There was an Operational Training Unit with Whitley aircraft and the Staff College with its impressive buildings loomed large over everything else. In the 20s and 30s, all RAF pilots were trained initially at Cranwell and the station had an aura rather like I mentioned previously, that of Lords Cricket Ground. We all felt that surge of pride at being privileged to be there.

Being located near Lincoln, the surrounding countryside was littered with aerodromes, mostly where Bomber Command operated, at that time, the more modest sized bombers such as Whitleys, Wellingtons etc, although the new four-engined bombers were beginning to come 'on stream'. It was an exciting place to be and we looked forward to our first flying experience. This turned out to be a short trip in a De Haviland Dominie, and six or eight of us, on November 13th 1942, took our seats with confident expectation. My impression was that the earth left us, instead of the other way round, but the wonder of the freedom of the air was paramount in my recollection of that day. For those who trained and became pilots, I can well imagine the thrill of their first solo flight.

Our air operating course was carried out in the Dominie, where some four cadets sat at individual radios and communicated with the ground station and also, and this was quite important, to be able to carry out direction finding procedures vitally necessary to get back to the home base in adverse weather conditions. We also flew in Percival Proctor aircraft, with one pupil seated next to the pilot and one in the rear, with his back to the engine. Flying in the Proctor was much more exciting and I recall a memorable trip with a Polish pilot who had some deficiency in the English language.

At take off, I was next to him, and as he opened the throttle, he took his hands off the control column and gestured to me to take hold. He either had a marked sense of humour or he perhaps thought I was a failed pilot—there were quite a few around, re-training for other aircrew categories. I politely declined his invitation and he resumed control, to my relief. He made amends in a super way, however. At about 5,000 feet there were a lot of broken cumulus clouds with clear blue sky above and we flew through and around the tops of these and also in the valleys between.

I remember so well the beauty of that experience, shared with this Polish pilot, one of the many who had made their way across Europe to fly with the RAF. They had a proud record in the air, with an exceptional motivation to destroy the enemy who had, in many instances, destroyed their families in Poland. Later on, with 254 Squadron, Polish pilots flying Mustangs accompanied us, as fighter escort, on our Strikes off Norway. On reaching the "enemy coast", they forgot their primary role and buggered off to have a bash at anything that looked faintly hostile. They were very aggressive and competent pilots and considering their situation, their country over-run and their families grossly ill-treated, who could blame them.

Our accommodation at Cranwell was Spartan and, in mid-winter extremely cold with only a pot-bellied stove for warmth. Service tradition had what was known as 'domestic night' which meant the hut had to be spit and polished to the satisfaction of the Hut Sergeant, a gentleman not easily pleased. Our beds comprised an iron frame of bars, and were, for some obscure but undoubtedly well-founded reason known as 'Churchills'. Whether or not this related to Winston I'm not sure but they were certainly grossly uncomfortable. At only eighteen years of age, most of us were staggered to discover that one of our number was all of thirty years old, virtually a grandfather, in our youthful reckoning. I recall him as a extremely pleasant type and regret that I afforded him little credit for fringing the upper age limit for volunteering for aircrew, when he could have so easily slotted into some other category with better long-term prospects.

Having tasted a bit of flying, in the Dominies and Proctors with a mate I am unable to recall, the OTU Whitleys caught our attention as a means of getting in a few more hours of air experience. The seemed to lumber huge and ungainly and had a fascination as the "real thing". We bided our time until the Sunday, when, after Church Parade, we were liberated for the rest of the day. Our approach to the OTU Crew Room was unofficial and with some trepidation, we spoke to one of the pilots, who, as a fully qualified 'flyer' was afforded the due deference of his status. Yes, they were about to take-off on a bombing exercise at a point just off the coast, and we would be welcome to join them.

We climbed aboard this black-painted, slow but sturdy monster and away we went. I stood behind the pilots in the cockpit and cruising at the almighty speed of 80 knots—literally take-off, cruise and landing speed—we reached the bombing area and commenced the exercise. This consisted of making a run up to the target, dropping a marker type bomb and wheeling—well, nearly in the old Whitley—around for another run. This was quite enjoyable and interesting for a while and the very modest 'g' forces provided a new experience in the air. However it then became my turn to retreat to the interior of the aircraft and let my mate see what was happening outside.

This soon became a bit dodgy, with no means of orientation and the aircraft constantly changing course and speed. The sickness came upon me quite suddenly, but fortunately at the rear of the aircraft was the Elsan chemical toilet, which I lovingly embraced for the remainder of the trip. The regular crew were quite amused, but I soon recovered and thought the whole of the exercise well worth it. I had actually flown in one of our bomber aircraft, although at one stage on the return flight to base I had thought I might not survive!

In these days of extremely sophisticated flight simulators, it is amusing to look back and recall what were known as "Harwell boxes". We had to spend some twenty hours sitting in these, which hopefully reflected the situation for the wireless operator in a real aircraft in real flight. A series of small and cramped cubicles, very dimly lit but with total blackness in the corners, were fitted out with the type of radio equipment that we would be using, the 1082/1083 transmitter/receiver. The *pièce-de-resistance* of the design was the horrible background noise, purporting to be the noise of aircraft engines. It was all pervading and totally numbed the sense, so that which was readily comprehensible outside, became a determined exercise in concentration, usually with indifferent results. With some ten boxes operating at the same time and each operator attempting to "communicate with base", this extraneous noise coupled with the whine of the many radio signals in the headphones, made the whole exercise appear like a medieval torture chamber.

But there was more... When entering the "box" and before "take-off", nothing worked because our sadistic instructors had carefully removed or disconnected vital connections between the equipment. It was very difficult to locate the faults, usually perpetrated in an obscure place on the floor, because it meant literally a grope in the dark. Having solved this, they then appeared to have a means of sabotaging something or other once the "flight " was under way necessitating further groping.

But it gave us confidence to communicate under difficult conditions and one of the aspects of a wireless operator's skills is the ability to read the signal required out of half a dozen or so, all at the same strength and a hairs-breath away in frequency.

We all came out of this type of training much better operators, but we still had a long way to go. Nevertheless, with all of ten hours forty-five minutes flying time in the log book, I felt that my 'knees were brown'—the RAF expression for having done a bit of time—despite the cold and dreary weather of Lincolnshire in mid-winter and I was ready to move on.

We were aware of the 'Empire Air Training Scheme' and knew that we were destined to travel overseas to one of the Navigation Schools in order to qualify in our chosen aircrew category.

If Lincolnshire was cold, then Manchester was even colder. We were put in Nissen Huts situated in the Park, with the usual single pot-bellied stove for 'central heating', to await our overseas posting. The stay was hopefully due to be a short one only and for all of us the shorter the better as there were almost no other facilities for recreation. The Park itself was quite a beauty spot in this somewhat dull city, centred on industrial activity, and although I do not recall any snowfall, Manchester lived up to it's reputation for never having many days without rain. But the anticipation of going overseas for navigation training eased the burden of our discomfort, and in a few days time, our move was due to take place.

However, there was a small fly in my particular ointment. In my early fiddling with radio—I will not justify 'experiments'—I had become pre-occupied, almost obsessed, with the North American continent, perhaps that voice of Radio Schnectady still lingered, when to my consternation found I was on a draft bound for South Africa. The Dark Continent interested me not one wit—my deep-seated feelings for that wondrous place came much later—and I was on the rather unpleasant horns of a dilemma. 'What to do to be saved?' as we used to say.

What followed has never since ceased to surprise me. I actually had a say in my future movements in the RAF. Mustering the full impressive appearance of my rank, a full-blown leading aircraftsman, I boldly ventured forth and requested to see an officer. I do not recall the details of the rather one-sided conversation, but he incredibly acceded to my request that I be allowed to join the draft to Canada instead of South Africa. I left his august presence a very happy little airman. A few days later, it was pack up the kit bag—a most ill-designed means of carrying anything—and we were on our way to the port of Glasgow to embark for sunnier climes.

WEST ACROSS THE NORTH ATLANTIC
JANUARY, 1943

The activities of the German 'U' boats hunting in what were known as 'wolf-packs' were producing dramatic losses in the Allied shipping fleets, but we were so delighted at the prospect of seeing Canada, with no rationing or black-out, and also other activities of a less serious nature, caused none of us any anxiety. We journeyed by train to Glasgow and then to Gourock or Greenock, I forget which, and went on board the good ship 'Andes', about 18,000 tons burthen, or so. This ship was relatively new but stripped of all unnecessary fittings and not yet equipped for 'trooping'. Accommodation was sparse and we had hammocks for sleeping. Perhaps this strange device may have served the navy for centuries but it did not seem appropriate for the use of airmen, who by then were known, in a cynical, but friendly way, by the other services as the 'Brylcreem Boys' who slept in pyjamas and sheets!

It was early January and freezing cold and once on board, it was apparent that this was no luxury trip. We were allocated to a 'mess', where we were to eat and sleep but with little chance of making merry. No bunks were evident and meals, somewhat 'ad hoc', were taken on the broad tables, mostly at random times, depending on the flow of the service men, not only RAF but a whole hotchpotch of sundry and largely unidentifiable types somehow caught up in the war. One particular group still stand out in my memory; these were a crowd of merchant seamen, with obviously great experience in sea travel. They were apparently travelling to the 'other-side' to pick up a ship for the return journey. With no pretensions to snobbery, I think to call them 'uncouth' would have been to flatter them.

We soon set sail, in rough kind of weather, and even a few yards 'down the track' running alongside the banks of the River Clyde the ship showed that it could do quite remarkable gyrations with little or no effort. The novelty of being sea-borne as against airborne soon proved to be just as trying on the digestive system and it was only a short time before a lot of us succumbed to the dreaded seasickness. Hunched against the ships rail, in the freezing weather, retching with great gusto, the magic and allure of Canada quickly faded from my mind, survival even became a not too desirable option. But the *mal-de-mer* was relatively short-lived and the constant motion of the ship took on an exhilarating effect as the coast of Scotland disappeared in the mist.

There were perhaps half a dozen tables in the mess, each accommodating a dozen men, and a pretty standard fare for most of the trip was hard-boiled eggs and rolls, a not too difficult culinary exercise in the obviously limited cooking facilities. Out at sea, the ship rolled and pitched furiously, and with every movement, unless you had a firm grip on your 'tucker', away it went down the table or onto the deck. It was a source of amusement for a short while. To compound this scene of mayhem, the aforesaid merchant seamen, perhaps to impress us airforce types with their total familiarity with seagoing, indulged in much inter-table banter, with much hurling of bread and eggs as missiles to establish a point of order. We watched in amazement and trepidation at this unseemly display, we, of course, being generally of more dignified nature!

We were not allowed on deck at night, somewhat strangely I thought, as I doubted we had on board anyone willing to signal to the lurking U-boats in his zeal for the Fuehrer' and thus find himself in the freezing sea with a life expectancy of only a few minutes. So it was early to 'bed' in that dreaded naval device, the hammock. Easier said than done, and any straggler who didn't 'sling his hammock' in concert with all others had a big problem. A hammock is designed for very narrow people, and for me, who liked sleeping on their 'tum', doubly difficult. With some twenty hammocks 'in situ' (and a very comical sight it is when viewed from below as all the bulging undersides swing in unison with the ship) to try and insert your hammock between two others, some few inches apart and with little co-operation from the slumberers, by opening it, getting into it about four feet above floor level and in a rolling ship, was well nigh impossible. Half the nights, I slept on a pile of life jackets on the deck, with the advantage that I had nowhere to fall!

Crossing the North Atlantic, at that time, meant either in a slow moving and vulnerable convoy of as many as fifty ships, protected by a screen of Navy destroyers and other escort vessels, or a quick, unescorted dash at high speed. The classic 'troopers' were the *Queen Mary* and *Queen Elizabeth*. The French *Normandie* operated for a while but caught fire in New York and was put out of service. Our ship,

Andes, had only been in service a short time, but was relatively fleet of foot, and we sped and zigged and zagged our way across those extremely turbulent and dangerous waters, on a westerly heading, with many and varied changes of course. We had no idea of our destination port—security was really secure in those days—but I think we made the crossing in abut four days.

Once accustomed to the routine, the wild motion of the ship became very enjoyable. It was so rough, that, walking along the deck, it would take a sudden down plunge and your feet would actually leave the deck. With the next huge pitch, the deck would rise with equal fury and the knees would almost buckle. We had great fun jumping around in 'horse-play'! The cold penetrated everything and everywhere, and as we approached our destination, which turned out to Halifax, Nova Scotia, it was early morning and all the ships rigging was coated with a thick skin of ice. Halifax was a very busy port, and in no time we disembarked and put on a train for our next 'port-of-call'—the Reception and Disposal Centre at Moncton, New Brunswick. The 'tang' of Canada caught in our nostrils—it is quite unique though not greatly dissimilar from Paris, France—but the vastness of the countryside gave a feeling of loneliness, and the distances were so unlike Europe where a train journey is almost over before it's started. We arrived at Moncton after dark in a blinding snow storm and climbing down from the railway carriages, also heavily coated in ice, one of our number fell and broke his leg; not an auspicious start to another vital stage in our long path to get to grips with the 'Hun'.

NO 33 AIR NAVIGATION SCHOOL
HAMILTON, ONTARIO, CANADA
JANUARY—MAY 1943

The train journey from Moncton, New Brunswick to Hamilton, gave us our first real taste of that vast country. I'm sure we all expected the famed 'Mounties'—the Royal Canadian Mounted Police to be in much evidence—but it was quite a long haul, about a couple of days.

The railway locomotives were huge compared with their European counterparts and we wound our way through the well timbered countryside in the comfort of the coaches of the Canadian National

Railways. During the day we sat in the open saloons, which at night converted into sleeping berths. One slept length-wise to the direction of travel, behind curtains and stopping and starting of the train produced a to and fro movement not unlike being on board the *Andes.*

At many wayside halts, the local people came to the train and offered us refreshments and wished us good luck and we greatly appreciated such kind thoughts as many had gone before us. But of course many young Canadians were serving in the armed forces, and the episode of 'Dieppe'—a Commando Raid on the French coast—resulted in severe losses of Canadian servicemen.

We relished the excellent 'tucker' in the dining cars, quite a change from the rations in England, and we were well cared for by the elderly railway stewards, who repeated warned us of the possibility of an attack by Red Indians at certain bends in the 'railroad'—a term which proved to us how far away we were from our own shores. At the end of each coach there was an 'ablution' compartment, for wash and brush up and this was done in matey style and conversation by four at a time. One wag professed to have found a toothbrush on a chain for the use of railway passengers!

Our route took us up to the north to skirt the State of Maine, and along, not too far away from Quebec, Montreal, Ottawa and Toronto. Perhaps my imagination is a touch better than my memory, in one respect, but I seem to recall 'The Heights of Abraham' where General Woolfe outwitted the French/Canadian Forces to win the battle. Hamilton is situated at the western end of Lake Ontario, and it's claim to recognition is as a centre for the manufacture of agricultural implements. It is proud of its 'Scots' connection and had some variation in height within the city which gave it an added attraction. It had little pretence to being a cultural centre, but the 'natives' were very friendly and treated us well.

The aerodrome where we were to train was some twenty minutes journey, and a bus service gave us good access to town when we were able to get away, but our courses, both classroom and flying was pretty full and not too many visits were possible. In any case, we had little energy enough to handle this quite intensive part of our training. The town was pleasantly laid out and our visits were orientated to catching up on the chance to indulge in pleasures of the appetite rather than the flesh—at least that is what we all maintained!

The Course content was most interesting, comprising elements of navigation, practical air navigation, astro navigation, air photograph, compasses, instruments, signals, maps and charts, meteorology, armaments, aircraft recognition, reconnaissance. The flying training was carried out in the good 'old faithful' Avro Anson. My total flying time, on completion of the course, was 80 hours (day) and 44 hours (night), so there was an indication here that we would be venturing into the night skies of Europe, rather than when the sun was shining.

We attempted a little astro navigation, but at some five thousand feet in a bucking Anson, and taking 'star shots' with a bubble sextant through the somewhat grimy perspex of the aircraft window, not a lot of success was achieved. In fact, there was great rejoicing when one bod claimed to have actually got one star position line on his chart! There is, of course the well known air force adage that 'only men and birds fly'—tempered by the qualification 'and birds don't fly at night...' It occurred to me at this time, that the possibility of navigating a bomber to Berlin by using a Bubble Sextant was expecting rather a lot.

The domestic arrangements were quite good, and we slept about thirty per hut in bunk beds one above the other. It was mid-winter and the temperature got way below zero, but the central-heating was fiercely efficient and we suffered more from heat than cold. The Dining Hall was close by and open more or less continuously, with flying going on. The food, of course, was much to our liking after the meagre rations of the UK, with ice-cream and chicken top favourites, and it was a pleasure to order a milk-shake at will.

I recall the softly scented atmosphere of these facilities, quite distinctive, and reminiscent of the Metro in Paris, and the never silent jukebox belting out the songs of the day. Top of the favourites was *Tangerine*, hotly pursued by *Moonlight, Becomes You*, and the inevitable Glen Miller's *In the Mood*. The latter reminds me vividly of one of our little band of 'mates'—Doug Holden. Doug was a little bit older than most of us, married and a Londoner, but somewhat superstitious. Anyway, it so happened that he was due to fly on a navigation exercise and it happened to be Friday the thirteenth. We were in the dining hall indulging in the customary chaffing and banter, and we expressed our fears for Doug's safety on such an ominous day to 'dice with death'. We began to regret our leg-pulling when Doug became almost distraught and only took to the air after our much reassuring that all would be well. Doug was certainly in no 'mood' to fly that day (I lost touch with Doug later and have often wondered if he survives to this day.)

In all service situations there is the inevitable grouping of kindred spirits, and at Hamilton I became mates with Jimmie Rodgers, Doug, Ernie Tebb and as the saying goes these days, we used to 'hang about together'. So when we were given a weekend off, halfway through the course, we all took the Friday night train to Detroit—we preferred the American pronunciation of 'Deetroit', with an adenoidal intonation—and were delighted to be in America for the first time. The hospitality as quite overwhelming and in the nightclub in which we somehow found ourselves, they lavished drinks upon us with little delay and with great regularity, every one of them referring to us as the RAF 'heroes'. Waking up the next morning in the Hotel Tuller where we had somehow come to rest, none of us felt at all like heroes, in fact it took me the whole of the following day to respond to stimuli of any kind.

Another memorable trip was using a Greyhound bus to visit Niagara Falls. (Little did I realise then that many years later I would have the pleasure of living almost within the roar of the mighty Victoria Falls in Rhodesia) At that time, for a dollar a day, up to ninety-nine days, a ticket could be purchased to travel anywhere in the United States, even allowing for cost standards those days, very cheap indeed. It was in February and it was a magnificent sight, with tumbling masses of ice, and little to detract from the grandeur. The journey took us through what is known as the 'garden of Ontario', with acres of horticultural activity. This was a sober trip, I think.

I think we all found the level of central heating, wherever we went just a bit too much and a complete contrast to the flying exercises when few of the aircraft heating systems seemed to work. The cold outdoors was a kind of crispness, and provided there was no breeze, quite bearable in plain uniform. We were issued with what were known as 'goon caps', having the main feature of large flaps which could be lowered to protect the ears against frostbite. I did, quite unknowingly, get a touch of this one evening, but a quick massage solved the problem. The pit of my discomfort from the cold came on my twenty-first birthday when I was flying as a wireless-operator, on the 22nd February. No heat was working, and I sat hunched up over the 1082/1083 radio equipment for three hours with, whenever possible, my hands pushed down into my flying boots, but to little or no improvement in circulation!

We were introduced to the sport of basketball and we all enjoyed the novelty of the game, but the time at Hamilton was occupied by very intense navigation lectures interspersed between a vigorous flying training programme and I recall no other form of organised physical training. The twenty-four hours was split into morning and afternoon lectures or flying and early evening flying and late evening flying. After a stint in the classroom, a quick 'din-dins', it was into flying gear and up and away. The Staff Pilots, who bravely flew us around Ontario, which by then they knew like the back of their hand, put in a tremendous number of hours.

Ground Training: Armaments

The emphasis in this field was the .303 Browning machine gun, the standard offensive weapon used in most RAF Aircraft, but as ammunition was expensive, we spent time at the 'butts', in the prone position shooting at the fixed target with antiquated SMLE (Short Magazine Lee Enfield) rifles—which I think were in service just after the First World War!

Having only a thin layer of meat on my bones, the noticeable recoil of this rifle gave me not only quite a jolt but also a deeply satisfying feel of aggression. I prefer not to think how Freud would have interpreted this obviously male-inherited instinct. I noticed recently that the services now have female combat troops—is this not a contradiction in terms?

We had to learn all the parts of the gun by name, dismantle it, reassemble it within a certain time and know how to clear stoppages. Interesting as this was—it certainly was grist to young and enthusiastic mills—when flying Beaufighters on Operations, equipped with a single Browning machine gun mounted on a very flimsy bracket behind my head, the vibration of the whole structure was such that any possibility of accuracy or damage to the enemy fighters was highly improbable.

We also had a chance, with 12-bore shotguns, to show our prowess at the clay pigeon shoot. Having grown up with pigeon fanciers who loved their birds, I made no mental connection between them and the flat discs of clay, and the exercise was to sharpen our reaction to a moving target as it emerged from the trap at high speed. A hit was very satisfying. For some reason, we also had the opportunity of throwing hand grenades, which produced a very merry explosion.

We learned about 'pyrotechnics', which covered various other explosive or dangerous devices, like the Very pistol, with which to fire flares in the 'colours of the day' for recognition purposes when overflying our own defensive positions or ships at sea, despite which we all later on experienced the frustration of what is now know as 'friendly fire'. Regrettably, there were many instances of our aircraft being shot down by our own forces when the 'colours of the day' were not used or were used incorrectly.

The whole atmosphere of the lectures in 'armaments' had a strong tinge of aggression, no doubt carefully introduced, as in those days of basic training when, with a rifle with fixed bayonet, we were encouraged to charge at the dummy targets with wild and uncontrolled screams and yells with which to subdue the enemy, or at least put the wind up him. Perhaps the present day tendency to run riot at football matches, get in the odd bit of 'road -rage' and paint everything not moving with scrawled 'graffiti' masquerading as 'self-expression', is not dissimilar in basic attitude. What odd — (I nearly said 'queer') creatures we human beings are.

Compasses

"Where do you come from?" said the Queen, "and where are you going?"
(Alice Through The Looking Glass)
The navigator's 'best-friend' came in for a real work-out, and we all found this subject very interesting. I found the quote at the beginning of the section of the text book quite evocative, as to me there is a strange magic and fascination with travel and the awareness of earthly position.

We became familiar with 'molecular magnets', how 'unlike' poles attract and 'like' poles repel (perhaps a bit like that strange chemical reaction between human beings) 'dip', 'dead -beat', 'isogonals' (lines on a chart with equal variation) and various co-efficients, etc. When we started flying, the properties of the magnetic compass became real to us, in the fact that flying around Ontario, the compass variation, to be applied to every dead- reckoning course calculated, and before being given to the pilot, was in the order of some sixty or seventy degrees !.

Woe betide the 'sprog' navigator who forgot to apply this staggering amount of compass adjustment. But there's more! It had to be applied in the correct direction, and with our early unfamiliarity with our navigation duties, coupled with the fatigue and the cold, the mind tended to play strange tricks. We all found that what was a simple mental calculation in the classroom, after some time 'airborne', became a very determined effort in concentration to arrive at the correct answer.

The above aspect of applying 'variation' was of less significance in Europe, where it was a matter of only several degrees, but other quirks relating to the compass reared their heads, resulting in some strange and dangerous outcomes. Navigators, in the heat of the moment, or experiencing a touch of panic when their position was a bit unsure, were known to have given the pilot the 'reciprocal' of the course 'to fly' — the wrong way round by 180 degrees — or even more remarkably, instead of the compass course, in a moment of mental aberration, the airspeed of the aircraft! Stories of such boo-boos are legion, but the worst mistakes have perhaps failed to be recounted because of he absence of those involved! The message here is that the magnetic compass is either a good friend or a source of potential hazard.

Photography

The fundamentals of photography were demonstrated, with emphasis that, as one of its long-standing functions, the Air Force was expected to provide vital photographic intelligence to the other armed forces. We were all greatly impressed by the high definition achieved, even from great altitudes, by reconnaissance aircraft, such photographs being used as a basic source of information for subsequent attacks by the aircraft of Bomber or other Commands. Even more impressive, and new to us, were the 'stereo' photographs, viewed through a special view-finder and clearly showing targets in three dimensions.

We were particularly intrigued with the actual cameras used in the air, one, the Hand-Held K24, and the other fixed camera, which was used to take what are known as 'line-overlaps'. Our practical work consisted of using the K24 to take photographs of selected points in the countryside of Ontario, such as bridges, railway stations or junctions, small villages, etc. Most of the countryside was covered in snow and the 'target' was not always easy to recognise from our height of about one or two thousand feet. Further, the side window of the Anson aircraft had to open, and with it's quite low sill, a firm grip had to be maintained to avoid being tossed from the aircraft when turns were being executed. The coldness of the slipstream making a short-cut into the plane was icy in the extreme, and our woollen mitts provided scant protection, in this respect.

More enjoyable was the exercise in 'line-overlaps'. The purpose of this technique was to ensure that a larger area could be photographed, in one run, with little possibility of any item of interest being missed. To do this, an overlap of 60 degrees of each of a series of photographs was taken. This involved several factors, including the angle of the camera, the speed and height of the aircraft, and the frequency at which the pictures wee taken. The aircraft, of course, had to be flown on a steady course, and this bit gave us a taste of real involvement in guiding the pilot along our target.

But first, having been given our 'target', we had to calculate the variables in the exercise, and set up the equipment in the aircraft. Mine happened to be an easily spotted new highway, known as the Queen Elizabeth Highway between Hamilton and Toronto, which ran pretty well in a straight line. It really was good fun carrying out the task, but whether I stood next to the pilot or lay down in the nose of the aircraft, I simply cannot remember, but I still have the photographs.

Meteorology

I think we all had a spot of bother with this subject as it involved better quality maths and physics, but we battled and overcame. What with 'adiabatic lapse rates', 'isobars', etc, the difference between stratus and cumulus, etc, there was much grunting and groaning. It all seemed so nebulous at the start of the course but as we got into it, it became very obvious that airy fairy wisps and lumps in the sky were of paramount importance to us aviators. Terms like 'katabatic' and 'anabolic' winds were casually tossed into our conversations, and we looked heavenwards with more interest, and in my case, I think with awe at the simple wonder of how it all worked.

The whole purpose of this subject, from a navigators point of view, was to be able to thread a safe course through this highly unpredictable environment, bearing in mind that perhaps even a simple mistake in planning ahead, of the course of the aircraft, could result in dire consequences, like having the wings torn off by a rogue 'cumulonimbus', or, equally embarrassing to the guiding hand of the navigator, failing to reach the point of desire on the terra firma of old Mother Earth.

Maps and Charts

Again, a delightfully interesting subject, which had gripped my imagination before joining the RAF and has since been a constant source of quiet and pleasurable 'browsing'. Next to my bed I have, at the ready, an Atlas and various maps for quick reference to places referred to in my general reading. Perhaps being favoured with a somewhat sharp-edged imagination, I am lucky inasmuch that I can, by gazing at a map, easily conjure a minds picture of the scene and circumstances of incidents, places etc. The now old-fashioned song *Far Away Places With Strange Sounding Names* still touches nerves untouched by almost nothing else and I'm away in spirit.

A basic point in this subject soon taxed our ability to think in 'spatial' terms, when the methods used to accurately portray the surface dimensions of the round earth onto flat pieces of paper which could be used for practical navigation purposes, were set out before us. We blessed the foresight of one 'Mercator' (a *nom-de-plume* for one Gerard Kremer, a Belgian map maker) and we spoke of the quirks of the 'conical orthomorphic' projection, this being done, apparently, by folding a piece of paper into a tube and sliding it over a sphere (the earth, illuminated from the inside) and drawing the lines of latitude and longitude on the outside.

The main distinction is that 'maps' are used to show physical features on the ground, such as railways, roads, rivers, towns, villages, landmarks, etc, so that by physical observation of the ground below the aircraft, a pinpoint may be established, with the cry, when uncertainty has produced some anxiety, 'Eureka!' or similar, whereas 'charts' enable bearings to be taken, courses plotted, calculations as to ground speed, a new course to the required destination, etc, then made.

For some of us, we enjoyed 'reading' maps as one would read a book. The fascination of scale, for instance, when with large scale maps, a whole lot of new detail of interesting features rose up from the map and bridged the gap between the map and the real thing. In the air, and gazing directly downwards through the navigation aperture in the aircraft, from several thousand feet, an added pleasure was to be deliberately conscious of the fact that there below were people going about their daily activities. Later, after the war, when flying with British Overseas Airways over Europe and India I spent many happy hours simply visualising the life going on so far below the aircraft.

All of us on the course found the distinction between 'great circle bearings' and 'rhumb lines' most intriguing. The former, being the shortest distance between two points on the ground and naturally being the most advantageous way to fly, with the problem that the compass course would be constantly changing and therefore impractical. The aforesaid Mercator chart, with it's parallel lines of latitude and longitude, allows an initial bearing to be taken, adjusted for the deflection due to the winds to be encountered, and thus provides a constant compass course for the whole flight, with only a slight increase in the miles to be flown.

Instruments

This aspect of the course dealt with the basic tools of the aircraft navigator, comprising;

The Dalton Computer,
Douglas protractor, and Dividers
Drift Recorder,

Airspeed Indicator,
Aeronautical 'Bubble' Sextant
Altimeter,
Astro-Compass

Looking at the above list, some fifty years on, the items shown appear primitive in the extreme, when compared with the present day simplicity of treading a path through the un-sign-posted atmosphere of the good earth! Peering even further back in the mists of time, when Capt. Cook was a lad, guiding a small collier around the east coast of England, and subsequently completing three circumnavigations of the world, there was even less tangible appliances to make a good 'landfall'.

It was only about 1775 that it was possible to know the time with any real accuracy, when a gentleman by the name of Hargreaves won the prize of about fifty thousand pounds with his 'improved Chronometer' and it became possible to determine longitude with a relatively simple astronomical calculation. All the successful sea-farers of long ago — and also today with those who, for sheer pleasure of the challenge, sail single-handed around the world, not only once but in one case three times non-stop, — appear to have that unique ability to sense, perhaps like migratory birds, their whereabouts at any given time.

The abilities of some Pacific Islanders are even more remarkable; in their ability to traverse vast tracts of the ocean, in extremely small vessels, using the stars, sea currents and the smell of the water and atmosphere as their sole means of navigation. The traditional knowledge of the stars and constellations, and their relative movement, is handed down by generation and taught by what appears to be a series of stones placed in various positions showing their movements. Several Western scientists have carried out practical tests by accompanying these hardy seafarers on their voyages and have been convinced that their techniques are as described and they have no modern 'satellite navigator' tucked away in a locker or other place.

Today, hand-held ground positioning satellite navigators are available at very reasonable cost. Perhaps by the year 2020 we will receive an inoculation at an early age, along with the one for whooping cough (which appears to defy scientific progress) so that if we blink, a series of figures will appear which will shown our global pin-point!

Aircraft Recognition

In retrospect this subject seems to be hardly worthy of the time devoted to it, when considering that today it is highly likely that the aircraft that will now deliver the mortal blow that has your name on it will arrive so fast that it's identity will be of little consequence. But in those days we struggled to sort the 'good' from the 'bad' as there was every likelihood of a tangled mass of 'us' and 'them' milling about the sky intent on inflicting severe hurt on each other and the need to exercise lightning judgement, based on a fleeting glimpse, as to fire or not to fire. Aircraft development by the opposing forces, had proceeded along similar lines of construction (knowledge of aerodynamics was based on empirical rather than tested lines of thinking) and the result was that several aircraft of each side had remarkable similarities to the other.

The RAF Beaufighter and the Luftwaffe JU88 are a case in point. Shortly after the end of the war, we flew into one of the aerodromes near Paris and we inspected a JU88, finding it a very smart and efficient aeroplane. It was, however, a strange experience to be sitting in the thing, as the possible sighting of one of these aircraft when flying on operations, had triggered a sharp flow of adrenalin!

Our course demand familiarity with a large number of aircraft, friend and foe alike, and from various angles and visibility. Most of the classrooms had the walls 'papered' with pictures of aircraft and scale models were strung from the ceiling. The Instructors in this subject appeared to particularly dedicated and paid little heed to our boredom and disinterest, but we later realised that some had done a tour of Operations and were acutely aware of the importance of knowing the subject in order to survive. Numerous instances occurred of losses, by both sides, of aircraft being shot down by 'friendly fire', and on ops we were conscious of the similarity of our aircraft to the JU88.

The hazards arising during the 'heat of the moment' were later amply demonstrated on my Operational Squadron, No. 254 at North Coates. Cine cameras were installed in the nose of the aircraft and these were synchronised to film when the four twenty millimetre Oerlekon cannon and machine guns were fired by the pilot. A 'strike' on an enemy convoy could involve almost fifty aircraft, all in relatively close formation and intent on attacking to best advantage. The prime duty of the navigator was to try to keep his pilot aware of the position of other aircraft, and, of course, both crew members were acutely conscious of the activity of the 'flak' heading in the opposite direction!

On return to base the films were analysed by the Intelligence Officers, put together into a continuous reel, and once a month or so we were assembled in the briefing room and given the dubious pleasure of re-living what we called our 'dice with death'. (In the relative tranquillity and safety of this re-run, their was much ribald comment and exclamation, but the hair still tended to curl just a wee bit.) The film showed, with the tracer inserts, the cannon and machine gun fire heading towards the target ships, but what caused our perhaps slightly hysterical reaction was the number of occasions that one of our own aircraft swept through the fire of our own attack. It seemed hardly possible that these unwitting targets could have survived, but I think we were lucky in this regard and much sarcasm flowed regarding the marksmanship of our pilots!

Signals

Our ability in 'signals', sending and receiving the Morse code by radio, use of the various three letter codes with which to send 'sighting reports' back to base when on reconnaissance flights, and the use of the 'Aldis Lamp' were all improved by refresher courses. The latter system, extensively used by the navy, involved the use of a relatively powerful lamp which could be switched off and on quite rapidly and to form the dots and dashes of the Morse code when aimed at a distant receiver. As we were heading to join Coastal Command we would be operating in close contact with the navy so we had to be competent in this form of communication.

Air Navigation: *Fundamental Principles*

We were destined to spend many long hours in the classroom getting hold of the art of this fascinating technique, still relatively novel, but based on a few very simple procedures. Most of us, although I do not recall this extensively discussed between us, having a deep-seated admiration for those pioneers of long distance solo flying in the twenties and thirties, like Amy Johnson, Alec Henshaw, Australian Bert Hinkler, and many others, who took off to fly to the other end of the world with little more than a school atlas. And this done in single-engined aircraft, frail in the extreme, and landing at intermediate points having little in the way of facilities or spare parts, etc.

Our course instructors were 'time-expired' pilots, Flt/Lt Heinbuck, a Canadian and Flt/Lt Edwards, brother of 'Jimmie' Edwards, who was also on the station and flew us as a 'Staff Pilot' on our actual flying exercises. (More of 'Jimmie' later). I think we started about thirty in number, and having got hold of the essentials by which to get an aircraft to its planned destination in more or less the shortest line, or as the 'crow flies', with the added luxury of knowing where it was a any given point in the flight, together with a reasonable accurate estimation of it's ETA (estimated time of arrival). This always being a desirable bit of information in case of running out of fuel, etc, we spent a lot of time on realistic planned classroom exercises.

It was easy to understand that if the bearing of the destination is taken of a chart, e.g. 050 degrees, the compass course, when adjusted for variation, etc, would also be the equivalent of 050 degrees, provided that there was no wind to deflect the aircraft from it's course, and of course, the pilot flew to the standard that pilots are supposed to fly to!

As with most things, however, there is a 'fly in the ointment'. The sky is a turbulent, restless creature, highly unpredictable and rarely in repose. An aircraft is merely a toy to be tossed and deflected by the slightest perturbation of the movement of the air masses. The recently expressed theory, regarded with suspicion and even ridicule by most, is the 'Chaos' Theory', but this captures the essential feel of the situation. This states, in effect that if a butterfly flaps it's wings in, say Tokyo, the eventual outcome could be a cyclone in the southern United States. Highly fanciful but it captures the vagaries and the unpredictably of our enveloping atmosphere.

So, in short, it is up to the navigator to be familiar with the territory into which he treads, by absorbing as much knowledge of the known variables as his capacity permits, and be deft enough to ply his trade with confidence and speed to combat not the 'enemy' but rather more like what is a sporting adversary.

However, the matter rests not there. Knowledge of what goes on is only the primary tool in the exercise. There are many more less tangible factors at play in this game of aircraft navigation, unfortunately not easily defined or set down for calm and methodical analysis. After easy familiarity with the 'air' is achieved there then comes, quite gradually, a feeling of comfort and understanding with these nebulous and invisible currents of the air, and an indefinable awareness of 'position' starts to become built into the equation.

However, the format of the bulk of our work in this subject, once we were acquainted with the basic procedures and the sequence of application, was to carry out long and increasingly difficult 'cross-country' navigation exercise in the relatively peaceful and quiet environment of the class-room. We were given detailed instructions for these imaginary flights, together with realistic 'weather reports', and had to firstly complete the 'Flight Plan', showing the courses over the different sectors, 'estimated times of arrival', etc.

Once 'airborne' however, the flight became somewhat complex, as the forecast winds were found to be the work of a most incompetent weather forecaster who was also, apparently, learning his 'trade'! Our early confidence and perhaps casual efforts soon became dispelled, and even a certain amount of panic ensued when we found our 'aircraft' to be miles off course without obvious reason. The vital and life-saving factor was to find, after being given a 'pin-point' en route, the actual winds experienced over the flight, and use this, plus our judgement on the winds over the next sector, to make fresh calculation of the course to fly to head towards our destination. Our desks were fairly close together, and although we were not the types to 'crib' (were we not the 'cream'!) there was much low key muttering between us about wind speed and direction available for those who were in real trouble and heading for disaster.

These exercises gradually became more demanding by introducing such things as diversions in mid-flight to an alternative destination, flying a series of complex courses to locate targets or missing aircraft etc, but we all enjoyed them immensely, particularly when our efforts resulted in arriving at our destination on course and the time we had estimated. I think none of us thought to complement the authors of these exercise, life was not like that in those days, but looking back, they must have put a lot of time and imagination into their preparation.

Flying Training

On February 2nd, 1943, in Anson Aircraft W1508, with our Course Instructor Flt/Lt 'Jimmie' Edwards as pilot, I had my first opportunity to be a real Aircraft Navigator. We took off at 0930 hours and landed 2 hours 45 minutes later having flown the exercise Base—Collingwood—Kincardine—Base. As in most of our trips, we flew at about 5,000 feet, airspeed about 120 knots, and the air was it's usual crisp and cold self for Canada at that time of the year. Also, as usual in these aircraft, after take-off, the undercarriage had to be wound up — 120 fairly strenuous turns of a handle not very well designed for this purpose — and happily delegated by the pilot to any other person in the aeroplane.

I had done well in the run of the classroom exercises described previously and attended the pre-flight briefing for this flight, with confidence, quickly completing my flight plan for the route and had my equipment stored and ready for action. Off we went, climbing for altitude over the aerodrome and a rapid check of my flight plan revealed the first course to give the pilot to head us to Collingwood. This done, I took up my duty for the next phase of the operation, that being to 'map-read' and find a pin-point on the ground that would enable me to check our course, find the actual wind (as against that given to us by the weather-forecaster), do my navigation tricks and keep us on course.

Peering intently at the slow moving ground, I soon recognised a prominent and unmistakable point. Good, I thought, but a quick reference to my chart to check our progress revealed that instead of being more or less on 'track' we were way off to one-side, and heading for where I knew not. At this point, my mind, despite the long hours of 'armchair navigation' which had given me a very good grasp of the technique, totally 'melted down' and I sat there like a 'stunned mullet', totally incapable of knowing what to do next, having what may be termed 'lost the plot'. Quite a few deep breaths later I came to my senses and took remedial action to bring us back on course, and although shaken by my 'moment of mental aberration', I have no memory of experiencing such a totally confused moment in an aircraft ever again.

Happy Birthday to Me

From then on, the flying programme was quite intensive, some kind of exercise or other being planned for almost every day, but it took some 'hours' in the air before we were deemed to be let loose into the air at night. A particularly memorable trip was on 22nd February 1943, when we took off at 10:05 hours, and flew the training route, Base — Barry — Port Perry — Milton West — Base and landed at 12:35 hours. I note that I flew as 'u/t Wireless Operator', and I recall the absolutely penetrating cold of the Canadian winter as I sat at the operating position doing my thing with the 1082/1083 radio equipment. Not able to move at all away from the set, all my bones, etc. seemed to lock solid, and to achieve at least a little respite from this agonising coldness, I stuck first one hand down the side of my flying boots and than the other hand. But to little noticeable relief, and at the end of the trip, it was considerable difficulty that I was able to 'de-plane'. It crossed my mind then that this was a peculiar way to spend my 21st birthday, when in more peaceful times, a party would have been in order and a 'key of the door' presented to me on attaining my maturity. Reflecting on the situation since, I realise that I was indeed very lucky, as a relatively early entrant to the RAF, to have reached the ripe old age of twenty-one, as it was not unknown for the more 'on-on' type to have reached the rank of Squadron Leader by then, with a large proportion of his vintage having 'got the chop' before acquiring maturity.

We flew the length and breadth of our little bit of Ontario and got to know it very well. So much so that it appeared that more often than not, those trusty old Anson Aircraft had a nose for where we were supposed to be going and were kind enough to make life a little more easy for us. However, one day great excitement spread around the camp when a night flying aircraft was reported overdue, The weather, not always correctly predicted, had turned 'nasty', with snow showers and winds, and 'one of our aircraft' with pilot and four trainees on board had not returned on schedule, and, more significantly, no radio report had been heard.

To us trainees, of course, this raised, some consternation, although not to a degree of anxiety but more of excitement or thrill about our activities in the air, with the reality that it could be dangerous. It was next day that the mystery was put to rest when news was received that the aircraft had become lost in the bad weather, and, with fuel running short, the pilot was obliged to make his difficult choice of action. They all carried parachutes and having detected signs of civilisation below in the form of indistinct lights, he instructed the trainees to 'bale out' — not an easy task from the Anson, which meant crawling through the side window and sliding down the wing — which they all did with no injury on landing.

The pilot, who would have had difficulty in getting to the rear of the aircraft to make a safe exit, decided to force land the aircraft, and was assisted by motorists, on hearing the aircraft circling overhead, using their headlights to give him a rough direction to land. He also 'got away with it' unharmed and I think we all benefited from this incident, in that we realised that all was not necessarily lost when things were not going to plan in the air.

By a remarkable coincidence, in about the year 1949, when living in Wimbledon, south west London, I was in the High Street going to the railway station when an approaching figure caught my attention. Out of uniform, we all looked less conspicuous but something clicked and I realised that this was one of the trainees who had baled out those years before. We had a chat, congratulated each other on having survived our operational flying and away we went our separate ways.

As we were training as 'observers', the old-fashioned Air Force term for the crew member who handled almost all other duties in the air other than flying the aircraft, on graduation we would, with due ceremony, have the insignia of a half brevet in the form of the letter 'O' and one flapping wing, pinned to our proudly thrust out chest, by a senior Officer — a great moment in an airman's life. (Alas, in my case, I was suffering from a heavy bout of bronchitis and was only vaguely aware of what was happening at our 'Wings Parade'.)

The aircrew category of 'observer' was shortly afterwards superseded by the title 'navigator/wireless operator' as the heavy bombers demanded even more specialisation in aircrew duties, with their crews split into navigator, wireless operator, flight engineer, bomb aimer and air gunners. Early in the war, there were two pilots on the heavies; the captain, known as the 'pilot in charge' and the co-pilot known as the 'second dickie'. This second pilot was later removed, with the introduction of the grade of 'bomb aimer', who was almost always an aircrew candidate who had not made the grade as a pilot but who had undergone quite an extensive amount of pilot training and who could, in an emergency control and possibly land an aircraft whose pilot had become incapacitated.

To cover the two main aspects of our aircrew duties, we flew more or less alternatively as either navigator or as wireless operator. Our part of Ontario was pretty flat so one of the principle hazards of flying, that of 'controlled fight into terrain' was not really a great problem. What was a problem was the cold and also the fatigue from which our 'staff pilots' seemed to suffer, with the intensive routine of flying day and night. This was amply demonstrated to me one dark night, when 'stooging' at about 5,000 feet and the usually unvarying 105 knots, along one of the training routes, all seemed to be going to plan and the required track being nicely maintained. I'm not sure what prompted my awareness — perhaps my guardian angel — but a slight, but significant change in the noise in the aircraft caught my ear. There was little lighting in the plane to facilitate observing the ground for 'fixes', but a glance towards the pilot revealed him slumped comfortably down in his seat with has head on his chest.

At our age, the possibility of a heart attack was as remote as putting a man on the moon, so a vigorous pummel brought him quickly around, with the aircraft just about to exceed the 'never exceed speed' tag fixed in all aircraft at a point very visible to the pilot. The Air Force motto *'per ardua ad astra'* — meaning, roughly, 'the way to the stars is heavy going' (and fraught with unforeseen snags, in my opinion!) should perhaps take cognisance of pilots going to sleep before you get there!

Our Anson aircraft were the very old Mk. 1s, the interior sparse in the extreme, with the tubular metal framework totally exposed to view.

Toilet facilities were somewhat Spartan also, the traditional procedure adopted by aircrew, perhaps from the most early days, was that one had a quick 'leak' beside — but not on! — the aircraft immediately before climbing on board (vital in our case, as the penetrating cold played havoc even with our young and presumably flexible bladders), with recourse, in flight, to a funnel and tube, which undoubtedly caused the good citizens of Ontario to exercise caution when looking up to observe aircraft passing overhead!

The intense cold produced an even more personal hazard, in that the funnel was not over-large and the tube to the outside of the aircraft was small in diameter. Having held on for as long physically possible — perhaps in the middle of a bit of tricky navigation — a sudden and rapid flow tended to hit the 'toilet equipment' at a volume not anticipated by it's presumably desk-bound designer, where it instantly froze and overflowed. Continuing the rest of the flight with wet and soggy flying boots was not very comfortable!

Our training routes were mostly 'dog legs' of about three hours duration, overflying such towns as Chatham, Owen Sound, Guelph, Sarnia, etc, but we made no landings at any point other than our base, Hamilton. The countryside was fairly well populated, with villages and hamlets and at night, it was a pretty sight as we plodded our slow path between these and other points. It took me a little while, strangely enough, to get the hang of being physically aware of our position, by noting an identifiable point on the ground and transferring this to the navigation chart and making the required alteration to the course to be flown from that point onwards.

The two aspects didn't seem to blend very readily but having overcome this strange 'mental block' I was fortunate in that I developed a good sense of 'location' which stood me in good stead later when navigating over the North Sea to Norway and the Dutch Frisian Islands with no tangible 'pin-points' available and recourse having to be made to the look and texture of the sea and the 'white-tops' or 'flying horses' as they were known.

The flying was quite intense, with many days involved in carrying out two 'sorties' each of three hours, which also involved the time to be spent on preparing the Flight Plan, and getting to and from the aircraft. I think most of us found it a bit of hard slog, particularly if one trip was done early in the evening, taking off at about 2000 hours, followed by another trip departing after midnight. I was about to write that in the total flying time of about 160 hours, I never experienced an engine failure in flight, but a look in my logbook shows one flight terminated through 'port engine u/s, returned to base'. Not bad considering the age of the planes and the problems of maintenance in such a cold climate.

Our intensely desired flying brevet was just about within our grasp, with the completion of the flying programme but we had the final hurdle of the written examinations. I think we all suffered — mostly in silence — facing the wide variety of subjects in which we had to achieve a certain pass mark. For some, of course their academic ability prior to joining the Air Force, was solidly based, but for the likes of me, and I think my ability was more like the average, these examinations were faced with much trepidation. We all felt competent to navigate in the air, but in such subjects such as meteorology, which in a written paper demanded a certain literary fluency, the spirit quailed a bit. Anyway, 'nothing ventured, nothing gained' so away we went to give of our best.

The elation of those of us who were successful was greatly tempered by the despondency of the six or so who didn't qualify, and the parting from such good mates, who we had known for a fair period of time was quite a wrench. It is hard to describe or explain the close companionship that we young men built up in relatively short space of time. Because of the sifting of the recruiting process, we were all of similar background, physical ability, general interests etc. and we bonded together like a swarm of bees! Those unsuccessful as navigators, however, had another chance, to become 'bomb aimers' and they went off to the bombing and gunnery schools where the specialisation was more narrow. In this grade they almost all wound up in Bomber Command on Lancasters, Halifaxes or Stirlings and suffered very severe losses in 1942 and 1943.

Some twelve of us moved on to the next phase of our training, half of us promoted to sergeants, including me, and the other half to the very smart rank of pilot officer. We were all extremely proud, and the drama of the Wings Parade, which no airman can ever forget, with the step forward to the Air Commodore for a congratulatory handshake and salute is still easily re-called. The Officer graduates wore the observer brevet only whereas we NCOs retained on our arm the wireless Operator's insignia and this somewhat unusual combination of aircrew qualifications raised interest from the more observant students of aeronautical matters.

Competent to guide aeroplanes over land, we were now called upon to achieve the same ability over the un-marked seas and to this end, we made our way to the East Coast of Canada.

CHARLOTTETOWN, PRINCE EDWARD ISLAND
NO. 31 SCHOOL OF GENERAL RECONNAISSANCE
JUNE/JULY 1943

Some nine training flights, in the faithful old Anson of a vintage perhaps even more archaic than those at Hamilton, each of about three hours duration, over the Gulf of St Lawrence, gave us the opportunity to learn to read the wind and the waves. The main technique, used by the 'ancient' aviators in the early days of long distance record-breaking attempts, was to master the art of 'track-crawling'. It is self evident that there is great benefit in flying along the desired track to be made instead of wandering off to either side and subsequently making many large changes of course to get back on track.

Careful and diligent use of the 'drift recorder' in all but dead calm and glassy seas, allows this to be done with ease. Practice is necessary, however, to also interpret the signs on the sea surface—the 'wind lanes', 'white horses' and general swell and surge of the sea, to deduce the wind direction and speed and so calculate the actual winds being encountered and from these deduce the 'ground speed' of the aircraft and the estimated time of arrival at a destination point, this latter point being very important as most flights involve several changes of 'track'.

Destined as we were, for searching the seas for enemy ships and attacking them and reporting back to base to enable further operations to be mounted, we were introduced to quite tricky bits of navigational techniques, known as 'creeping line ahead', 'square search', and an even more precise exercise 'radius of action to a moving base'. These terms all have, to me, a quite adventurous ring, but it was necessary to work at high speed to do all the intricate calculations to carry out these well designed and proven techniques. The basic principle was to sweep the sea in a regular and ordered fashion to ensure that all the area was covered within the limits of the visibility appertaining at the time, and this involved many rapid changes of course.

Remarkably, when the full might of the Allied Forces was assembled for the invasion of Europe on 6th June 1944, the 'creeping line ahead' technique reared it's head as a vital part of the whole massive exercise. In order to extend the 'decoy' plans to fool the enemy as to where the landings were planned to take place, the four-engined aircraft of Bomber Command, mostly Lancasters, flew an extensive area of the English Channel, using the creeping line ahead navigational technique and dropping, in a specific pattern, 'window' to simulate the approach of a vast number of ships. It all added to the confusion of that historical day, and may have, knowing the strange quirks of such seemingly small or even insignificant parts of large puzzles, played a more than credited part in the success of this mammoth movement of men and machines perhaps never before achieved or likely to be repeated in the future.

It was mid-summer, and despite the limited time that we were off-duty, we managed to get some short glimpse of the delights of Charlotte Town. Not a very big city, and I am unable to recall little other than having a swim in the very cold water on a sandy beach. As usual in the Services, places and people are quickly awarded nicknames or abbreviated names, some pleasant and acceptable, with others of a more scurrilous ring. This City was known as 'Harlot Town' but, as I recall — and I think it would have stuck in my mind — I could neither prove or otherwise the veracity of this moniker!

The *pièce de resistance* of our training at Charlotte Town was the 'Dawn Patrol'. 'Dawn Patrol?' I hear you say, 'On an island tucked away in the Gulf of St Lawrence? Shades of the 'Battle of Britain? With Anson aircraft? Well it wasn't as absurd as it sounds, as not a great deal of publicity had been given to the situation on the eastern seaboard of North America, of events after the entry of the United States into the conflict. The USA and Britain were ill-prepared, strangely enough, for the far-reaching strike abilities of the German Navy and a vast amount of shipping, plying the east coast was sunk very quickly and efficiently by submarines and surface raiders.

Oil Tankers took a particularly severe hammering and within a relatively short distance from the coast and the Gulf of St Lawence (the entrance to which we had diligently learnt to 'track crawl') was a happy hunting ground for enterprising German skippers whose dedication and 'risk-taking' was, by then, legendary. However, the tide eventually turned against them and it was established after the war that of some 30,000 men who had served in 'U' Boats, approximately 28,000 were killed.

Having regard to all the above, we approached our 'dawn patrol' with some seriousness, and even a touch of 'lets get at 'em'. With pilot F/L Thwaites, we took off at 0403 on 7th July 1943, with two 500lb depth charges under the wooden wings of our Anson to our patrol 'cross-over to North Point' and landed 2 hours 45 minutes later with 'nil' sighting report. It was a start, after all.

Once more it was to pack up the old kit-bag and tackle the next phase of our training, but first we had to head East back across the North Atlantic, and our transporting ship awaited our pleasure in its berth at New York.

EAST ACROSS THE NORTH ATLANTIC – JULY 1943

Troop movements in the services are based on long experience and higgledy-piggledy, ad hoc kind of 'sideways' trips avoided wherever possible. So to get to New York, we were routed back to the not inspiring 'disposal centre' at Moncton, New Brunswick, to join the throng of the output of newly qualified aircrew of all designations, and from many parts of Canada, to make up a 'draft' and then be on our way.

The train trip from there, to New York, although not very comfortable physically, was most interesting. Passing down through the maritime states of Maine, New Hampshire, Connecticut, in glorious summer weather, with so many old and interesting things to see was quite an experience. I recall seeing the towers and buildings of Yale University and the countryside was mature and green. Our approach to New York was somewhat circuitous and we skirted to the west and arrived at some railway sidings, with a relatively long view of the skyscrapers (a lovely word, when you think about it) and in 1943, with most of the world still unsullied by rampant tourism, we were greatly impressed to see what to all of us had been hitherto only a dream. Little time was wasted, and we were soon on board our 'ocean liner', by means of 'lighters' to cross the short span of water, but as we got closer to this 'leviathan of the deep', it's immense size became more apparent.

It was the good ship *Aquitania*, a bit long in the tooth, but still capable of giving the dreaded *unterzeeboots* a run for their money. Probably 40,000 or 50,000 tons burthen, we soon discovered that it held a *lot* of people. We RAF men were overwhelmed in number by the arrival of the American servicemen destined to become part of the invasion force of 'D' Day on June 6th, 1944 who joined us soon afterwards. When we set sail I would estimate that there were some 15,000 men on board. I have many times since, wondered how many of these men, who appeared to me to be mostly young and naive farm boys, survived that decisive day and the subsequent thrust through Europe before the battle was finally won.

Once on board, we RAF were allocated our 'quarters' for the trip. The ship had many promenade decks, almost circling the length of the ship, with an area and width of perhaps ten feet across, and this was where we set ourselves up. In an almost continuous line next to the bulkheads, and around the ship were two rows of bunks, four beds high, with a gap between the bunks and the bulkhead of a couple of feet. This small space held our kit bags and other personal bits and pieces. This was to be our lot for the three or four days voyage. Ablutions were carried out whenever and however the very basic facilities allowed, but with the immense number of personnel on board, the eating arrangements were the most fundamental. It was not possible to sacrifice space to provide a mess, so the procedure was to get in line, grab what was offered and hunker down to eat at the most suitable spot available. The whole voyage, seemingly, was spent in this queue, which was never-ending.

The departure from New York was very stylish. We were all thrilled to see the Statue of Liberty as we sailed down the Hudson River in glorious September weather, and we soon became 'buddies' with the Yanks. The decks were literally a sea of that subtle shade of brown of the American Army uniforms, sitting, lounging, lying everywhere and on anything which offered a vestige of comfort.

But the predominant emotion was excitement, as can only be felt when enveloped in a large crowd of young men, all spurred on with the infectious drive that results from feeling confident in the training completed and the physical well-being of youth, and all heading for the unimaginable adventures of war that lay ahead. It also seemed, however, a long way to Europe, but a sea cruise like this, which our respective governments had so thoughtfully provided, free, gratis and for nothing, was not to be sneezed at!

Naturally, we provided a juicy target for the dead keen 'U' Boat commanders, as we sallied forth on the initial part of the trip, with their promotion guaranteed and the honour of the Knight of the Grand Cross—or similar—to be pinned up by Admiral Raeder himself, no doubt, if we could be held in their periscope's cross-wires long enough for a decent shot. The broad area of the approaches to New York, was the obvious place to hang about in this hope, but we Allies were also a touch cunning, and as we entered the open sea, we were escorted by a number of semi-rigid 'dirigibles' that circled around us.

The whole affair was a glorious sight as we settled down to 'ship-board routine' in somewhat restricted space. As on all sea voyages, a strange ripple of empathy, perhaps, flutters around the fellow sailors, and like finds like in a quite unerring fashion. The dominant pastime on this trip was the game of 'craps', otherwise known as 'dice' or 'seven-eleven'. Groups sprang up all over the decks and there was much shouting and excitement as, to us poor 'erks' in the RAF, money in unimaginable amounts changed hands at lightning speed. The rules of the game are fairly basic and simple but I for one found I could not keep up with the dice rolls, the calls and the constant exchange of dollars. Many groups continued in this fashion throughout the voyage, with no apparent break for food or other requirements.

I have no clear recollection of seeing other ships, in the several days it took us to reach Glasgow, I think we docked at Gourock or Greenock, but travelling at very high speed, with regular changes of course, it would have been difficult for even the fastest navy ships, like destroyers, to keep up with us. What had a long lasting impression on me, however, was the apparent miniaturisation of British trains and railway carriages that seemed to have taken place while I was away in

Canada. The tiddly little things that met us on the docks after the massive beasts of the Canadian Railways, struck me as totally absurd.

Postings, movements and transfers (call them what you will) in the services never operate in a 'straight line', or even from A to B. It almost always involve a detour through what was known as a 'disposal centre', perhaps not the most sensitive term, but there was not really a great deal of time for delicate feelings in those hectic days. So our next place of rest, while the paper work was sorted out was to Yorkshire.

AIRCREW RECEPTION CENTRE
HARROGATE, YORKSHIRE — JULY 1943

And what a dignified place this was, despite the rigours and wholesale commandeering of stately homes which had taken place to house the thousands of men now under arms. After our sea passage and the somewhat brash Canadian way if life — and the climate — it was like a step back to Victorian times. Our billet was a huge mansion, perhaps built by one of the early canny Yorkshire mill owners. It was, of course, denuded of any hint of the finery or the luxurious fittings and paintings which gentlemen of that era thought necessary to establish their place in society (not that I blame them — they deserved the fruits of their enterprise).

It looked as genteel as those pictures on chocolate boxes, and the behaviour and appearance of the many airmen who strolled about appeared to be in keeping with the general ambience of the place. Brand new brevets, which denoted a future role as aircrew, were much in evidence.

I think it was at this point in training, after overcoming the early rigours of training and the harsh words of our drill instructors, and 'keeping our heads down' to pass the many courses of instruction we had so far survived, that I became aware of an unspoken respect — perhaps gratitude — reflected in our contact with the general public. This is not to say that all was rosy, there were 'dust-ups' of course, when the favours of the more attractive (and desirable) young ladies were open to competition, between us and the unfortunate young bloods who wore neither uniform or, more importantly, had the status of potential flyers.

Maybe we had about us that heady hint of danger, and it was well established by this time, that the young ladies referred to, were not averse to being more generous with their favours, when regaled with stories—and some were extremely fanciful—of our adventures in the air. I am almost embarrassed to recall some of the more questionable techniques, employed by the more boastful, in order to 'have their wicked way'. I personally thought this to be a touch unscrupulous and undeserving conduct of a future 'officer and gentleman'. Whether the ladies thought this too, I am still not sure.

To occupy our time while the 'postings ' were finalised—the Administrative people must have had prior advice of our arrival date—we went, in squads of about twenty men, on not too long route marches into the delightful countryside around Harrogate. These I greatly enjoyed, with a 'sing-along' as we went and our discipline sergeants at ease with us now we were well into the service routines and relationships. The leafy lanes and the bird songs and the rhythm and cadence of our marching brought about a wonderful feeling of unity and relaxation, and this phase I remember with particular pleasure.

There's 'many a slip between cup and lip', and one of these nearly ended my long journey to fly in action. My good mate Les Gee and I had been training together for some time, and with a bit of time off, we ventured to nearby Knaresborough, a small village where there was a river, some rather nice waterfalls and one could go punting. It was pleasant on the water, poling ourselves along in grand style, but in an unguarded moment, Les swung his pole and clobbered me in the eye with the end of it. I thought, with the impact of the pain, that I was seriously, if not mortally wounded, but fortunately the end of the pole must have had a small cavity and that saved my eye from serious and perhaps permanent injury. Nevertheless, the variety of colours which emerged the next day were startling in the extreme.

Our stay here was quite short, perhaps just over a week and the next posting was to complete more flying training, but it gave opportunity to adjust to the austere kind of life in Britain, in food only simple in variety, blackout, congestion, and weak beer, etc...

NO. 3 SCHOOL OF GENERAL RECONNAISSANCE
SQUIRES GATE, BLACKPOOL, LANCASHIRE
SEPTEMBER—OCTOBER, 1943.

For me, this was a return visit to the environs of Blackpool. The airport is some few miles to the south of that city, and it was a poor navigator who could fail to glimpse the landmark of the tower when heading for home, as it rather gave the game away.

The basis of the flying exercises was a very similar to those carried out at Prince Edward Island in Canada, although with the different weather conditions to cope with in the Irish Sea. The major hurdle was to carry out navigation and radio operating duties at the same time. After a couple of familiarisation trips it became very apparent to me that this was a full time job—no time to waste. On take off, after setting up the radio frequencies and establishing the first course for the pilot to steer, it was our duty to wind up the undercarriage—a damn chore!—let out the radio trailing aerial, and almost simultaneously send a radio departure message to aircraft control station.

Our training routes took us around the Irish Sea, with the Isle of Man more or less the dead centre point, with Ballyquinton Point on the coast of Northern Island seemingly a favourite target for the route planners. The Irish Sea is notorious for its roughness—few survive a crossing without recourse to the paper bags or a quick dash to the rail of the ship—but our trips were pleasant enough in the mildness of the English autumn. From my log book, I see that some relatively involved navigation was on our programme, including;

- Diversion to fictitious vessel (I trust I found that space in the sea where it was reputed to be.)

- H/F D/F Sighting Reports (be one of our principal duties on 'ops' when on reconnaissance flights, to report enemy ships)

- Most importantly, radio exercises to obtain 'radio fixes' and the universally known QDM, that course to steer which will take you back to your aerodrome.

The use of the 'Flashing Light Beacons' and 'Pundits' at fixed points on the ground and coast line, sending Morse Code letters to provide identification and so a 'fix'.

The practical use of the aircraft camera—another important part of our main duties—by taking 'twelve oblique photographs of the coast of the Isle of Man.'

This phase passed pleasantly enough but it seemed a long haul away from my earlier visit to Blackpool, the massive throng of recruits in the initial stage of training and the jam-packed dance floor at the Empress Ballroom, the rendezvous point for young and lusty airmen and young (and also lusty) lady mill workers from Lancashire. A more volatile mix would be hard to imagine!

I was pleased with my assessment on completion of the course, and then, as always in the service, it was time to 'pack up and go'—and away we went to our next station, this time to experience aeroplanes with some real punch, and also to meet our pilots.

NO. 132 OPERATIONAL TRAINING UNIT
EAST FORTUNE, EAST LOTHIAN, SCOTLAND
NOVEMBER, 1943—JANUARY 1944

By comparison with my last years 'wintering', at Hamilton in Ontario Canada, where the temperature went way down below zero and, provided there was no wind it was comfortable to walk around in normal uniform, this new abode was punishing to the point of sheer misery. The East winds off the North Sea swept across the station with little respite, perhaps it was the dampness that exaggerated the cold, and unlike the more 'civilised' way of living across the Atlantic, there was no central heating. In fact there was little heating of any kind.

But many things compensated for this shortcoming, and although difficult to define I can only conclude that it was the discovery of my affinity for almost all things 'Scottish'. This empathy became more pronounced, with further time spent in Scotland for more training, and is still strongly felt even today. With no attempt at psychological analysis, I feel, nevertheless that it stems back to about 1935. At that time, as a 'nipper', with my family being railway employees, they were able to obtain, when taking their annual holiday, free travel to anywhere in Britain.

Living in the centre of England, at Derby, the furthest distance to take advantage of this munificent offer (their wages were not overly generous), was to either Lands End or to the top of Scotland to the small village called John o' Groats. Perhaps they spun a coin, perhaps to the North offered a better bargain, so off we went and wound our rather slow way—I think it took a couple of days—up and across the Scottish hills and highlands, in our party of half a dozen intrepid Uncles, Aunts, Granny and Grandpa. The luxury and delicacy of my first taste of fresh smoked salmon — we lived somewhat austerely at home — still lingers and, like the salmon returning to spawn in it's home waters so the call of Scotland lingers within my spirit.

For we sergeant navigators, the first part of the exercise after 'settling in' was to meet the group of pilots with whom we were to 'crew up' and commence the flying exercises. This point of our lives was most significant. Here we were, two disparate groups of men, from many different countries, many different backgrounds, ages, experience, education, etc, and with greatly different training, ability etc, in respect of flying, but being obliged to cast our lot together for the good (and survival) of each other and the best operational performance that we could achieve.

This was a 'moment in time' for both our groups, so much so that I was constrained, in the recent past, to try to express the strength of feeling that became evident in trying to 'pick a partner' with whom to face the rigours of the next bit of our lives, operational flying itself. Some years ago I wrote an article entitled 'It Took Two to Tango in a Beaufighter' and was honoured when it was published in *Air Mail*, the Journal of the Royal Air Force Association, resulting in world-wide distribution. Several personal letters were sent on to me, from readers, also re-counting the delicacy, and humour arising in the matching of pilots and navigators to best advantage. I need say no more on this particular aspect other than I was extremely fortunate to be blessed with a 'happy marriage' by crewing-up with Jeff McCarrison of the Royal New Zealand Air Force, to whom I owe a very great deal and of whom more will later be written.

We started our Operational Flying Exercises (OFEs) at the end of February, 1943 and these consisted largely of flying quite long distances out over the North Sea, in large triangular format, in order to consolidate our ability to 'track-crawl' and at the same time doing all the other things that were pertinent to our type of operational demands. This included such things as taking photographs of specific points on the coast, carrying out fairly complex search procedures, many radio exercise, importantly the ones to be able to get back to base in bad weather, etc.

One exercise comes vividly to mind. Our role was to attack ships, using torpedoes and 20mm cannon, and to get practice in this somewhat skilful operation. It required much finesse by the pilot but none by the Navigator, other than he had to watch out for other aircraft pursuing the same objective and rather prone to forget the fact that their near neighbour was in the line of fire, unless he yelped rather excitedly to advise avoiding action. The target for these 'dummy runs' was a stately old Royal Navy cruiser, which submitted to the onslaught of a gaggle of earnest young Beaufighter pilots, all intent on recording with their cine cameras the proof of their prowess. And what a wonderful sight this cruiser made, a decent bow-wave in evidence and the blue of the North Sea, and the winter sun shining.

Perhaps the attacks were a bit ragged—it was, after all, early days for our pilots, still getting used to handling a somewhat difficult aircraft to fly—and they had been warned of the 'high speed mush', which necessitated care in pulling up out of a diving attack. Sitting in the back of the plane, it was really exhilarating, with aircraft seemingly coming from all directions, and the high speed run in close proximity to the ship, and the pull up and away really gave a tremendous kick.

Very sadly, one of the new crews was killed when carrying out night 'circuits and bumps'. I am, even today, still impressed with the adaptability of our pilots of those days, who generally had not too many flying hours, all in aircraft of fairly simple characteristics, with initial training done in dual-control cockpits. There were no dual control Beaufighter aircraft, which were a dramatic step up in sophistication and noted for their idiosyncrasies in handling, particularly a strong tendency to 'swing' on take-off, demanding instant corrective action, which could only be learnt from personal experience of this phenomenon.

As I recall, the new pilots were given a run-down of the cockpit layout, a few trips standing behind the instructor and then, presumably with a casual wave of the hand from the instructor, taxied to the end of the runway and gave it 'stick'. Remarkably, it seemed to work and I salute the 'on-on' spirit of those earnest young men who became capable of handling what was, for it's day, a very potent aeroplane.

The pilot of the crew that was killed very soon after we arrived, had, at this time, very little experience. He stalled at point down the runway and the aircraft flipped and dropped on top of a hangar, killing them both instantly. The navigator was younger than most and his parents came to attend his funeral, with burial arranged in the local churchyard, which was redolent of times gone by, with tombstones dating back many years and a place of peace and quiet in some contrast to the lively bustle and noise of the aerodrome. Being about six feet in height, I found myself delegated to be one of the pall bearers, which was of course a totally unexpected new experience, but all part of the happenings of those times.

The weather was, unfortunately, most unpleasant for the occasion, with rain falling in a steady drizzle, and when our burial party arrived at the grave-side, we were thoroughly wet and not a touch miserable. The parents of the navigator were young, their son being perhaps hardly twenty years old, and they were extremely distressed, standing by the side of the freshly dug grave. Grief, and the need for us not to show too much emotion — in those days the 'stiff upper lip' was really the only way to cope with the stress of the ever present dangers — provided a strange mixture.

The outcome of this provided a memory that is still remarkably vivid even today. At a point in the ceremony, the RAF bugler raised his bugle to sound the 'last post'. All would have been well, but unfortunately the steady falling rain had entered his bugle unbeknownst. Instead of the clear and ringing notes so well known to all, the effect of the rain was dramatic and unexpected. The noise was not of this world, in pitch, clarity or substance but a kind of half strangled cry of a wounded animal.

Next to me, a fellow pallbearer was a New Zealand pilot, and it would not be unkind to describe him as a 'not overly sensitive' person. On hearing this grotesque parody of the first note of the solemn piece, he started to quiver. At first I thought it was perhaps the emotion of the occasion. But then I realised that it was mirth being restrained with a superhuman effort. Fortunately, it did not infect the others of our party, to the same degree but I'm sure we all had to grit our teeth to hold it in.

It was, of course, partly a response to our own hidden fears — after all to attend the funeral of colleagues at that point in our careers could have been no boost to our general morale. However, the human mind is full of nifty tricks to fool the conscious part of the brain, and some mechanism emerges to cope with the fear of annihilation. The flying part of the services had been very forthcoming from the early days, when to take to the air in the most flimsy contraption was asking for trouble. As a consequence, many euphemisms had been invented and by this point in our training, we had adopted them as a protective shield It was infra dig to speak of being killed, you had the choice of: 'going for a Burton', 'getting the chop' 'caught by the Grim Reaper' etc.

East Fortune was quite a historical aerodrome. It had been the point of departure of the Airship, the R.34 in 1932 on its flight to the United States and return, which was very successfully performed, not, however, without some drama, as it was necessary for some hardy crew members to crawl onto the tailplane in mid-Atlantic to repair rents in the fabric. The Station had about it the feel of aviation activity, and was more sprawling than most. To get around we were able to use bicycles, over the not inconsiderable distances and with the blasts of the icy winds, arrival at the destination was usually with numbed hands and face and tears streaming from the eyes.

The long distance exercises over the 'uncharted' North Sea were taxing for both pilot and navigator. 'George' the automatic pilot was not fitted in the Beaufighter and this demanded constant concentration by the pilot, with a careful watch of the instruments and engine performance. This latter aspect was vital, as the ability of the 'Beau' to maintain height, over a long distance on one engine was not of the best, although Mac and I never lost an engine in the whole time that we flew together, a credit to the design of the 1650 horse power

Hercules radial engine. Whether Mac, sitting at the front exercised much worry as to the possibility of trying to return on one engine, I never discovered but I have no recollection of ever worrying about that happening.

In view of our ultimate role, that of attacking enemy ships at low level, and carrying out reconnaissance duties along the enemy coasts, we flew mostly at heights below a couple of thousand feet. The North Sea is almost always a boiling cauldron of turbulent air, with cloud going up many hundreds of feet and we had to maintain a view of the sea in order to observe and also to navigate. Just under cloud is not the place to be for a smooth passage, and the tossing and bumps which constantly rocked the aircraft were violent in the extreme. It was very difficult to put pencil to navigation chart with any degree of touch, as the point was either plunged into the chart or left above the paper. By this time, we all had a few hours under our belt and we coped pretty well, although one trip found me, for the second time in my flying career, ninety-nine percent incapacitated by air sickness.

After nearly five hours of hefty buffeting over the North Sea, it was necessary, on reaching landfall, to take oblique air photographs of a small railway station near our base aerodrome. This meant half a dozen or so high speed runs at low level, with the aircraft been thrown around for each consecutive run for the next photograph. This was the straw that did very unpleasant thins to my old gut, and with a heave and a ho, nature took it's course.

Mac was very sympathetic and found our way to base with me taking no interest whatsoever, death being preferable to the agony which overtook me. However, this seemed to purge my body and soul of the dreaded 'mal-de-air', and I thereafter enjoyed the rough and tumble of bad weather flying, even more so than any stately procession when flying conditions were literally as smooth as the proverbial babies bottom.

That turbulent and lonely North Sea is now a very different place. The end of the war marked a vast need for oil and to the amazement of many, there it was, lying about waiting to be 'reaped ' on our doorstep. After much and presumably difficult negotiations, and agreement to divide the spoils, that lonely sea is no longer lonely but alive with activity, with helicopters buzzing like bees over the solitary paths that we so earnestly traversed in our trusty old Beaufighters. We had no guide marks to find our way, the navigation aids did not stretch far across, but now the oil rigs, with massive superstructures, are like beacons beckoning across the waste of empty sea. Regrettably, there has been considerable loss of life, oil rigs and drilling down so many feet poses hazards which even the best of modern technology fail to eliminate. The loss of some 180 lives in the oil rig 'Piper Alpha' in the 1980s, shook the industry and brought about a system of commuting to and from the rigs, in an effort to reduce the dangers. The North Sea claimed so many lives during the war years, and now, perhaps, the continuing loss of life is it is a penalty that we humans have to pay for the demands of more and more material possessions.

The end of January 1944 marked our completion of the course, and with the magnificent total of sixty-five hours flying time behind us — I was again pleased with my Assessment — we were ready to move on, and Mac was due to learn the not very well known art of 'how to drop an aerial torpedo with the objective of sinking a ship'.

NO.1 TORPEDO TRAINING UNIT
TURNBERRY, AYRSHIRE SCOTLAND
FEBRUARY — MARCH, 1944

This was rather like a 'finishing school', to put the final touches on both pilot and navigator, although we really had no specific duties to learn, or perform and went along mostly for the ride. It was quite an exciting ride, to sweep along around the Firth of Clyde, with our pilots manoeuvring to get that desired optimum position from which to drop the deadly torpedo.

The 'torps' dropped, in these exercises were not, of course deadly, but known as 'runners'. They were 18 inches in diameter as opposed to the 21-inch diameter naval torpedoes and the head was filled with water, to get the correct balance. They were fitted with a small plywood tail to ensure the correct trajectory in flight, and set to 'run' under the target ship. After a suitable time interval, the air was automatically expelled from the nose and the torpedo rose to the surface, to be recovered by a team using a small motor boat.

The pilot had to fly to very strict parameters to ensure a successful drop, and this, together with the rather obvious need to have the correct position in relation to the target, demanded a flying skill rather more than most types of operations. The whole process was carried out at extremely low level, the initial approach to the target being made at some fifty feet above the sea. Each drop demanded a full supply of adrenalin and sweaty palms were not entirely unknown, particularly as the view from the navigator's seat in the back revealed the deadly dangers of the rapidly moving sea seemingly just beneath one's bottom.

The best approach to the target was from sixty degrees off the bow of the ship, in order to get the best 'comb' — if I remember the correct term — in that the closing angle of ship and torpedo would provide the best possibility of a hit. The aircraft had to be flown at 195 knots, 150 feet above the sea, straight and level, and the torpedo released 1,000 yards from the target. Put all this together as a 'workload' for the pilot and it is safe to say that he had his hands full. To determine the accuracy of our pilots in this intriguing technique, our aircraft were fitted with several cameras synchronised with the torpedo dropping mechanism.

Of course, on actual operations, while all this was carefully being established, the gunners on the target ship would not be idle, and would by this time have 'drawn a bead' on the rapidly approaching foe in order to check up on their marksmanship skills.

Another thing became apparent. With the aircraft flying at 195 knots, it took about ten seconds to cover the 1,000 yards to the ship, so there was no possibility, after dropping the torpedo, of turning tail to retrace the approach path as the gunners on the ship would have had a sitting target. The plan was, therefore to keep going over the target in the hope that the gunners would have by this time 'chickened out' and got their heads down. More of this in a later chapter...

The runway was situated right on the coast, with take-offs immediately over the sea, and into the broad expanse of the Clyde. It was pleasant flying, and I see from my log book that Mac and I did 35 'sorties' in just under one month (on one day we did five very quickly in a row). The Isle of Arran was a good backdrop to our flying, with the 'sugar lump'— the small island of Ailsa Craig always very close to our 'dummy runs'. The target ships were not large, but in true naval tradition they had the imaginative names for ships which reflects the perhaps more intellectual or sensitive standards of the naval officers. In this regard, there are many legion stories of the semaphore exchanges between ships, often in the most disastrous or hazardous situations, which capture so pertinently, the humour and inimitable style of the naval officers. Perhaps this is a legacy of the naval heroes of the past, like Cook and Nelson, who exercised with little apparent effort, a management and leadership style which could only be the envy of us lesser mortals.

To return to the theme of target ships. I see that we 'attacked', in quick succession, His Majesties ships, *Malahne, Heliopolis, Cardiff, Ramillies* and *Dido* — and what naval encounters of the past such names evoke. On return to base, the cameras were quickly relieved of the exposed film, which was processed and then analysed by several young, and I must say, very attractive, well educated and intelligent Womens Royal Air Force Officers. (I think there was not one man of our Course who did not harbour intense feelings of desire for these young ladies, who, though professing not to notice, would have been dumb in the extreme not to be aware of our tongue-tied flushes when they debriefed us after the drops.)

For simplicity, each exercise had an abbreviation. ALT (Attack Light Torpedo) was innocuous enough so we progressed to ART (Attack Running Torpedo). We then tackled the more difficult flying (for the pilot) in the FALT (Formation Attack Light Torpedo). When this exercise was done with running torpedoes, the abbreviation FART was, for it's day somewhat rude, particularly when uttered in the presence of these sweet and desirable young ladies. Their innocence remained unproven — at least by any of our course members, as none admitted to any liaison, innocent or otherwise.

Our activities on joining an operational squadron in Coastal Command, would entail close cooperation with naval forces, and to further our knowledge of the Navy, it was arranged that we would visit a Navy submarine at the docks in Glasgow. This was looked forward to with pleasure, as a break from the flying and a close look at a submarine greatly interested all of us. We were a mixed group, Mac and I were both NCOs at the time, but the hospitably of the navy, usually fairly rigid in the distinction between officers and 'other ranks' held no sway in the welcome we were given and the tour of the submarine.

There was not one of us who would have willingly ventured to the depths of the ocean in the vessel that we saw; just to be on board while it was still tied to the bollards made some of us squeamish. Narrow access ways, cramped working conditions and the area in the bows where the torpedoes were in their tubes was unbelievably cramped. To crawl through the watertight doors, aware that one could be trapped, in emergency situations, made the blood run cold. The Navy men responded to our perhaps obvious concern by gallantly suggesting that our role in the hostilities was far more life-threatening, but I 'had ma doots'.

Having been thoroughly scared by all this, then followed the good news. We were all, irrespective of rank, invited to the 'wardroom' for drinks. The crew obviously had our measure, no doubt by previous visits from Turnberry trainees, and the drinking that followed was a most unequal contest. Perhaps they had the edge, being on their own ground, so to speak, but what followed is still a total mystery to me, beyond any hope of recall and perhaps better left in that alcoholic limbo which protects us all from too much embarrassment.

Another 'contact' we had with the navy was during our low-level flights, playfully dropping torpedoes at our target ships. This area was the scene of much activity, being the entrance to the major port of Glasgow, and shipping movements were heavy and constant. Occasionally we would come across a Royal Navy Aircraft Carrier. Our aerodromes had runways mostly at a minimum of 1,000 yards in length, and this, to the navigator, who took no part in the delicate process of getting the 'bird' — as the Americans would say — on to the ground, seemed not overly generous on some approaches in poor weather or cross-winds.

To see the Aircraft Carrier decks of some 200 yards as a place to land an aircraft seemed to be a bit irresponsible, and more so given that surface was performing gyrations in all planes. The skill of the Fleet Air Arm pilots, to make a precise approach, at the right speed and height and with the nicety of making connection with the arrester wires, made us respect our counterparts. I could well understand the practice in the navy of the navigator being regarded as the captain of the aircraft. I was certainly of no maturity to adopt this role, which was based on the aircraft performing reconnaissance and tactical functions, rather than the expectation that we in the Beaufighter Wings would get very aggressive and display brutal and ruthless destruction of the enemy with never a qualm.

One Australian pilot, and his navigator had a most unpleasant experience. Each of our flights was of short duration, being to take off over the sea, manoeuvre to position to carry out the drop and return to the aerodrome. This crew taxied round to the end of the runway, the pilot opened the throttles to get airborne and the aircraft gathered speed down the runway. As subsequently recounted by the somewhat shaken (read 'traumatised') pilot, the aircraft failed to respond to him pulling back on the stick. With the end of the runway fast approaching, he resorted to fairly hefty trim on the elevators to raise the nose.

It did raise the nose but so violently that an immediate application of downward trim was demanded. Realising that the elevators were not performing normally, this unfortunate pilot had to maintain control solely with the small amount of trim available to him. He flew an erratic circuit and managed to get the aircraft back on the deck but he was extremely fortunate and displayed great skill in emerging from a situation which has undoubtedly been the downfall of many pilots.

To escape from the Beaufighter by parachute was a not very attractive option in the light of day but perhaps the final recourse to survive, both pilot and navigator were each provided with a hatch to the rear of their seats. This was hinged, to be forced open by the action of the slipstream when a wire was pulled. They were somewhat prone to open, untouched in flight and with a mighty bang and, of course, to the immediate concern of the crew. We very seldom, in this part of our training, ventured up to a height of more than several hundred feet and to save time and effort, we tended not to bother putting on our parachute harness, I usually threw mine onto the hatch at the back of my seat.

One day just after take-off, as we crossed the coast and were over the sea, my hatch flew open in a cloud of dust and debris and my harness was sucked out and disappeared into the Irish Sea. After this incident, it seemed prudent not to stand on the hatch unless duty necessitated, such as a quick tune up of the radio equipment, the

Marconi 1154/1155. However, the formalities of service discipline and the strict application of rules and regulations demanded that, despite what could have been my early and tragic demise, the ponderous application of investigation, findings, etc, should be carried out. The outcome was that I was charged with 'loss of Air Force property', found 'guilty as charged' and made to pay for the lost parachute harness — I think it was worth about six pounds.

The verdict rankled somewhat and for a long time I felt hard done by, but in later maturity, I accepted that such action was proper to the maintenance of order. Nevertheless, I could not help but compare this extremely modest loss of equipment, due to my misdemeanour, with the loss of a complete Beaufighter due to 'finger trouble on the part of a casual type pilot.

Our accommodation was a bit Spartan, I recall we were housed in Nissen Huts, with ablution facilities consisting of outdoor troughs, but the Ayrshire coast in this vicinity was delightful. The famed Turnberry golf course is close by and the town of Ayre some few miles away. During the war years, in the service, one of the first priorities after moving to a new 'camp' was to reconnoitre to find a good source of food and, of course alcoholic refreshment. The former we found close by our quarters, in a quaint little village called Maidens — no, I make no comment on the high improbability of any such a find there, food being the object of the exercise — where we were able to get supplementary food and relaxation when not rostered to fly. We had by this time 'bonded' not only with our pilots but also with other crews, and this phase, of relaxing together in this small village is recalled with particular pleasure.

A photograph in my log book refreshes my memory of that time and captures the smiles of pilot Merv Thorburn, RNZAF and his navigator, Charlie Brown, pilot Harry Bennet, RNZAF and his navigator, Nick, myself with Mac my pilot and another RNZAF pilot whose name I cannot recall. Fate is strange in the game it plays, it tosses us hither and wither and no rhyme or reason is ever discernible. Looking at this photograph, taken over fifty years ago brings back the instant of it's capture and all the warmth of feeling and comradeship that is reflected in this fading print.

Merv and Charlie survived the war, Merv to marry a young lady from Maidens, raise a family and become engaged in trawler fishing on the coast nearby. After many happy years, including obtaining a degree from Glasgow University, he succumbed to sickness while still comparatively young. Charlie, who married whilst with 254 Squadron, raised two children and built up a successful chicken farming business, but at an early age was struck with Multiple Sclerosis and condemned to spend nearly twenty years in a wheelchair. He died at the age of sixty four. Double tragedy was to fall on Charlie's family, with his son Mervyn also contracting MS, condemned to a wheelchair in his mid-twenties and dying very young.

Harry Bennett and his navigator Nick were posted to the Far East and were lost in the jungle there without trace. The remaining pilot of that group was also posted overseas and I have no information as to his fate.

Having been polished to the utmost degree by so many training courses, we were now adjudged ready to go into action, and we awaited the details of our posting to a Squadron with much expectation.

For me it had been a particularly long haul from October 1941 to March, 1944. I had seen and experienced just a small sample of being on the receiving end of the 'horrors of war' but I looked forward to giving the Hun a taste of his own medicine. My role as a navigator would not demand that I personally 'pull the trigger' but I would certainly be getting good view from my rear seat a Beaufighter.

I remember not whether, at this stage, I had built up any great animosity towards the foe. Our type of air warfare was, in any event, somewhat impersonal and a far cry from the trenches of the First World War when the louder the shriek when going into action the more likely the prospect of successful bayonet charge.

I saw no need to practice screaming.

NO. 254 SQUADRON, RAF
NORTH COATES, LINCOLNSHIRE
MARCH, 1944—MARCH, 1945

After so long a journey I was at last on the 'front line' so to speak, and face to face with the enemy, although the North Sea still stood between us. The first impression was one of organised, purposeful, flying activity, and the initial settling in, in finding quarters, the whereabouts of the Sergeants Mess, etc, completed, time to assess the situation more objectively. Then the need to get navigation and flying equipment together, to locate the Crew Rooms, the Briefing Room, and Air Crew Dining Room, where the 'before' and 'after' operational trip traditional egg and bacon meals were served.

The aerodrome was on the edge of the coast, totally exposed to the persistent East winds off the North Sea, everything flat as a pancake, as most of Lincolnshire, with one runway East and West, the end almost on the beach, and a large expanse of grass for North and South take-offs. It was approached down a typical English country lane, about a mile or so, from the pub on the main road, and the nearest place of more normal activity was Cleethorpes, itself not of startling beauty, with Grimsby a larger town with more attractive and varied recreational pursuits.

The beach was very shallow, with a very small range of tidal height, and taking off, to the East over the North Sea, it was either about half a mile of mud flats or high water. Just inland were some Bomber Command aerodromes, equipped mostly with Lancasters. On several occasions, when in the Mess or sleeping, there would be a deep sounding rumble, with the ground giving a noticeable convulsion. I soon realised that this was no natural phenomenon but some unfortunate crew who had 'gone in' on take-off with their bomb load of up to ten tons being detonated on impact.

North Coates had an interesting beginning as an Army Camp in 1914, when the first aircraft landed there with the pilot 'taking breakfast' at one of the nearby farmhouses. It became a place of more activity after Zeppelin L-22 bombed nearby Cleethorpes in March, 1916, killing 29 and wounding 53 men of the Manchester Regiment. De Haviland DH6 aircraft were then stationed there to repulse such 'dastardly' attacks, as they were invariably described, and at the end of that bout of hostilities, in 1918, the field reverted to agricultural purpose. In 1927 it once again became active, being used by the RAF as a base for bombing and gunnery practice at the ranges of Donna Nook and Thedlethorpe. In 1934, an Air Observer School was opened and air displays were held in the years immediately before the war stated in 1939.

It's distinguished record as an operational base started on February 22nd 1940 when the station was transferred to Coastal Command, No 16 Group. The Blenheims of Squadrons, 248, 235 and 236, began to carry out offensive patrols and shipping reconnaissance over the North Sea. However, these squadrons were soon re-located to other stations, to be replaced with Beauforts of No. 22 Squadron. This squadron was to suffer losses probably higher than any counterpart, the Beaufort was hardly suitable or equipped for the arduous and hazardous role of low level attacks on well armed ships, they were in fact, almost like 'sitting ducks'.

The role of the 'Strike Wings' — a quite imaginative description — is more fully explained in an Appendix to this memoir, but put very simply, their main function was to inhibit the movement of shipping around the whole of the European coast and so deny the Axis Forces of supplies for their various armed forces and to prevent war supplies and raw materials to be moved around in the process of manufacture. Close co-operation was maintained with the Royal Navy and aircraft of Bomber Command were largely engaged in 'gardening', the dropping of sea mines in the shipping channels. It was not the role of the Strike Wings to attack purely 'land targets', other than those such as harbours, jetties, etc, where the prime target was the actual ships.

Tactical demands meant that the three Wings were frequently re-deployed, and later, Mosquito aircraft replaced Beaufighters on some Squadrons. However, in March 1944, when Mac and I arrived at North Coates, our wing consisted of three Squadrons, 143 and 236, whose primary role was attack with four twenty millimetre Oerlikon cannons and six sixty pound rockets fitted under the wings, with 254 normally the carrier of the eighteen inch torpedoes fitted under the fuselage, and also having the four cannon for offensive fire.

The style of each operation was tailored to meet the character of the enemy forces, their defensive capabilities and strengths etc.

Intelligence information came in from a wide variety of sources — the movement of shipping is readily observable from any coast — and probably a courageous part in reporting such movements was played by the underground patriots. With constant air activity by the various commands of the RAF, including the Photographic Reconnaissance Unit stationed at Benson, it was difficult for the enemy to make many shipping movements before detection was made and the Strike Wings were called to intervene. It was all a bit 'cat and mouse', and each and every day it brought it's own excitement, with the call over the Station Tannoy System for "all crews to report to the ops room" bringing that instant surge of adrenalin.

An Appendix hereto will describe a Wing Attack in detail, with emphasis on the personal reactions and emotions that I certainly experienced but that almost all of us forbear to recount even to our 'best mates', or perhaps acknowledge to ourselves. Human psychology of fear in war situations is complex and not a great deal has been written. Embarrassment seems to wrap a discreet cloak around the fact that when in imminent danger of 'getting the chop', strange factors emerge, quite startling to the recipient, but an experience which is embedded in the subconscious probably for all time.

Euphemisms for anxiety were the order of the day, the most common being 'flak happy'. It stemmed from a condition when a surfeit of worry peaked and a kind of euphoria set in when all risks and dangers were subdued to a point when they no longer disturbed. It was manifest in a determination take part in every operation, beyond the normal ration, and an aura of bliss seemed to envelope the sufferer. Perhaps it wasn't a bad state to be in but with the loss of the sense of vulnerability — they assumed an air of invincibility — they were prone to lose their professional expertise and attempt foolish and reckless manoeuvres to the detriment of their own safety and also to expose colleagues to unnecessary danger.

Now perhaps, a brief comment on the aircews that had the privilege of participating in what were some of the most exciting war-time operations.

The Crews

What I found very noticeable was the total lack of conformity to what is now known as a 'role model', with characteristics, in personality, education, background, etc, ranging so far and wide as to indicate that the urge to take part in air operations had no common denominator. Perhaps it was the fickleness of fate that provided the vehicle which brought us all together, but together we were and the training which we had endured for so long dominated all other differences of character and made the instinct to perform our flying duties with competence and verve, the over-riding motivation. It was unthinkable, at this stage that we could possibly not live up to the general standards, or more importantly, let down our colleagues by failing to face up to the risks that combat flying entailed.

The three squadrons were comprised of men from a large number of counties. From recall, most were from the British Isles, but also a pair of New Zealanders, Mac and Merv, with whom Charlie Brown and I flew, a Dutch crew, who were properly Dutch Naval Officers and wore very dark blue uniforms, and were shown on the crew availability list under the name of 'Bierundbroodspot'. It struck me as being a rather strange name, and it was only later that I learned that it meant, translated literally, something like 'beer and bread'(it was, of course a *nom de plume*, in case of capture I imagine.)

There was an Aussie, Hefferan, a South African, a very diminutive pilot from South America — I forget which country, but he needed a cushion to reach the rudder bars of the aircraft — a pair of Canadian pilots who were twins — sadly almost at the end of their tour of 'ops', one was lost shot down and killed.

A Danish pilot, quite dashing, who had been at a University in Scotland at the outbreak of war and had done a spell with the Royal Guard at the Danish Palace. He spoke English with style and class that put marked contrast to the colloquial tones that I and many others from either the north or central counties tended to utter. Such differences were of no real consequence and added touch of spice to our conversations and relationships. I recall no instance of personal animosity, even when circumstances were rough and stress levels a bit above average.

On arrival at the Squadron, Mac and I were flight sergeants, and with a couple of others, shared a room. We had no duties other than flying, and life in the sergeants mess was uninhibited to say the least. The food and accommodation was typical of wartime, better perhaps than the other services, and apart from the several hours of regular operational flying, we enjoyed a pretty comfortable routine. But it was in the evening, when no flying was taking place that life took on a quite different hue.

A party in the sergeants mess on an operational station was an unforgettable experience. The beer flowed freely, the songs became more and more lurid and total mayhem usually erupted, to be continued until the early hours when fatigue took over and the route back to sleeping quarters negotiated with considerable difficulty.

The Mess piano took dreadful punishment, it was frequently 'abused' by having pints of beer poured into it's works, but it was the focus of our revelry, there was always a pianist of sufficient talent to hammer out the tune, and it took us no time at all to learn the words of the traditional Air Force songs. Most of these consisted of repetition of the most pungent phrases, repeated often and gradually becoming louder and louder, until the final verse when we always collapsed in helpless laughter. Even the most prim of us took enormous delight in mouthing what would normally be regarded as obscenities of the highest order, and it is to be remembered that many sons of 'men of the cloth' were attracted to the flying branch of the services. Their pleasure was obvious and perhaps it compensated for a life that had previously been a touch prim and proper.

Many of the songs were as old as the Air Force itself, many were parodies of well known songs, and religious themes did not escape the witty pen of the unknown authors. It was rumoured that many of the latter were composed by notables, such as Ivor Novello and Noel Coward but the biting wit and the exquisite rhyming put them in a class far more 'catchy ' and memorable than the usual compositions. At unguarded moments, I still tend to recall snatches of those delightful parodies and have to guard against giving audible voice!

(These songs have now been gathered together in a book edited by Harold Bennett, a former WW2 flying instructor at Medicine Hat, Alberta under the title *Bawdy Ballads and Dirty Ditties of the Wartime*

RAF, published by Woodfield, the publishers of the book you are now reading, at £9.95)

We also had Sergeants from the regular Air Force, who had done time all over the world, particularly in the Middle East, like Mesopotamia. They had their own brand of humour and the songs to go with it, and these gave all us young and relatively inexperienced youngsters particular pleasure in the link with the 'old RAF'. Not only did they have an almost endless repertoire, liberally laced with snatches of Arabic, but in addition to the vastly entertaining lyrics, they had the pantomime of actions to illustrate the story. The polish of the performance reflected the many times it had been previously done, no doubt in isolated Air Force stations in the sandy wastes of the Middle East far from the company of the 'gentle sex' and subject to the onset of sandstorms or intervention by 'hostile locals.'

The Station Commander was Group Captain Braithwaite, a mature and dignified pre-war regular officer, who exercised discreet restraint and kept a watchful eye on general morale. It was with deep, regret, some years after the end of the war, that I learned that he had been tragically killed in an aircraft accident involving an Anson. It seemed a particularly hard way to go after such a long flying career.

Wing Commander 'Paddy' Burns was the officer in charge of flying, and he invariably led the Wing on operations, when some forty aircraft were involved in a mass attack. He was an imposing leader, with that indefinable air of authority and leadership, complete with bushy moustache to complete the image. If he said 'jump', then one jumped without hesitation, and it was men like 'Paddy'— I always addressed him as 'Sir'! — that provided the driving force to direct the crews to perform aggressively, sometimes when the instinct of self preservation made 'flight' seem a very much better option than 'fight'!

'Paddy' had a stutter. Not very pronounced, but apparent over the intercom when the Wing was nearing the target and coming up into more precise formation to carry out the attack (with the large number of aircraft, the 'anti-flak' aircraft at about 1,500 feet and in 'vics' of three, and the torpedo aircraft in line abreast at about 150 feet, it was necessary to marshal the whole Wing to achieve the best results) Paddy's voice would come over the radio with the demand to 'close-up', but it came out with a delightful staccato 'C-C-C- Close U-U Up'!

When in position to perform the actual attack, it came over as 'At-At-Attack!' But we all greatly respected him and he was an inspiration to both pilots and navigators alike. He always took over the most difficult and dangerous operations and I recall him with affection.

Later in the year, Wing Commander Doug Cartridge took over from Paddy Burns and he also had considerable experience of operations against enemy shipping. He exhibited the same easy leadership as his predecessor and led from the front. These type of officers demonstrated the essential core of discipline, and, most important, they had that unusual knack of knowing how to distinguish line between command, and that point of familiarity with those that they led, which usurped the essence of their control and leadership, and provided that quality to make us, of lesser character to follow them without question into highly dangerous situations.

The qualities referred to above are difficult to express, but were exercised with verve and style at our parties in the Mess. These tended to be extremely wild an uninhibited affairs, and a perfect medium for getting rid of what we now know as 'stress'. The games were rough and consisted of 'rugby', with the mess furniture taking a beating, challenges between teams for downing the standard half pints of beer in the best time, and, usually when diverted to other aerodromes for the night, the 'footprints on the ceiling' trick.

A 'volunteer' would have his feet well an truly dirtied with ash from the stove, and then he would be hoisted to the top of a very unsteady group of slightly hysterical friends and walked up one wall, leaving his footprints across the ceiling and down the other side. The result was always viewed next morning with quiet satisfaction, rather like the marking of territory by some of those in the animal kingdom! Our 'senior' officers knew exactly when and how to either participate or not and also to know that point in time, at any party, to suddenly not be present. Looking back, I realise the skill and maturity in how these gentlemen, using the term in the proper sense, conducted themselves.

The Sorties

After several local flights and a couple of 'Navex', early in April 1944, interspersed with several 'Ops Briefing' for actual sorties that did not materialise, Mac and I carried out our first countable operational sortie on the 10th of the month. This consisted of a 'Wing Sweep', along the Dutch coast, between Ameland and Borkum, with the result 'nil attack'. Anyway, it was start and we came back with mixed feelings as to the outcome. It was the first time that we had flown in a large group of aircraft and Mac handled the somewhat arduous demands with notable skill and calmness. Being one of the group, surrounded by aircraft with the physically aggressive 'expression' of the Beaufighter — the bulldog style of the protruding engines — and aware that we had lethal ammunition on board with the high probability of using it, stirred the blood just a touch. Sitting in the rear, perched high in the cupola, and being carried along with those 1650 horsepower Hercules Engines', gave a beautiful clear view of all the other aircraft, the sea not too far below and the broad horizon which then gave way to the 'enemy coast', was a unique experience.

Four days later came my next sortie, not with Mac, my regular mate, but with a young English pilot. (Mac was away for some reason, and this was the only time that either of us flew with other crew members). It was a reconnaissance of the coast off Den Helder, a hotbed of enemy shipping activity, and demanded that observations be made close in. When my temporary 'skipper' took up the station of the patrol, he then proceeded to constantly make rapid changes in height, which took me by surprise, but which was the obviously sensible thing to do as we were within range of the coastal anti-aircraft batteries.

Although I have no really vivid 'picture' memory, this was the first occasion when someone deliberately tried to do me serous harm and the bursts of 'flak' were proof of that intention. However, the long training in use of the radio stood me in good stead as it became my urgent duty to transmit to base a 'sighting report' concerning the several ships which hove into view. This was done using a 'three letter' code, based on the navy procedure, but what the outcome was of our sighting and my urgent efforts to inform base I never learned.

The principle danger to us, in these flights close to the coasts of Europe, was the ever present possibility of crossing paths with the Luftwaffe fighters, the ME109 and the FW190 who disposed of any unwary Beaufighter in double quick time. There was a tendency for us to relax once away from the other side and on the way home, but many

RAF aircraft were caught short on the approach to their home base and were shot down, which, to me seemed an even more rough way to get the 'chop'. Perhaps the most dramatic loss of Beaufighters occurred during a strike off Norway in February, 1945, when the Wing was attacked by a swarm of these fighters, with the result that ten Beaufighters out of the attack force of some thirty, were shot down. Not without cause is February 13th known among Beaufighter crews as 'Black Friday'.

Mac and I were reunited and carried out several reconnaissance flights off Holland and then a new factor became apparent with sorties known as 'Conebo'. This, although it was not divulged, was a preamble to the invasion of Europe, when the activities of the enemy shipping had to came under more rigid surveillance and our efforts were towards locating the movement of the enemies 'E' Boats. These were extremely efficient, high speed launches with torpedo tubes and bristled with 20mm cannon. In fact they were so deadly that it was an operational instruction to our aircraft that a single aircraft was not to engage them in action, but two might have a go!

It was around March/April of 1944, that a major exercise in the use of Landing Craft for the Invasion Forces, was being carried out on the south coast of England at a place called Slapton Sands. A couple of thousand men were involved, mostly American, when purely by chance a group of 'E' Boats, apparently just 'stooging around '', came across this fairly large and unsuspecting fleet and wrought havoc amongst it, with no loss to themselves. The tragedy was hushed up and only recently, through the tenacity of one man, the details came to light, with the result that a suitable memorial was established to record what was a very sad episode.

Early in June, 1944, all aircraft were suddenly given black and white stripes on the wings, and many theories were expressed as to the purpose of what seemed a strange happening. It is to be remembered that even in the front line of the services, security was zealously guarded, with severe action taken of any detected breech. It must also be appreciated that with the massive amount of post-war detail of the momentous events of those days, that there is scarcely a point of even modest significance that any reasonably well read person can not give a pretty accurate run down on the events of any period, in sequence, with reasons and detail to boot.

But we lived each day by day, with little indication of what was around the next corner, and with no 'over-view' of the relationship of events that were occurring over most of the globe. We all know the benefits of hindsight, and so many 'arm-chair warriors' have told us how the affairs of those days could have better been handled. My answer tends to be curt to the point of obscenity.

On the 5th June, 1944, at 2340 hours, Mac and I took off in Beaufighter NE577 (X) to carry out a 'percolate' in the vicinity of the Hook of Holland. We landed at 0305 hours in the morning of 6th June, having not seen or attacked anything. The momentous occasion of 'D' Day' had started to operate while we were Airborne unbeknown to us. After a short snooze we went off on one of our usual periodic three days leave and it was only a chance encounter early that morning with an American soldier that I heard the news that our forces were in full assault of what at that time seemed 'the Impregnable Fortress of Europe'.

The squadron's operational activity hotted up after this event and the prime objective was to establish a dominant presence in the Channel area and along the Dutch and German coasts to inhibit the attacks on Allied shipping busy building up the bridge head already established on the coast of Normandy.

Receiving the Kings Commission

At this time, Mac was a warrant officer and I was a flight sergeant, but having regard to the nature of our training and operations, there being only two of us in each crew, etc, the Air Ministry were apparently generous in allowing a higher than normal ratio of commissions to us. After a quick trip to some Headquarters in London, and what appeared to me to be an even brisker cross- examination by an Officer of exalted rank — I forget his precise status — I was deemed not too unsuitable to 'Hold the King's Commission' and in due course, off I went to be kitted out as an 'Orficer'.

The very thin and almost indiscernible blue stripe of my new rank of 'Pilot Officer' — a bit of a misnomer as I was a navigator — seemed a poor swap for my three stripes and crown, together with, in the form of the hand grasping a bunch of sparks, the visible evidence that I could operate radio equipment. But the pay was better, the privileges of the officer rank extensive, and, in the event of becoming a prisoner of war, a more comfortable life in the Stalag Lufts.

I make no bones of the fact that it was with some trepidation that I ventured forth, after being fully kitted out, with one of my elderly Aunts' in Derby, into the public domain to receive, instead of give, my first salute. I well recall her absolute pleasure and pride in my achievement in reaching officer rank — and it was a sailor who 'through me one up', strangely because they were disinclined to recognise the RAF in this way — and my Aunt was so carried away that I almost had to restrain her from also acknowledging the salute. A happy memory of Aunt Margaret. But the time I spent in the Sergeants Mess also provides many happy memories.

I was 'promulgated' in Air Force Records as a Pilot Officer with effect from 20th June 1944, shortly after 'D' Day, and given my new Identification Number, 179350. From my entry into the Service on 31st October 1941, I had always thought of myself as '1433827' and to discard this old and what I thought to be a 'friendly' sounding series of digits caused a bit of a pang, although the increase in pay put paid to any real remorse!

On reflection, although Mac and I made little tangible contribution to the events of the historical and momentous occasion of the start of the invasion of Europe, to have been 'airborne' in the vicinity at the time that the Liberation Forces swept into action gives cause for a touch of pride and pleasure. In an earlier Chapter, I gave a brief description of a Navigation technique known as a 'Creeping Line Ahead', a type of search over the sea to find a target or to locate for the purpose of rescue, individuals lost at sea.

Interestingly, in the early stages of the offensive, Lancaster aircraft of Bomber Command used the basic format of this to drop what was known as 'window' (short metallic strips) to simulate, in an area away from the real target area, the movement of ships, with the intention of luring the enemy forces to that point. This called for very precise positional flying by a large number of aircraft, with no errors to be made in the complex and frequent changes of course otherwise there was the possibility of the 'cat being let out of the bag'. Despite the bad weather and the huge scale of operations, with the inevitable breakdown of some of the plans, it was a remarkable achievement to grasp a foothold on the heavily defended continent, although at certain times, a successful outcome was far from certain.

Many historians of modern times, with their well-developed sense of hindsight, often seem to be oblivious of the fact that history is always poised on a delicate sense of balance, with destiny so often decided by trivial incidents, which they fail to take into account when preparing their learned tomes about past events. They also show little hesitation in pointing out how the affairs of those times could have been affected far more efficiently. Perhaps, in the face of uninformed criticism, our best excuse is that we had no computers those days!

The majority of our 'sorties' (is this a French word?) were carried out by individual aircraft, taking off at intervals, usually about 20 to 30 minutes, and traversing the same area, in order to provide the maximum opportunity of locating the enemy, and either mounting an attack or reporting the information back to base. We usually carried a torpedo, or around the time of D-Day, two 500lb bombs and two 250 lb bombs. Code names were always used to identify the sortie, such as 'Conebo', 'Percolate', 'Purblind' etc, with, also, the obvious 'Recce'.

When the whole Wing operated, some thirty to forty aircraft, the usual term was a 'sweep', a rather nice and appropriate name, I think. These were highly exciting, being swept along in a seemingly irresistible way, with a sense of irresistible power, and, as far as the navigator was concerned, no specific navigational duties, the navigator of the Wing Leader carrying out this chore. The procedure for the 'take-off' of such large number of aircraft from North Coates with relatively limited runway length, is described in the Appendix, but once over the sea, then the really exhilarating dash across the North Sea stirred the blood.

To avoid the enemy radio detection devices, which were, by then, fairly sophisticated, it was necessary for our pilots to get down as close to the sea as possible, and the standard type of altimeter in the Beaufighter was the 'Kolsman Sensitive Altimeter', which responded to changes in the local atmospheric pressure by indicating the height on a dial. It was not easy to discern on the dial, changes of some twenty feet, and furthermore, the atmospheric pressure, influenced by the general meteorological conditions, varied considerably even over short distances.

To overcome this problem and allow pilots to virtually skim the surface of the sea (sitting in the navigators position, on occasions it certainly felt as though this was happening) the aircraft was fitted with a 'Radio Altimeter'. This enabled the pilot to fly with confidence at fifty feet for long periods and so minimise the chances of detection by enemy radar. Some sorties were up to five hours duration, with a lot of this time spent at low level. As the Beaufighter was not fitted with 'George' (the automatic pilot), this imposed considerable strain on my good friend and pilot, Mac.

After departure from Base, the aircraft spread out over the sea, in several 'lines abreast' and at as low a level as possible, for the run of an hour or so to the enemy coast. Precise formation-keeping was not feasible or necessary and the sight of this fairly large number of aircraft, gently moving back and forth in their positions relative to each other was a stirring sight. Also fascinating (to me, at least) was the surface of the North Sea so near to our underside. Although not to be compared to the almost overpowering majesty and power of the North Atlantic, the wave tops frequently rose to heights sufficient to make comparison. It was the random pattern of movement, first one way and then another which intrigued, with the 'white horses', the spume from the wave tops, blowing hither and thither and the 'wind lanes' etched on the sea surface that provided me with a diversionary wonder prior to encountering whatever hazard faced at the end of this seaward dash.

With such a large 'gaggle' of aircraft, trying to maintain a cohesive relationship, at such low level, it was inevitable that the odd 'blip' arose, calling for some smart evasive action on the part of one, or because of the closeness involved, several pilots. There was, of necessity, some give and take by all pilots and little difficulty normally occurred. However, on one occasion, a somewhat startling, and in afterthought, amusing incident occurred...

A Canadian Pilot was experiencing, in an erratic and unpredictable manner, the slipstream of an aircraft preceding him because that pilot was fluctuating in height and course to a more than usual degree. This resulted in some loss in safety and imposed on the Canadian an even more arduous task in keeping station. Flying the heavy Beaufighter was, Mac assured me, quite taxing physically, and this was evident as I spent quite a lot of time perched on the main spar immediately behind the cockpit, particularly when on the way home after an operational trip and, hopefully, beyond the possibility of an encounter with the dreaded ME109 or FW190.

The Canadian pilot tolerated the situation for some time but his patience began to wear thin, and, with 'radio silence', he was not able to point out to the leading pilot the error of his ways. He was, in any event, a bit of a 'hot head' and noted for his 'on-on' spirit, as we called it, perhaps in a slightly envious way for we less enthusiastic airmen. Nothing daunted, he let loose a burst from his 20mm Oerlikon cannons, over the wings of the recalcitrant aircraft in front of him with the intention that the tracer content would alert the wayward pilot to the error of his ways! Whether or not this somewhat drastic action solved the problem for the run out to the target I do not recall, but the Wing Commander Flying did not take kindly to the possibility of loosing our own aircraft to what is now know as 'friendly fire' and gave the Canadian a real roasting. This chastened pilot nevertheless, had a good record and survived his tour.

The summer of 1944 was warm and pleasant and on one short leave Mac and I visited my folks in Spondon. Granddad Marshall was, as previously mentioned, inordinately proud of my attaining aircrew status and to meet Mac my pilot gave him much pleasure. Granddad was born in 1875, in a small rural village and for most of his life he was a farm labourer, with neither the resources nor the opportunity to travel or make any change in his way of life. He was very much in tune with the natural things in life, his 'allotment' garden totally occupied any spare time available and with his kind and gentle nature, I remember him with great pride and affection. He passed on to me a love of the pleasures of the unsophisticated aspects of life, his knowledge of the flowers and trees, his habit of walking in the then unspoilt English countryside and that he always had as a constant companion, a Fox Terrier dog invariably known as 'Spot' or 'Frank' or similar.

The visit of Mac and I was an occasion of some importance and to do the thing properly, Grandad had managed to get the loan of a 'pony and trap' from one of his farmer friends. The trap held, in somewhat cramped conditions, four people, and Grandad, his son Tom, Mac and I sallied forth into the crosspatch of narrow, leafy, meandering country lanes, littered with simple 'pubs' some few furlongs apart, and within the stamina range of what was quite a small, but not delicate pony, to saviour the pleasures of the rural hospitality.

Our 'itinerary' had little indication of pre-planning and our subsequent course around the countryside was a navigation exercise gone horribly wrong. For most of the time, I think none of us were really sure of our 'position' only that the next 'pub' was becoming visible over the ears of our very willing pony, with the delightful thought of yet another ale and the casual and easy conversation and companionship of the 'regulars' of that particular halt. Standard fare in those days was rough bread, a hunk of cheese and a very large onion, long before the fancy 'ploughman's lunch' became the vogue, and the pubs were as they had been for many long years, even centuries.

It was rural England at its best, despite the impact of the war, and it provided Mac and I with a short but memorable escape into a world remote from the pressures and hazards which were then our lot.

A strange phenomenon occurred immediately after all the aircraft in a 'Wing Strike' had completed their attack. On approach to the target, and having formed up for the actual attack, the sky seemed to be congested with aeroplanes, in reasonable order initially but almost immediately appearing to be flying in all and even conflicting directions. Then suddenly Mac and I were alone in the sky, with a great feeling of loneliness and vulnerability. It was a touch like the lines from the poem: 'I must away to the sea again, to the lonely sea and the sky'.

The sea, however, was not completely lonely, as a successful effort by the Wing left evidence of destruction, and death, of course, for any observer to witness. Our instinct of self-preservation came to the fore very strongly during the short duration of the attacks we mounted and we had little time to consider the consequences of our actions. The thought that human beings were on the receiving end of our cannons, rockets or torpedoes and that injury and death would almost certainly result, was kept firmly at the back of one's mind until the whole matter was over and we were returning to base.

Once clear of the 'enemy coast', Mac and I had developed a simple procedure to settle down for the run home to base. From my position in the rear, under the cupola, I could lift my small navigation table, crawl over the butts of the four 20mm cannon, over the pilots hatch and perch on the main spar of the aircraft just behind Mac's seat. I had stopped smoking in 1943 when in Canada, but Mac was still a slave to the 'pernicious weed' and in any event, I always thought he deserved a 'drag' after the rigours of the attack, particularly as he was at the sharp end and would have copped whatever was coming before I did.

In view of the relatively short duration of our sorties, and the restricted nature of the Beaufighter for any fancy preparation of food or drink, our 'flying rations' consisted of small tins of orange juice — otherwise only issued to mothers with new babies — and bars of chocolate, also not generally available in wartime Britain. So, after lighting up a 'fag' for Mac, and being careful not to inhale, we had our little 'feast' and felt much better with another trip virtually in the bag. It was a pleasant formality and enhanced the already strong bond of fellowship between Mac and I.

Making landfall after flying over the sea has a significance that is hard to express, being a mixture of apprehension and inquisitiveness as to where the first glimpse of terra firma will be. After all, flying over the sea involves man in two unnatural environments — air and water — so the return trip always had an element of intrigue, despite my reasonable confidence that my navigation was not too far amiss.

The journey was usually not too long, an hour or so — a bit longer from Norway. A height of one or two thousand feet was usual and the prevailing wind westerly, with aircraft course being based on the general appearance of the surface of the sea, as previously mentioned, the spume, windlanes, etc.

Our good friends Charlie Brown and his pilot, New Zealander Merv Thorburn, on the return from one strike had to use a bit of 'lateral thinking'. It seemed that on this occasion Merv was more than generous in the use of his 20mm cannon fire — the breeches of which were only a couple of feet from the Nav's feet — and the vibration was most vigorous throughout the aircraft, with the heady smell of cordite wafting into the nostrils of the Navigator. The vibration did unpleasant things to the aircraft compass, and when they emerged from the melee of the attack, it was almost dark.

All sense of direction at this time had been lost, and they both became aware of the need to decide a compass course for the way home. A glance at the compass revealed a wild and erratic needle that showed little or no inclination to conform to its proper purpose of indicating magnetic north. Fortunately, the sharp, and probably anxious eye of Charlie, detected a fading glimpse of light on the horizon. It was the rapidly setting sun in the west, and enough to point the general direction home.

Lincolnshire, where our base aerodrome of North Coates was located, is remarkably flat from the Wash in the south to above the mouth of the river Humber, so on the return trip, 'controlled flight into terrain' — to use current terminology — was not a desperate problem, particularly as our height was normally below a thousand feet or so. After the anxiety and rigours of the action of the day, the comforting appearance of the coast and the security embodied in the gently rolling green pastures, so old and apparently untroubled by the actions of war, induced a warm feeling that I remember with pleasure.

That first sight of land was all important and as to where we were and any later complications was another issue, to be dealt with in the way our competence as aircrew had trained us to do.

If the weather conditions were such that visibility was very limited, land would make an appearance almost below the aircraft, and with a limited range to relate to the map features of the area, it was not always easy to find a specific 'pin-point'. Fortunately, there were two predominant promontories in the area, Spurn Head at the mouth of the Humber and Flamborough Head some distance further north. These were extremely good points over which to make landfall. There must have been many thousands of airmen, of in many types of aircraft of all Commands of he RAF, the American Eighth Airforce and many others who felt a surge of relief at identifying their whereabouts from these particular landmarks.

In this general area, off the east coast, the sky was literally swarming with aircraft. Our flying objectives with the Beaufighter Wing meant that we operated at any time of the day or night, and we frequently approached the English coast either at morning twilight or evening twilight. Coming back in the morning coincided with the departure of the B17s and Liberators of the US Eighth Airforce and evening twilight was departure time for the Lancasters, Halifaxes, Wellingtons etc, of RAF Bomber Command.

It was a wondrous sight, to see the sky darkened by often nearly a thousand aeroplanes, all travelling in different directions while gaining height before crossing the English Coast. By contrast, our crew comprised only pilot and navigator and looking up at the vast horde of aeroplanes it had to be appreciated that each had at least seven, or even up to twelve men aboard as crew. On one occasion over ninety Lancasters were lost on one raid. The emotional impact of such huge losses only became clear in my mind in much later life. They were all brave young men.

It is difficult to fully comprehend the loss of human life on the scale mentioned. A comment by one speaker expressed his way of relating the tragedy of the Holocaust, by modifying the generally accepted figure of six million people dead into six million and one people dead. He found that in this way he could put the incredible tragedy into human terms and so obtain a better awareness of the suffering of each and every individual who was killed.

Mac and I witnessed many of our colleagues being shot down during the course of our operations, it was usually quick and overcome by the pressures of the moment, but one incident remains vividly in my mind of the actual destruction of an aircraft and its crew.

We were carrying a torpedo, operating at night and looking for any target that may present itself in the full moon. Our area of patrol was along the Dutch Fresian Islands and round the German Island of Heliogoland. The moon was full and a lovely sight over the water. We were just 'stooging' along and I was very conscious of our exposure to the attentions of the German Night Fighters. The cupola gave clear and good vision all around and the procedure was to maintain a constant scanning motion. There was, however, a small glow from the radio equipment that, at one very narrow angle became reflected in the perspex of the dome and gave the impression of an approaching aircraft, to much immediate concern and utterance of coarse expletives!

Matters seemed fairly well under control, but on one scan, I became aware of a bright light quite high in the sky, which then became split into two lights. It appeared to pose no imminent threat to us, but as I watched it slowly fall through the sky, I was puzzled as to its origin and purpose. It was something we had not seen before, but we quickly realised that it was a shattered and burning aircraft, more than likely a Lancaster. We imagined the agony of the crew, either shattered, like their aircraft, in the initial assault by fighter or flak, or coming down slowly in the falling aeroplane. We wished fervently that they had sufficient time to take to their parachutes.

The incident was a sudden and unexpected drama unfolding before our very eyes, and it remains for me, an unforgettable symbol of the determination and courage of the crews of Bomber Command, who probably witnessed such occurrences on most of their operational trips, but 'pressed on regardless' until their 'tour' of 30 trips had been completed or they were, themselves, shot down. The Command lost 55,000 aircrew, most of them around 20 years old.

July and August, 1944 were busy months for the Wing and we took part in several 'strikes' against well defended shipping convoys along the Dutch Fresian Islands, Heligoland and the Norwegian Coast. The targets were different in composition, but usually a small number of Merchant ships carrying war and other cargo, surrounded by a protective screen of quite war-like and aggressive naval vessels. The most feared of these was known as a 'Sperrbrecher'—which means 'mine sweeper'—but these were equipped with large calibre anti-aircraft guns which could put up an inordinate amount of 'flak' when aircraft such as ours were sighted.

The trip over to Norway, in loose formation, and good and clear weather conditions was pleasant enough, culminating in the sight of the magnificent Norwegian coast with its hills and inlets. So far so good, but it struck me as being somewhat unkind of the convoys and the coastal batteries to open up with deadly intent, and spoil the whole beauty of the sea, the coast and the ships. Anyway our business had to carried out and in no time the 'game was on' and no quarter asked and none given.

On one occasion, when the whole of our force of aircraft was about twenty miles from the coast still low over the water, and getting ready for the 'run-in', I spotted a small rowing boat ahead. Standing up in the boat were two men, with arms raised in token of surrender. They had probably gone out for a few hours of quiet fishing when, with an almighty roar, some thirty or forty Beaufighters approached at about fifty feet, in a highly aggressive manner, to disturb their tranquil activities. I trust they survived the ordeal, although with the build up of the pilots urge, during the trip over, to shoot at something, they must have offered a terrible temptation!

Frequent changes were made to the aircraft equipment for navigation and that used by the pilot. Perhaps the most useful was a device to relive the pilot of the need to assess one of the critical parameters in performing a successful drop of the torpedo. The whole of this skilful procedure included the need to drop the weapon at a distance of one thousand yards from the target. This ensured that, after entering the water, the torpedo stabilised and ran sufficient distance to turn a small propeller fitted in the nose which inserted a small explosive charge into the main explosive and so on impact with the ship the whole charge exploded.

The technical development of radio and electronic equipment swept along at an ever increasing pace, largely by the demands of Bomber Command, which was involved with the Luftwaffe in a cat and mouse, tit for tat, battle over Europe with measures and counter measures to win the air battles. The device for the Beaufighters was probably an offshoot of one such development and consisted of a scanner fitted in the nose of the Beau, which picked up the presence of the sea-borne target and translated this to an audible warning horn for the pilot and also gave a visual indication.

In November, 1944, Mac and I again spent a couple of weeks at Turnberry in Scotland to attend a 'Refresher Course' at the Torpedo Training Flight. This involved a dozen short trips, dropping dummy torpedoes at various angles of attack and also in formation with several other aircraft. It was a pleasant and relaxed break from the operational flying at North Coates and gave our pilots an opportunity to polish their technique to an even more stylish performance. There was a group of crews there at the same time doing their initial course, preparatory to joining an operational squadron for the first time, and we, including the navigators were treated with a modest amount of deference, perhaps as it should be!

The occasion arose for our 'skippers' to indulge in a little showmanship, when we returned from one dropping exercise. I think Merv Thorburn, the New Zealander pilot of my close mate, Charlie Brown triggered it off, he flew with great verve, and when we arrived back over the aerodrome, our four aircraft had been tucked up into extremely close formation. Sitting in the rear seat, when in such formation, was greatly stimulating, with our wing tips almost overlapping and the lower aircraft, in the 'box', edging up very close. Chas and I were so close that an exchange of 'hand signals' was carried out, and our visual expressions readily understood. Sweeping across the aerodrome at fifty feet or so, achieved what the performance was supposed to ... impress the 'sprog' crews!

In February 1945, our squadron was require to undertake an unusual task, that of 'Fighter Escort'. Mention has been made of our shortcomings in relation to the standard fighters of the Luftwaffe, the ME109 and the FW190, but fortunately any attack would probably only have eventuated from a less formidable foe.

During the war, certain essential and highly prized metals and materials were vital to the antagonists, in the production of war equipment in many different forms, such as aircraft, tanks, ships, etc. One of these, some kind of special steel ball-bearings, were produced in Sweden and it was of the utmost importance that a regular supply of these reach England as any failure in this regard would have had severe impact on the 'war effort'. They were transported in fairly fast and small ships across the Baltic and North Seas under cover of darkness for as much of the journey as possible, which depended upon the time of the year.

The plan was for aircraft of 254 Squadron to take off at intervals of 90 minutes, head across the North Sea towards the Baltic, locate the speeding ship with it's vital cargo and then circle it in a protective way to ward or fight off any hostile aircraft. The first onerous aspect, for the navigator, was to trace a path across some three hundred miles of sea, with no external navigation aids and one bit of the sea looking remarkably like any other bit. The 'fall-back' technique in such circumstances is to study the forecast weather report with more than the usual concentration, then bring to bear whatever knowledge and experience seems appropriate and utilise the simple method of 'track-crawling'.

By this method, provided the course and position of the target ship is fairly accurate, a 'meeting' somewhere in mid-ocean should be achieved. How far along these two converging paths that the rendezvous would occur, depended on other intangible aspects, such as vagaries in the predicted weather, the accuracy of the aircraft compass and the course flown, and, of course, the accuracy of the navigation of the 'target' ship. General weather conditions, in terms of visibility at sea level, could easily mean failure to spot the small vessel, particularly if a heavy swell was running. (This sortie demonstrates the incredible advance that has been made possible by the advent of the Global Positioning Satellite system, where an instant fix can be made anywhere in the world to an accuracy of a few feet; it even gives height above the ground!)

Airmen, in all types of aircraft and Commands, learnt very quickly that to approach any surface vessel was very dangerous, perhaps the 'foe' being slightly more dangerous than our own Royal Navy. Regrettably, many instances occurred of RAF planes being shot down by 'friendly fire' and RN vessels being sunk by the RAF. Areas of operation were defined and intelligence provided to both arms of the Service, but it was difficult, in bad weather etc, to conform to what was known as a 'no go area'.

Airmen appreciated that when an aircraft — not readily or easily identified — approached a ship, it was prudent of the Captain to take action, with the onus on the aircraft to take avoiding action. The general outline and superficial appearance of a Beaufighter closely resembled that of the Luftwaffe JU88, so we faced an even more acute hazard of falling to friendly guns. However, in the several instances that Mac and I made an unexpected approach to one of our own ships, we were dealt with kindly in the form of warning shots 'across our bows'!

Our trip to provide 'fighter cover' went very well, keeping on our intended track, and constantly reassessing our 'ETA' (estimated time of arrival) at the rendezvous point. I must admit that I derived much satisfaction, when we sighted the ship dead ahead exactly at the time calculated. We then spent 90 minutes circling this lone vessel with its valuable cargo of war material, ploughing its speedy way across the empty North Sea. We parted with a friendly waggle of the wings!

However, the pilot was still left with the demand of precision in the other criteria previously mentioned, such as height, speed, and relative angle to the course of the target, etc, together with an acute awareness of the position of fellow attacking aircraft. The danger of collision was ever present in the hectic final moments of a Wing Strike (tragically, during an attack into Den Helder harbour on January 17th, 1945, our squadron lost four colleagues, when the two aircraft collided at very low level, and burst into flames.)

With no extraneous factors to deflect the concentration of the pilot, it could be safely said that this was a more than adequate 'workload', but the defensive activities of the opposition were by this time intruding somewhat and I hold in high regard the skills shown by all the pilots of Coastal Command Beaufighters.

Some aircraft were fitted with a single 303 Browning Machine Gun mounted on a flimsy bracket at the rear of the navigator's cupola. When fired to 'test the guns' the whole thing started to rattle and vibrate in an uncontrolled manner until the trigger was released. The thing was obviously a greater danger to the well-being of the Beau than to the enemy, and in any event, it only fired to the rear of the aeroplane. It could not, therefore be used during the run-in to a target, and in the short time of hasty retreat, after passing over the ships, with aircraft in some disorder, 'jinking' (changing course and height very quickly). Any attempt to fire the Browning at the rapidly receding target would have been totally useless.

The Beaufighter had a cruising speed of 180 knots, with a flat out straight and level speed of about 350 knots. Whilst known as a 'Beaufighter', its manoeuvrability in respect of the fighters of the Luftwaffe, such as the Focke Wolfe 190 and the Messerschmidt 109 — those in operation in the same operational area as us — was totally inadequate in comparison. The possibility of the Navigator using the single barrel 303 Browning to inflict any harm on those swift and agile machines was zero and we assumed that the device was merely a 'toy' and installed largely as a morale-booster for the navigator. Pilots, for their part, were always apprehensive about the possibility of the navigator accidentally shooting off the tail of the aircraft.

The outcome of a serous clash between Beaufighters and the skilful Luftwaffe pilots in their truly 'fighter' aircraft was amply demonstrated on 9th February 1945 during the course of a Wing Attack on the Norwegian Coast by the Dallachy Strike Wing.

The Strike Force was made up as follows:

455 Squadron RAAF	11 Beaufighters
404 Squadron RCAF	11 Beaufighters
144 Squadron RAF	9 Beaufighters
489 Squadron RNZAF	1 Beaufighter
Total	**32 Beaufighters**
65 Squadron RAF	10 Mustang fighter aircraft (as cover and protection)

The target was towards the end of a fiord, with high hills on either side, and once the force was committed into this course towards the East and into the dead end, they had little room for manoeuvre or evasive action. Moreover, the target was very well defended by the firepower of the ships and also land-based anti-aircraft batteries, who shot down several of the attacking force as they flew up the fiord.

Worse was to come. The approach of the Wing had been monitored by radar and at this time, several squadrons of Luftwaffe fighters had been established in this vicinity of known activity by our aircraft and were alerted to repulse the attentions of the Wing. A force of FW 190s with the Beaufighters committed and virtually trapped in the 'one-way' route, stormed in from the West and created mayhem among the attacking aircraft. The outcome was inevitable and losses horrific in the following air battles that ensued, with the sturdy versatile, well-loved Beaufighters no match for the agile 190s.

Nine Beaufighters of the 32 that attacked were shot down, 404 Squadron RCAF losing six of their 11 aircraft, and one of the escorting Mustangs of 65 Squadron RAF was also lost. However, it was not all bad news a five of the FW 190s were also destroyed in the battle, including one flown by a Luftwaffe 'Ace', Lieutenant Rudi Linz, credited with 69 aerial victories (mostly in Russia but including a few British). Remarkably, considering the violent action took place at very low level, several crew members survived, either crash-landing or ditching in the sea and were re-united subsequently when being hospitably treated by their German captors.

Not without good reason did this encounter become known in Beaufighter circles as 'Black Friday and it lives on vividly in the memory of those fortunate enough to have survived such daunting odds.

Despite the fragility and clumsy operation of the navigator's single Browning machine gun fitted in the cupola, as mentioned above, a post-war reconstruction of the events of that tragic day was closely researched, with the paths of the various aircraft that were lost in the action plotted on a map. This revealed a remarkable result of a tussle between a Beaufighter and a FW190. A 144 Squadron aircraft (pilot F/O P.C. Smith and navigator F/O Holly) had completed their attack and were heading away from the target area, when Holly, to his consternation, became aware that a FW190 was only a short distance behind his aircraft, so close, in fact, that the radial engine was most conspicuous and obviously sizing up the situation before the 'kill'.

In what was perhaps an act of desperation, Holly 'pooped-off' — a term then current — some shots from his Browning, almost at the same time being severely blasted by the cannon fire from the pursuing aircraft. Holly was so severely injured that he lost consciousness, and shortly after this, his pilot ditched the plane in the fiord. After ten minutes in the icy water, which resulted in severe hypothermia, they were rescued by two Norwegian fishermen and taken for medical attention. They both survived the ordeal.

The reconstruction of the incident revealed the high probability that Holly, with that random burst from his 'morale-boosting' weapon had, in fact, shot down German Air Ace, Lieutenant Linz!

Diversions on Return Flights

The varied nature of the operational trips and the location of the target between the Dutch and Norwegian Coasts, together with the somewhat unpredictable weather over the North Sea, frequently resulted in diversion to other than North Coates after the duties had been carried out.

This resulted in some inconvenience to our personal comfort, having no 'over-night' change of clothing, toilet equipment, etc. but there was, as adequate compensation, the novelty of visiting another aerodrome, visiting the Mess, meeting the other airmen and comparing notes over beers at the Mess bar. An overnight stay was more than enough excuse for vigorous 'horseplay', with the traditional games established from the early days of service flying as an excellent means of getting rid of those little tensions brought about by our fairly hazy long-term life expectancy.

In mid-summer 1944 we were diverted to Manston in Kent and saw a strange sight—an aeroplane without a propeller. The development of the Gloucester Meteor, for that was the name of this mysterious machine, had been a well-kept secret and none of us had any idea of the principles involved, being familiar only with the internal combustion engine, either 'in-line' (as in the Rolls-Royce Merlin) or the large and bulky 'radial' engine of the Beaufighter, the Bristol Hercules.

At that stage, the Meteor was not allowed to fly over enemy territory in case one was shot down and the secret revealed. It transpired, however, that the German Airforce had already developed a jet fighter of comparable efficiency and they were in combat shortly afterwards and took heavy toll of both RAF and American bomber aircraft. It is true to say that the invention and development of the jet aircraft engine, which has led to travel and communication at a speed hitherto undreamt of, has probably been one of the most significant factors in mankind's path into the future.

On one occasion, a diversion found me in the mess at Banff, in Aberdeenshire, Scotland. This was then the base for one of the other Strike Wings which had converted from Beaufighters to Mosquitoes equipped with rockets. These were largely utilised for attacks off the Norwegian Coast. I wandered, a touch lonely and with that feeling of being far away from home (Mac was probably around somewhere) into the mess bar, where several others were drinking. A voice hailed me to come and have a drink, and I turned to see a well-decorated Wing Commander. I still treated one of his rank with due deference, but responded with alacrity, and became aware that this was the famed Max Aitken, son of Lord Beaverbrook the Minister of Aircraft Production.

He personified the qualities of leadership, which sat comfortably on his shoulders and led his squadron with great verve. The leaders of repute always seemed to have a few 'gimmicks' (they are seldom recognised as such!) and Max had the spinners of his Mosquito aircraft painted red and no doubt the members of his squadron responded to the subtle way that this simple action raised a couple of fingers at the enemy and invoked a feeling of invincibility!

On one occasion, we were diverted to Thorney Island, near Portsmouth on the south coast of England. It had been a rough sort of day, and the following morning, after an indifferent nights sleep, we were gathered in the Briefing Room for the operational requirements of the day to be assessed. The weather was pretty grim and it appeared that no sorties would be mounted, when Wing-Commander 'Paddy Burns' took a telephone call on what was known as the 'scrambler phone', coloured red to show it's purpose and a direct line to Command Headquarters designed to make 'tapping' impossible.

We were all somewhat lethargic and not at all enthusiastic about undertaking any flying, operational or otherwise. The caller, judging by Paddy's half of the conversation apparently demanded that we all get airborne and do something, exactly what we obviously pricked up our ears to ascertain. The conversation, tolerably polite from Paddy's end at the start, rapidly became more animated and impolite, culminating in Paddy, brooking no argument, slamming down the phone after saying "My chaps have had enough and I'm not prepared to send them out in these conditions."

Such a stand against Command Headquarters, even by a Wing Commander, bordered on being a mutinous act and we all sat there with bated breath while it was happening. Needless to say, Paddy immediately rose to dizzy heights in our estimation and after that we would have followed him, had he asked us, into 'the Valley of Death' like the gallant six hundred!

It was only many years later, I think, that the incident came to mind and a thought occurred. Was that conversation a real one or was there, perhaps no one on the other end of the phone from Paddy, who very convincingly, and being conscious of our subdued spirits, simulated the dialogue as a boost to our morale? Either way, it did us all a power of good and illustrated in simple terms how leaders show their leadership.

North Coates, being exactly on the shores of the east coast, was also the recipient of diverted aircraft from other Commands who were in trouble and looking for a place 'to roost'. Not a lot of runway length was available, particularly in bad weather and for four-engined aircraft experiencing some difficulty in control or the crew suffering from fatigue or recent attack, was over-run on several occasions by B17s of the 8th US Air Force. Aircrew have a more than sharp interest in getting a good look at any stricken aircraft lying about the aerodrome and an up-ended Flying Fortress at the end of our runway invited immediate inspection.

I think most of us were impressed by the design and facilities of that great machine, but I doubt that few of us would have willing tackled the dangers of trips over German, at the twenty thousand feet and more, that was required. Despite the number of bristling guns — they had machine guns of point five calibre, against our .303 — with the ventral turret just big enough for a small man to sit with his knees up and operating the gun though his legs, the odds seemed to be a bit unfavourably stacked. They were called upon to operate in daylight, in large and unwieldy formations, at fairly slow speed and for deep penetration into enemy territory. The individual groups were known as 'boxes' and it became the practice of the Luftwaffe fighter pilots to single out one such box — no doubt to the relief of the other crews in the immediate vicinity — and focus their attention and fire-power to split up the formation and then pick off the disorganised individual aircraft virtually at their leisure.

The crews of these Flying Fortresses had our respect and they also caught our interest in their behaviour, dress, etc. Having trained in Canada, we were familiar with the style of the North American continent, although, of course, there are significant differences in the ethos of the Canadians and the Americans They seemed to us to be much more varied in physical appearance and character than other members of the Allied Forces. Also, having been unexpectedly diverted, they had only the clothes that they wore, usually, because of the extreme altitude of their operations, thick and woolly 'Irvin' flying jackets, trousers, set off by thick and cumbersome flying boots.

What we 'stiff upper lipped' British found most strange was the tendency for them to endorse their flying jackets with various statements, like 'I've been to Berlin,' etc. In conversation with one such flyer, some time later, I commented on this practice and his reply was to the effect that we in the RAF, with our unwillingness to extol our courage and to play it 'cool', probably derived the same kind of internal satisfaction by doing so as they derived from their, to us, flamboyant approach.

But I still recall the look of amazement on the face of our pre-war Station Commander, Group Captain Braithwaite, on encountering airmen so dressed in our mess, but being the gentleman that he was, quickly averted his gaze to a more acceptable vision of standard type RAF officers at home in their mess!

Some Observations from Operational Sorties

Extraneous to our direct activities to try to engage the enemy, and, of course, occasionally succeeding, various other matters of interest came our way when traversing the many square miles of the North Sea. Almost the whole of the flying time was spent in solitude, with, as described previously, the sight of Bomber Command and the US 8th Air Force occupying a lot of the sky over the East Coast of England as we returned to base.

Natural Phenomena

A marked attraction of just simply flying, is the constantly changing pattern of clouds, from the stratus or sheet type, to the more interesting cumulus or convection, with their form made in individual 'lumpy ' shapes and which their formation and dispersal can frequently be observed at the time of happening. The progress of an aeroplane on it's course through the sky provides a moving panorama of the natural forces of Nature in visible form. Although aviators study the science of Meteorology as part of their profession, which explains these natural phenomena in down-to-earth terms, there exists, when actually in the environment of the sky, a kind of magic that only a most unimaginative soul would not be conscious.

Returning after dark from one individual sortie and about half way back across the North Sea, Mac and I became aware of a kind of eerie glow around the aeroplane. It was quite startling at first, as our senses were, as usual when on 'ops', highly sensitised for any unexpected change in the performance of the aircraft, or any external intrusion on what may be described as our 'privacy'. Enemy fighters were, of course, foremost in the mind of every crew from take-off to landing and dispersal. The glow appeared to have attached itself to the tips of the propellers and the small radio aerials and was soft and delicate, with little indication that it could pose any danger. This curious and unusual effect stayed with us, to our fascination, for quite some time and then disappeared as discreetly it had appeared.

This was 'St Elmo's Fire', an unusual occurrence only produced under highly specific meteorological conditions. Whatever the technical explanation, it was a privilege to have seen this soft and mysterious light in the loneliness of that dark night over the North Sea.

Operating in the English Channel shortly after 'D-Day', our minds alert for any possible eventuality, Mac and I saw, at a little distance, a strange kind of column connecting the cloud, which was not very high, to the surface of the sea. Weather conditions generally were a bit indifferent, with the sea in an agitated state, and an occasional lashing of rain. What we saw was puzzling at first but we soon realised that this was a 'water spout', quite uncommon in the area in where we were. Like St Elmo's fire, it was produced by a strange quirk of the prevailing meteorological conditions. The power of nature to produce updrafts of air capable of lifting such a large volume and weight of water gave us another glimpse of the wonder and magic of forces beyond the control of man.

Man-made phenomena

A heavy loss of life in a major accident or incident in war when the expression 'act of God' has no application, always wrenches the emotions. Even after the event, the sight of the inert and distorted remnants of what was once a building, an aircraft or a ship can greatly sadden any onlooker and may prompt deep thought as to the circumstances that led to the catastrophe.

On patrol, almost at sea level, in the English Channel in late Autumn, carrying out a fairly complex type of search involving many changes of course—the aircraft was fitted with a 'G' Box, which simplified the navigation load—the sky was devoid of any other aircraft and nothing was sighted on the sea. It was all very relaxed and after several changes of course, already an after briefing report of 'nil sighting' was beginning to come to mind. Then, straight ahead, loomed a dark and at first indistinguishable object which reared out of the water to a considerable height. A closer inspection revealed that this was the bows of a fairly large ship, which, due to the quite shallow waters of the Channel, may have had it's stern resting on the seabed. The details of the sighting were duly reported, but Mac and I never learned the ship's identity, the circumstances of the loss or any known casualties. Nevertheless, the image of that ship's bows, thrust up though the lonely waters of the Channel, remain quite clear in my memory. In just one of the early years of the war, the Allies lost over eleven million tons of shipping. Did the bows we saw, pointing skywards like the visible part of an iceberg, form a fractional part of similar losses incurred in 1944? Or was it one of 'theirs' that had come to grief. The sea gives up its secrets with great reluctance.

In June 1944, the first wave of V1 flying bombs—quickly nicknamed 'doodlebug' (for what reason, even now, I'm unsure)—were launched against Southern England. Visiting London around this time was an interesting experience, with the raspy discordant note of the pulse engine reverberating all over the city. Everyone waited to hear it cut out, with the knowledge that when this happened the thing would fall to earth somewhere soon. The one-ton warhead produced much loss of life. The loud detonation, together with the eerie note of the air-raid warning sirens heralding its arrival, are firmly etched in the memory of all of those who experienced onslaught by this 'Vengeance Weapon', as dubbed by the Fuehrer himself. On one occasion a land-launched V1 fell in the crowded East End of London, killing 170 people.

Attack by this weapon appeared to be one of surprise and countermeasures were some time in evolving. There is little doubt that the V1 unchecked would have had a serious impact on the progress of the war, the outcome of which, at this stage, was far from assured. The problem was tackled in two ways, the establishment of a huge anti-aircraft force in Southern England, as a protective belt to shoot down the missiles and secondly, use of the fastest aircraft the in operational use to knock them out of the sky by pursuing them on their inwards flight.

It was the anti-aircraft belt that afforded Mac and I a view of what was entailed in this countermeasure. We were operating in the Channel, at low level, with our area of activity carefully specified, when, to our amazement, we saw this huge display of 'flak' covering an arc in the sky. It was of breathtaking intensity, the guns aimed not an individual target but they simply put up a 'wall' of shells with the hope of downing a flying bomb. It seemed improbable that anything could have flown through this sheet of shells, and it was shown, in the final analysis of results that the 'diverse belt' achieved very good success. Heaven help the poor airmen who unwittingly flew into this wall of steel, but the glow in the sky that was produced gave fair warning of it's presence.

A modest flexibility in the use of the V1, which normally took off from a very long ramp lined up with the large target of Greater London, together with the ingenuity of German scientists and the courage and skill of Luftwaffe pilots, gave North Coates a bit of fright one dark night in late summer. A group of us were in the mess when to our astonishment, we heard the strange and distinctive sound of a V1 in flight. First thought was that it was perhaps a stray that had overshot the target of London and drifted North, but it was heading inland on a course from the east, apparently towards the industrial cities of Leeds and Sheffield. Subsequent information showed that it had been launched from a Heinkel III bomber aircraft at some distance from the coast. I am unable to recall how many such launches were achieved, or the casualties involved, but it demonstrated the vigorous and unending quest for more and varied weapons by which to strive for the upper hand in the balance that existed until almost the end of hostilities.

In the autumn of 1944, the North Coates Wing was deployed in the eastern end of the English Channel, searching for any type of hostile ships posing a threat to the cross-channel bridgehead which was pouring in more and more Allied men and equipment to further the sweep across the continent with Germany the final objective. Our part was small but it is said that the 'sum of parts is greater than the whole' so we felt our contribution was not amiss. It was on one such reconnaissance mission, fairly near to the Belgian coast, that Mac and I were astonished to see a thick trail of smoke rising from the land and soaring vertically to a height beyond sight. Several plumes — the only way that I can describe them — followed, and the incident was fully described to the de-briefing officer on our return to base. We had witnessed the early launches of the Nazi's second 'vengeance weapon', the V2.

The vision recalled my youthful fascination with the writings of H.G. Wells, read with great avidity by youngsters in the pre-war years, which focussed on sending men to the moon. He had imagined a cannon of huge diameter and power as the 'launch vehicle' and had caused our young and impressionable minds to boggle and boggle... and then boggle some more. Now I had witnessed with my own eyes the beginnings of the real technology that would take Man into space. If I had one wish to be granted, it would be to watch, at reasonably close proximity, a launch of the Space Shuttle from Cape Canaveral. Such a sight, even on television always brings about a wonderful soaring of the spirit and a renewal of confidence in the better qualities of mankind.

By autumn 1944 Mac and I had quite a few operational trips under our belt, including several what are now known as 'firefights' — engagements involving an exchange of fire with the enemy, with the consequent likelihood of serious damage to the health of both of the warring parties — and had become relatively senior in the hierarchy of the Squadron. Many crews had, by this time, come and gone in the almost standard, and accepted, routine of the way of life on a frontline Squadron. It was an easier time for us, having attained this status, but, of course, the underlying stress was always there, but subdued to a lower level.

Our initial plunge in to real flying that involved the threat of 'the chop' by flying accident (Bomber Command lost more men through flying accidents than were lost due on operations) was now behind us, as were the dangerous low-level attacks against well defended targets, to the enhancement of our general confidence. By now we knew what to expect when setting out on a 'trip' and had developed an easy harmony when in the air — and on the ground — and the danger, large in the first operational flights, as statistics showed so clearly, of succumbing to inexperience, had been reduced considerably.

The loss of a senior and well-experienced member of the Squadron, nevertheless, was always acutely felt, but a practical remedy to the inevitable depression and impact on morale, had been established from the very early days of service aviation. It was quite simple and involved a gathering in the mess, the consumption of drinks to a point of uninhibited joviality, followed by vigorous, and dangerous horseplay, largely a form of rugby, forming a large pyramid, which eventually collapsed with everyone in a laughing heap on the floor and two teams in line to compete in drinking contests. A good boost to morale was a bus trip to some of the country pubs in the near vicinity of the aerodrome, with song and general inhibited behaviour, led by our senior officers.

These activities blunted the edge of the loss of Squadron members, and despite our deeper feelings when a particular friend failed to return, it was 'bad form' to express any overt feelings of loss. Only many years later did the true sense of the tragedy of the loss of those well-loved and respected colleagues surge into the memory, but even these later feelings were tempered by that inbuilt defensive mechanism, fostered in those days, of accepting the fickle nature of the 'Grim Reaper'.

Nearing the end of the tour

During the latter part of 1944, the frequency of sorties increased due to the greater movement of enemy shipping. By now, the North Coates Strike Wing had lost 236 Squadron, which had converted to Mosquitoes and transferred to Scotland to join the Banff Wing at Tain. The two Wings in Scotland were fully engaged in furious activity along the Norwegian coast, but their targets were in the protective cover of the fiords and invariably tied up close to the fairly high cliffs, which made the run in to the attack very difficult. The losses incurred by these squadrons became very heavy, whereas operations from North Coates, with a couple of exceptions, proved to be acceptable.

The most serous of these was on 17th January 1945. It had been reported, after a reconnaissance flight that there was a significant amount of shipping gathered in the Harbour at Den Helder, renowned for the volume and pungency of its anti-aircraft batteries, consisting of both heavy and light 'flak'. No doubt Bomber Command crews were well aware of the heavy stuff and took good care to cross the enemy coast at a more docile spot. Beaufighter attacks had been mounted on Den Helder on several occasions late in 1944 and the mention of the name tended to tickle the hairs on the back of the neck. Many aircraft had been lost and we saw the reason when were treated to a glimpse of some excellent photographs taken by one intrepid navigator as the Wing made their close approach to the Harbour. One of the RAF 'lines' was that "the flak was so thick it was possible to walk on it". The photographs, with the thick wall of exploding shells and the stream of tracer from the light flak, almost gave credence to this assertion.

After the run across the sea, the Wing came up into formation, at the usual low level, for the attack. It was blue skies all the way, and the harbour was sighted with a considerable distance still to run, which gave time for thoughts such as "What am I doing here?" One symptom of what is now called 'stress' is a marked increase in the rate of pulse and breathing, not unknown to aircrew under such circumstances, and a flow of adrenalin that gives a zest to life which is normally hard to find.

The arrival of the Wing found the defences ready and more than willing and able, and they quickly made their intentions known to us. The line of attack had been decided, which was straight in, with a later swing to the south, back to the coast and so homewards. The congestion of aircraft, and the need for the navigator to keep a sharp look-out and 'advise' his pilot—perhaps yell to his pilot is more correct—seemed more hazardous than usual, and regrettably the results of the strike were disappointing, with little real damage to either ships or installations being confirmed. Six of the thirty Beaufighters who attacked were lost, two from 254 Squadron colliding immediately after crossing the target and bursting into flames.

In recalling those times, memory plays odd tricks in selecting what comes readily to the 'top of the pile'. Some incidents I remember with almost full re-call as if they had happened within recent days, whereas only a faint glimmer of others can be summoned up. However, if mulled over and played with in the mind with some perseverance, they often emerge with sufficient detail to be set down in a cohesive way.

One such incident, to me of considerable poignancy, was the loss of three young (we were all young, come to think of it) Australian pilots. It was a couple of months before the end of the war and these chaps had not quite completed their Bomber Command operational training, at a station somewhere not far from North Coates. Like all Aussies, they were dead keen to 'give it a go' and thought they had little likelihood of doing any real operations before hostilities ceased. Somehow or other they came to our aerodrome on a visit, perhaps through an Aussie friend, and 'cadged' a flight in a Beaufighter that was doing an 'air test' (a short local flight to make sure the aircraft was all in order). The three of them managed to cram themselves into the aircraft, standing in the well behind the pilot, all totally against regulations, and they took off. Unfortunately for all concerned, visibility deteriorated while they were flying. On the final approach to the runway, the pilot lost control, the aircraft crashed and all on board were killed. Many thousands were lost in a similar way, but these circumstances struck me as being particularly sad.

Towards the end of 1944, Allied land forces were making satisfactory progress across Europe on their way to the 'Big City' (as Berlin was known to Bomber Command); Paris had long since been liberated to recommence some semblance of 'the pleasures of the night' in such places as Pigalle (known to the American Forces as 'pig alley'); and the Russians were fast approaching from the East.

January 1st 1945, however, saw a remarkable and determined attack, early on New Year's morning, by the Luftwaffe. They swept in, in force, and 'clobbered' the forward aerodromes of the allied forces, inflicting severe losses on the aeroplanes sitting on the perimeters. It reminded everyone that the war was far from won, and that the Germans were 'in for the long haul'. Very heavy ground fighting took place in the Ardennes, between Luxemburg and Belgium, despite the incredible amount of war material available to the Allies and the pounding of the German war machine that had been going on for so long.

For most of us at North Coates, the situation on the continent was far away and of remote academic interest. We had our sorties to fly and our particular enemy, the heavily defended coastal shipping still plied up and down the coast and offered targets of opportunity. Despite indication that matters were going well for our side, the flak to be encountered had not lost it's dangers and tours end was still a goal to be attained through experience, hope and a touch — perhaps a bit more than a touch — of Lady Luck.

It is not easy to describe the thoughts that came to mind in the run-down to completing a 'tour of ops'. When the tour began, my mind appeared to block out the cold fact that it was necessary to complete 200 hours flying or to survive for nearly a year hence. Not a conscious act; it was simply by-passed in the thought processes. Preoccupations were with the sortie just completed and the knowledge that the next one was not too far distant. The longer-term implications were, perhaps, just a little more than the average mind would be prepared to safely accommodate, without imposing unacceptable strain. I recall no instance of hearing any discussion between crews, except between crewed pilots and navigators, of the number of trips they had achieved. The odds of completing a tour was a taboo subject.

The sturdy Beaufighter, with it's two massive Bristol Hercules sleeve valve engines of 1650 horsepower, had served us well. After every trip Mac and I inspected the wings and fuselage for damage by flak and invariably found evidence of success by the enemy gunners. The largest piece entered the fuselage about one foot to my rear and embedded itself in some unit or other (it probably still resides in Auckland, New Zealand, in Mac's junk box!). It is not productive to make any delicate mathematical calculations of, for instance, the time lapse by which that particular projectile failed to bury itself in my rump, thereby sparing me to live on to a relatively ripe old age. There were not a lot of engine failures in Beaufighters, either from enemy action or mechanical failure, but Mac and I never had the slightest problem in this regard.

We did get quite a fright, however, as we turned for home after one strike off Norway. Twenty miles or so off the coast, the aircraft suddenly started to fill with thick, pungent smoke. Such a happening was never far from the mind, but the source was quickly apparent. The navigator sat on a pedestal-type seat, with head and most of the shoulders above the general level of the fuselage. The feet more or less rested on the breeches of the four 20mm cannon, and it was the duty of the navigator, when airborne on an operational sortie, to 'cock' the cannons ready for the pilot to fire on command.

On this particular occasion, on top of the cannons, a tardy member of the servicing crew had left a couple of tarpaulins which were used to cover and protect the engines from the weather when on the ground. During the attack, Mac had been liberal with the use of his cannon-firing button and the resultant heat had set fire to the tarpaulins. Self preservation is a very strong instinct and rose sharply to the top of all other inherent attributes, and it was with great gusto that I tackled those burning tarpaulins and beat out the flames with my bare hands.

Aeroplanes have a delightful and distinctive smell of many compounds, fuel, oil, machinery, aircraft dope and paint, etc, which I can, even now, recall to memory, even though my sense of smell has all but faded. But my dominant memory of being in the back seat of a Beaufighter, is of the vibration and sense of power when the guns were fired and the heady smell of the cordite from the shells which filled the aeroplane and persisted for a long time on the way home. Modern day 'Rambos' eat your heart out!

We edged up to the 'last' trip', though I recall no specific discussion with Mac that we were nearly there. On 9th March 1945 we took off at 1615 hours in Beaufighter 'W' RD354 for a 'night rover' into the Heligoland Bight. It was the time of full moon, and our task was to fly along pre-determined tracks, looking out for any target. The objective was to get 'down moon' of any ship we spotted so that Mac could get a clear view of it in the light of the moon and so perform the attack. We did our patrol, which involved three and a half hours flying, but no target was found. We had to land at another aerodrome—Langham in Norfolk—as the weather had clamped down at North Coates. The engines stopped and Mac and I got out of our seats and stepped out of the aircraft.

I think we shook hands. There were no histrionics, no anti-climax, just an overwhelming sense of achievement and relief. Perhaps tucked somewhere in these emotions was the feeling not so much as being alive but of 'not being dead'. Suddenly, the whole world seemed to expand to unknown horizons, but this was tempered by the knowledge that the wonderful sense of comradeship and companionship that had been established between Mac and I now had to end. That moment in time, standing by that trusty old 'Beau' with so much shared experience, the good and the not so good, remains in my mind with great clarity.

We took off early next morning and returned to North Coates, where Mac performed the standard 'beat up' of the 'drome at very low level, permissible by crews at the end of their tour. That afternoon we both went our separate ways, on leave, and were not to see each other again until we met at Auckland Airport, New Zealand—43 years later in 1988. Neither of us looked a day older... (well, that is what we both generously decided!) but while I recognised my 'old cobber' instantly, Mac, somewhat embarrassed, later, and with his ingrained sense of honesty and decency, admitted that as our group of passengers had emerged, he had approached a gentleman, apparently not too dissimilar to what I was likely to look like after that huge passage of time and had greeted him with some enthusiasm, much to the consternation of that elderly gentleman!

In 1986, the opportunity arose to visit what still existed of the aerodrome at North Coates. It was an eerie experience to drive down the country lane from the nearby village and approach the guardhouse. Emotions began to surge in an uncontrollable way, as with all 'old soldiers' who tend to spill the odd tear with little provocation, as the memory of old comrades, the throaty roar of those Beaufighter engines, the high spirited sounds of a party in the mess and the memory of numerous individual kindnesses began to become almost real again. These thoughts and feelings were the subject of an article I entitled '*The Runway*', which is included in these writings as Appendix.

My last act at North Coates, on 10th March 1945, was to send a telegram to Carol to let her know that I was 'tour expired'. We both looked forward to a less stressful existence in the future, with more time together and without the possibility of her receiving a telegram of the other type of news.

A BIT OF INTROSPECTION

Coincidentally, Mac and I hit, almost on the button, the requirements of achieving an operational tour, which was one year on the squadron or 200 hours operational flying In almost precisely one year, we flew 58 operational sorties for the total flying time of 200 hours and twenty minutes. Could it be that during that random fraction of twenty minutes, our fate to survive or not was decided?

Fate is fickle in the extreme. Are there such beings as guardian angels? Some crew members flew with confidence and a feeling of security that somehow or other, they were being watched over and would survive. Others exuded an aura that their demise was only a matter of time. Marriage when on an operational squadron appeared to be the touch of doom. Most flew with a 'talisman' a rabbit's foot, a scarf, or even more obscure items to ward off the 'Grim Reaper'. To suddenly find themselves 'airborne', having changed quickly before a trip and forgotten the lucky charm, provoked agonies of apprehension until the trip was over. I know, because it happened to me once when I realised I had forgotten my own talisman.

We search for explanation of such things, beyond our direct control, and although not conscious of it at that time, in retrospect, my inclination has been that I was favoured in surviving, by the aura of care by my immediate ancestors. The family bond, particularly with Grandad Marshall, was strong in the extreme. I just had to survive; his pride and pleasure that his grandson was flying on operations with the RAF was so strong as to be almost tangible! Who can deny or dispute, that in the mysterious ways beyond our ken, that this factor perhaps tilted the balance on more than one occasion, when things were looking a bit unfavourable for Mac and I when we were 'dicing' over the ever-waiting waters of the North Sea.

Remarkably, throughout our time flying together, Mac and I suffered no bodily injuries, not so much as a scratch, quite remarkable in view of the type of operations that were our 'lot', with the chief danger being 'light flak'—and on some occasions the heavy stuff—which chucked shrapnel randomly about the sky.

One crew took a direct hit to the bottom pivot of the control column, with the result that the pilot could only turn the aircraft in one direction. Somehow they managed to return across the North Sea and make a safe landing. The pilot, was more than thankful that his own 'vital personal equipment', which was in close proximity to the point of impact, had been spared for use on another day!

As mentioned earlier, our most serious hit was just behind my navigation seat, where a substantial, and certainly lethal hunk of flak came into the aircraft from the side and embedded itself in a piece of radio equipment. As it was only about two feet behind me, and as our speed was over two hundred knots, the time interval between it striking me instead of the equipment probably amounted to a couple of microseconds. Still, as the saying goes, 'a miss is as good as a mile!'

It was my proud boast for many years that I was 'never hurt in a Beaufighter'. Ironically, this changed 28 years later, in 1973, when a Beaufighter 'bit back'. By this time, most wartime planes had either been scrapped or were lost in remote places, etc, and it was only much later that it was realised that these aircraft were valuable and collectable relics of a type of warfare never to be repeated, so much so that 'vintage' aircraft now constitute a massive and lucrative worldwide industry. Every discovery of a crashed plane is cause for excitement, with 'bounty hunters', with an eye to a bargain, vying for first pick.

Carol and I were on holiday in Lisbon, Portugal — where the approach to Portella airport still entailed a very low-level passage over the centre of the town — and a couple or days before we were due to fly back to Rhodesia, I learned, in casual conversation, that there was a Beaufighter aircraft at the Portuguese Air Force Base just a few miles away. Despite the lack of time available, I could not resist the opportunity to go out and once more take in the sight of one of my old friends, so after a train journey I arrived at the entrance to the base. The NCO on duty had little English and I had no Portuguese with which to converse, but he willingly and cheerfully called the officer of the day. This smartly dressed young officer, in the engineering branch, spoke excellent English and reacted with great interest and enthusiasm when I explained that I had been wartime navigator on 'Beaus'.

"Yes." he said, "we do in fact have a Beaufighter, and it's in good condition, having been recovered from a beach where it force landed many years ago." He apologised, saying that the plane was some distance away in a secluded part of the airfield, and we set off across the base, and by this time I must confess to mounting excitement as we drew near where it was standing. As it came into view, up came the lump in my throat and memories began to surge. There it stood, still proud and in what appeared to be very good condition. With typical courtesy and reflecting that empathy which Latin people exhibit in any personal contact, he quickly discerned my emotional condition and, to my relief, said that he would leave me to wander around the plane and familiarise myself once again, after so many years, with the cockpit and navigators station.

I recall that after a good walk round the outside, which bore little evidence of age or damage after lying exposed to the elements, I lifted myself into the plane through the pilot's entrance beneath the fuselage. I then perched on the main spar behind the pilots seat, as I did on the way home from a trip, when the main danger was passed and pursuit by enemy fighters unlikely, to light a cigarette for Mac, open a small tin of orange juice and reflect on defying the 'Grim Reaper' once again.

Everything was there, almost as I remembered it 28 years ago, and I then crawled through the fuselage, over where the four twenty millimetre canon blasted away with the tang of cordite, and through the armoured doors to 'my' seat under the cupola. By now the experience was taking on a quite unreal aura and I sat there for a long time letting a flood of past impressions surge through my mind until such memories took over from the real world and I went into a kind of limbo, totally unaware of where I was, in Portugal, in a Beaufighter, in 1973.

Gradually, I brought myself back to the present time and reluctantly decided that it was time to go. To do this, it was necessary to crawl back through the fuselage to drop down through the front hatch. Still in a bit of a 'dwal'—a South African term for 'mental fog' is about the closest translation, I can offer—I leaned forward to go and really brought myself back to the present by hitting my head on one of the top fuselage spars.

I immediately felt the blood run down my face, and my handkerchief quickly became saturated, but fortunately it stopped the flow. Making my way through the various aircraft on my way back to the Main Gate, 'bloodied but not bowed', I was only conscious of how fortunate I had been to once again make the acquaintance of my old and reliable friend, the Bristol Beaufighter.

Arriving back at our Hotel in Lisbon, Carol saw my injury, enquired what had happened to me, to which I replied, truthfully but quite extraordinarily, "I finally hurt myself in a Beaufighter!"

AIRCREW OFFICERS SCHOOL—CREDENHILL, HEREFORDSHIRE—MARCH-APRIL, 1945

The subsequent leave was greatly enjoyed, with spring in the air and new territory to explore with my next posting. Perhaps the pre-war 'salad days' were about to start all over again, but life's experiences thus far had been more than rewarding and left me little room for complaint. There was, of course, a background feeling of relaxation, with no likelihood of the torch in the face in the middle of the night and the whispered words, "Briefing in the Crew Room in twenty minutes," so a kind of calmness permeated to most of my body's nooks and crannies.

The next phase of my life in the Air Force was soon mapped out. Having being commissioned as Pilot Officer in June 1944, while still on ops, had hardly transformed me into what may be termed 'a real officer'. There were many of us in the same situation, in many different aircrew categories, and we needed to be 'licked into shape' at what was known as ACOS (Air Crew Officer School). It was flattering, in some ways, to be selected for this hopeful transformation, as it implied potential for continued service after the cessation of hostilities. Even better news was that Charlie Brown, my very good mate, was also to join the same course.

Of course, it may well have been the case that our group had been selected on the basis that we were a touch 'beyond the pale' in our general behaviour, deportment, style or what have you, and a large dose of training in etiquette would do us little harm! I must admit that we tended to be a bit 'stroppy', sloppy in dress and regarded our sole duty to the Air Force as one of flying activities. Moreover, none of us had any idea of the administrative responsibilities or procedures that seemed to be such a large and important part of service life.

The camp was situated at Credenhill, fairly close to Hereford and not far from the lovely River Wye, a well known beauty spot. The camp was certainly not one of beauty, being the standard collection of wooden huts, and, somewhat ominously, a very large parade ground. When we assembled for the usual introductory welcome by the commanding officer, a glance at my fellow students revealed that we comprised all categories of aircrew, with a heavy splattering of medals, including many Distinguished Flying Cross and Distinguished Flying Medal, visible evidence of the number of 'ops' that had been collectively achieved. I think that, in fact, we were all 'tour-expired'. There seemed to be also a fairly large number of NCOs lurking at the rear who seemed to eye us with what appeared to be a touch of relish! We were soon to realise why.

I recall very little what 'officerly characteristics' we imbibed on the course, but what I remember very vividly are the hours we spent on that huge parade ground under the dominion of the aforementioned NCOs! At the start we were issued with overalls which had no badges of rank or category. This, in itself, was a bit of a come-down, as few humans do not inwardly enjoy showing their achievements by an outward show, such as rank, special attributes, etc. in the form of badges, braid, etc.

The first objective was to get us in better physical shape, after previous slackness and the effects of those beery sessions in the mess bar, and the NCOs set about this task with quite disgusting enthusiasm. They were a group of remarkable men, all mature in the service and had had their will with many previous groups as ours. Obliged to address us as 'sir', they could, nevertheless imply a degree of stupidity to the recipient of a dressing down, when a drill movement had gone awry, that had such a fine balance of skill that no officer could ever fault them for overstepping the mark.

Once the initial shock of doing 'square bashing' for long periods had been overcome, many of us settled down to enjoy the rhythm, the sense of unity and purpose that has to be experienced to be understood. The synchronised steps, the instinctive response to the drill instructor's commands and the awareness of the common bond of fellowship with all others in the 'squad', invoked an almost hypnotic state of enjoyment. In some ways, it could have almost become 'habit forming' and I confess that it was a wonderful sense of relief after the previous flying activities, to 'get fell in' and simply do as bidden with no decisions to be made and feel a physical sense of well being.

Those with an inherent lust for power and dominance—my lust (in this respect) was quite low on a scale of one to ten—also enjoyed frequent opportunities, when the vocal chords of the instructors gave an odd quiver of over-strain, to take over control of the squad and give the members a hard time with rapid and often conflicting drill commands. It was a favourite trick to let the group march off into the far distance until almost out of earshot, and when they were on the point of leaving the Parade ground, thunder out with distended lungs, "A-Bowat-Turrrn!"

One evening turned out to be highly entertaining, if not down right hilarious. One way of distinguishing between 'gentlemen' and others is the way they handle their cutlery when eating. The very obvious 'give-away' to sort out the Northerners from the Southerners, is the way the knife is used. 'Ooop north' the knife sits over the thumb and 'down south' it rests below that digit. To bring us all into line in such important matters in order to avoid later embarrassment in the more traditional behaviour of our post-war service, we all had to undergo a 'formal dining-in night'.

General response to this course requirement brightened considerably when we learnt that we would be 'paired off' with the some young lady officers of the Women's Royal Air Force. Where they came from escapes my memory, but our eyes lit up quite noticeably, to by dimmed a touch when it was emphasised, in a polite and discreet way, that the 'pairing process' implied nothing beyond a meal together. The more incorrigible amongst us, however, regarded such a restrain as a challenge to their manhood, and, perhaps, an already very successful track record.

The evening was nevertheless very pleasant and as we, in line and in pairs, escorted 'our' ladies into the ante-room and later, after drinks, into the dining room, it brought to mind vivid images of the countless occasions, in far away countries all over the world, over many hundred years of service life, that such a delightful procedure had given pleasure to the participants. We were dressed in standard uniforms, the more elaborate 'dress kit' was not available to us, but the ladies had made the most of their dress and all in all, were a 'pretty sight'.

The unforgivable 'faux pax' at a dining-in night was to pass the bottle of port that went round the table after the meal, to the left instead of the right (or was it the other way?). I think we all passed muster during our evening and perhaps even learned a thing or two about how to behave like a real officer!

A week or so into the course, after rigorous physical activity, we were all feeling pretty fit and another excursion was on the programme. Although it was April, when the weather is still unpredictable and always cold, we were taken off into the 'bush' somewhere close to the River Wye. Our wooden huts suddenly appeared not unattractive, as we found that the purpose of this exercise was to spend several days under canvas and 'rough it' a bit.

For most of us, camping in tents was to be a completely new experience, even for me, despite the fact that my pre-war life in rural England had provided intimate contact with 'country life', involving exploration of the highways and byways, ventures into dark and almost impenetrable woods to gather bunches of bluebells, climbing hills of not too difficult challenge, swimming in the rivers and canals, etc. My bicycle had provided many excursions of sheer delight, drifting through the lanes and green fields of northern England, with a deep sense of its history. All around, one could still stumble upon the sites and sometimes the evidence of ancient battles or of the incredible engineering feats of Roman road building with their magnificent symmetry and long straight lines over hill and dale. On top of these 'perks' was the feeling of physical well being from the effort of the pedalling, the hum of the tyres, and, after the long drag up the hill, often necessitating dismounting and pushing the bike, the wild exhilaration of the long freewheel, downhill ride, with feet up, when a yell or song not to be resisted!

However, the RAF had omitted to provide bicycles at our tented camp, presumably to ensure that we continued to receive the large dose of exercise that was one of the principle objectives of our course. So it was away on 'Shank's pony' up and around the beautiful countryside that blesses Herefordshire. We took it all willingly and felt all the better for it. One of the benefits, in austere Britain of the day, was being able to visit some of the local farms and buy fresh eggs, to be later cooked by those on duty in the camp kitchens. Local pubs appeared to be in short supply, however, and I recall that at day's end, usually pretty whacked from the day's exertions, we were quickly down for the night on our rigid beds.

The River Wye, despite it's great charm, with it's twisting course and deeply sloping banks, was, in April, 'as cold as charity'. Even in mid-summer it was hard to imagine much improvement in the temperature, but it represented a challenge to the more adventurous and foolhardy, not unlike Mount Everest to a certain New Zealander. One thing lead to another and the outcome was that some half dozen ill-guided persons decided to have a swim. One of these — me — was of slender construction, with not an ounce of fat to ward off cold, and obviously a highly unsuitable participant in the venture. But given my constant need to prove that I could 'run with the best of them' to 'chicken out' was unthinkable. The river was fast flowing and after we took the plunge we were quickly swept along at a rapidly increasing pace. The water almost literally froze the blood (and everything else) and a horrible numbness quickly set in.

It took most of us to the limits of our strength and endurance to make our way to the side of the river, many yards downstream from our entry point. Perhaps the 'tingle' as the blood again began to circulate made it worthwhile, but important to me — and I do not hesitate to disclose it — was the sense of achievement and adventure that made life at that stage so wonderful and exciting.

Another important exercise had to be undertaken, this being the 'assault course', but mercifully. this ordeal took place towards the end of the course, probably in deference to our obviously unfit state on arrival, being tarnished by the laxity of squadron life. We undoubtedly looked very pale and insipid and hardly up to this highly demanding physical challenge, devised for the more brutal members of our armed forces, who were likely to be called upon to storm ashore, up high cliffs if necessary, with wild shrieks to frighten the defenders and slaughter them without compunction.

Few of us appeared capable of this kind of activity, but although there were individual unspoken qualms it would have been unthinkable not to tackle the course with a zest and enthusiasm befitting men who had flown in the face of the enemy and emerged unscathed. We would show our instructors that we were not just 'Brylcreem Boys' who slept in pyjamas and sheets...

The first sight of the course, however, made short work of any bravado. The whole area was wet and muddy, and the obstacles — high fences, low tunnels and all kinds of devices designed to impede movement — soon extinguished our wish to show our courage. Of more concern was the tangle of scaffolding, set in a most awkward style and high enough off the ground to ensure that a slip would cause considerable personal injury. On top of each of these structures, separated by a considerable gap, was a very narrow plank, its purpose not, at first, obvious.

We were clad in overalls, heavy Army boots and carried a rifle, and after being assembled, the instructor pointed out that we would climb up the first 'tower', run along the narrow plank, jump the intervening gap to the next one, and so and so on. Most of us considered such a feat to be impossible, but it seemed a pity to deprive the instructor of his bit of fun. In any case, we were officers who led men and unfortunately it seemed that the time was now upon us to show how.

Once up and running, however, this part went quite well, and as I recall there were no broken limbs. But there was more... Some distance away stood a high tower constructed from poles joined together, probably about sixty feet high, and hanging from the top was a kind of knotted rope ladder. It had certain air of fragility, as though a stiff breeze might topple it to the ground, but 'in for a penny, in for a pound'!

Running from the top of the tower was a long cable, at about thirty degrees below the horizontal, and ending attached to a support some two hundred feet away. Again, the Instructor took his perverse delight in explaining how this device worked. The object of the exercise was to climb this indifferent rope ladder, stand on a small platform at the top, grasp a small bar attached to a wheel that sat on the aforesaid descending cable, and, with a shout of 'Geronimo' — this was optional — launch off into space to be conveyed, in comparative comfort, down the cable to the ground. The style of landing was one of personal choice, but it was apparently important to decide this before hurtling into the cable anchorage post at the end of the downward slide!

Remarkable, and not very well-known, is the fact that most aircrew have a poor head for heights. Only under certain circumstances in the air is there a sense of having a long way to fall, and I was no exception to this quirk. It so happened that the trainee immediately preceding me up the tower, was more than usually afflicted by this fear. On arrival at the top, an instructor was there to ensure that nobody merely fell off, but performed to the satisfaction of the organisers.

Sticking my head up through the hole in the platform revealed that the sergeant was trying to loosen the grip of the preceding trainee, who had utterly panicked and would not let go. Wishing to take no part in this argument, and already 'fired up' to take the required death-defying leap, I brushed past, grabbed the handle and was away before anyone could say 'Jack Robinson'. And what a lovely sensation it was! A swift and smooth glide to earth with a plunge into soggy earth at the end of it. To my regret, however, I completely forgot to yell 'Geronimo!' Perhaps a dry mouth prevented me uttering this symbolic American challenge to the gods who look after people doing silly things on high.

Amazingly, what we had done was comparatively tame compared to the antics of ordinary civilians in present times. Nowadays young and old, able-bodied or physically handicapped, take to such challenges with great gusto, abseiling down tall buildings or cliffs, 'bungee jumping' from heights of three hundred feet or more (such as the Victoria Falls Railway bridge), free-fall parachuting (one aficionado is 83 years old!), white-water rafting, and so on. The best of luck to them all!

The course was near the end and Charlie Brown and I were hovering around the Administrative Office trying to glean the nature of our next posting. With so much shared experience, we were now very close 'mates' and it was important to us to know what the Air Force had in store for us. Perhaps the course had done us both a power of good, toned up our physical senses and injected a new zest for further challenge — it mus have dome because we were seriously contemplating two alternative courses of action — one was to get in a couple of trips or so with Bomber Command, and the second, perhaps more audacious, was to volunteer for the Paratroop Regiment. Maybe such enthusiasm was the objective of those who designed the course, but we genuinely wanted to do something along such lines. However, we soon found that our 'dies' had already been cast, and it was back again once more across the now familiar North Atlantic.

WEST ACROSS THE ATLANTIC — MAY, 1945

Now being 'qualified' officers, we anticipated that our sea voyage this time would be under much more comfortable conditions. It was also likely to be less dangerous as it was apparent that the war in Europe was nearing its end and attack by enemy shipping fairly remote. Already, although it had not been made known, the horrors of the concentration camps in Eastern Europe had been revealed and the whole of the continent was in a sate of turmoil, with massive movements of refugees, prisoners of war and others, trekking in all directions.

The war in the Far East, had, to us in Europe, an unreal remoteness, but the fighting was far more vicious than that in Europe, with prisoners suffering torture and brutality under conditions of terrible squalor and degradation. Shot down airmen were as often as not killed, frequently by beheading. Suddenly, we found that eastern war more pertinent, as it appeared that we would be ferrying aircraft across the Atlantic to Europe, with the possibility of continuing to that 'remote' theatre of operations.

This time the 'good ship' *Ranchi* would be our transport and we were housed about six to a cabin. As ever, most of the fittings to provide 'cruise-style' comfort had been removed, but it was nevertheless a great improvement on the absolute austerity of my two previous voyages. This time we sailed from Liverpool, the historic port for Atlantic crossings, and the weather appeared 'set fair'. The interest and pleasure of another crossing, with more comfort, deflected our thoughts from the major and historical happenings in the wars general progress, and in any event, to return to Canada was viewed with anticipation of another taste of the hospitality previously enjoyed.

Life aboard troopships had a kind of surreal atmosphere. It was rather like being suspended in time and space, and the slow passage of the sea, with its endless swell and rhythmic movement, gave little indication of progress. Furthermore, there was absolute secrecy as to destination, our course to that point and our actual position at any point during the trip, consequently, the ship was alive, all the time, with the most wild rumours as to where we were, etc. This time, instead of the obvious direct passage, we would, perhaps, call in at Gibraltar, or even Capetown, and our departure route would be either north or south of Ireland, with a course up in the vicinity of Iceland or Greenland, not to ruled out.

These circumstances put Charlie Brown and me in a state of some demand. For reasons I am unable to recall, we had with us our astronomical sextants and the various tables etc, with which to calculate a position by 'shooting the stars'. Above us, in the Atlantic heavens we had an impressive array of stars, with the weather to give good viewing, through the eyepiece, to capture the heavenly body in the centre of the 'bubble' and then proceed to ascertain the position. Resulting from this, our cabin became a kind of supplementary 'navigation room', with streams of inquisitive callers requesting our latest position.

I think we were even able to advise our 'ground speed'—always an important factor for aircrew—but all had to be done under a cloak of secrecy. This meant tucking the sextant under a jacket, skulking up on deck and surreptitiously selecting the appropriate stars, and then taking the shots. Using a 'Bubble Sextant'—the bubble provides an artificial horizon as a datum line—was not easy even on the gently wavering decks of the ship, but we professed absolute confidence in advising our position, at any time, and in any case, who could dispute our reckonings! Conditions were also vastly different from our previous mid-winter trip, when progress around the ship had been dependant upon locating suitable handholds. These activities gave a bit of spice to the trip, but I cannot remember whether we Charlie and I achieved the goal of all aircraft navigators, that is to arrive at one's destination exactly on course and at precisely the time estimated.

Almost exactly in mid-Atlantic, however, the day that all had been praying for arrived. It was May 8th 1945, 'VE' (Victory Europe) Day and it was so difficult to realise that at long last, it was all over. The senses seemed numbed by the knowledge that a momentous era had drawn to a close and the ever-present sense of foreboding that had always been there in the wartime years, despite the outward jollity and carefree attitude—could now lift and be gone. Our ship-board circumstances, however, gave little opportunity for the wild celebrations and totally uninhibited parties we had promised ourselves when this day arrived and had to be 'put on the back-burner' to await a better time and place. Alcohol was a prohibited substance on most ships, but the Captain, from some probably secret storage deep in the bowels of the ship, produced enough bottles of beer for each of us to toast (one bottle per person!) the fruits of our efforts.

Such restrained exuberance, however, had not applied in the port of Halifax, Nova Scotia. Although most of the debris had been cleared away when we disembarked there a couple of days later, we learned that the crews of the ships, dock personnel and others had run amuck on that fateful day and done a large amount of damage. Inexcusable perhaps, but our only regret was that we had not been there to join in the fun!

Once again it was time to enjoy the hospitality of the Canadian Railway system, and to the sound of "all aboard"—what a delightful call this is, drawled and deeply resonant—and the 'clang-clang' of the sonorous bell, away we went on the long haul through the undulating and well-wooded provinces of Nova Scotia and Quebec, skirting the great St Lawrence river, to our next posting, Montreal.

313 ATLANTIC FERRY UNIT, 45 GROUP, MONTREAL, QUEBEC & NORTH BAY, ONTARIO JUNE—SEPTEMBER, 1945.

Halifax to Montreal by train is a fair haul and on arrival we had to report to the RAF Headquarters at Dorval Airport, a relatively short distance from the city. To our surprise and pleasure we were told that we could find our own accommodation in the city and would receive appropriate expenses for what was to us quite 'high living'. The first sally in this new found independence was to locate the 'Y'—the Young Men's Christian Association Centre—for accommodation, on the basis that it was cheap and any surplus balance of funds between our allowance and the very modest cost at the 'Y' could be put to far better use than merely providing somewhere to sleep. It was a huge building, with single rooms for many hundreds of inhabitants, austere, but still an improvement on many of the facilities provided by the services.

But it had it's oddities. Charlie and I, ever on the look-out for new adventures, decided to explore all the facilities on offer in our new 'billet' and found that in the basement of the building there was a swimming bath. 'Whacko!' we said, and rushed off to get swimming trunks and towel. But at the entrance to the pool our way was barred and we were told that all swimming had to be in the nude. Though not endowed with figures styled on the Greek Gods, neither of us were prudes, but we jibbed at exposing what nature had kindly chosen for us so our swim had to wait for another day and another place.

We soon found that our inexpensive quarters were not really to our liking and through, I think, an advertisement in the newspaper, packed the old kit bag and moved into a huge flat. The resident 'landlord' was one Peter Carter-Page, said to be, and I think we believed him, a member of the well-heeled and well-known family of the English firm of Carter's Seeds. A most flamboyant character, large in stature and almost overwhelming hearty manner, he was an artist who had been working on Walt Disney cartoons. Years later, in Africa, I found he fitted precisely the mould of what was known as the 'remittance man' — sent abroad when he became an embarrassment to the family and kept out of sight and harm's way by regular payments of cheques. To look at, he resembled the actor Peter Ustinov in his mature years.

A muster of the residents of the flat revealed, apart from Peter, Charlie and me, another former Beaufighter navigator, John Knight, and an RAF pilot known as 'Pancho' who had done a tour early in the war and was now involved in Air Traffic Control. The latter was of the same ilk as Peter, heavily moustached and wild and reckless in character. He and Peter were comfortably ensconced, receiving regular visits, mostly overnight stays, of ladies exhibiting similar lifestyles, and the whole flat was in a constant state of hilarity and turmoil, with unexpected happenings all the time. It became immediately apparent, however, that funds to pay for this hectic lifestyle were not in abundance and our contribution in the form of 'lodging money' was needed to make ends meet.

For us young airmen, after the austerity of Europe and the way we had lived, the contrast of life in the flat and in free and easy Montreal was most marked. However, flying duties pressed and first we had to undertake a 'refresher course' at Dorval to accustom to the technique of long distance trans-Atlantic navigation. With a distance of some 1,700 nautical miles to be flown, as a yardstick, our previous sorties of a few hundred miles paled into insignificance. This was a long air journey in those days, difficult to remember in the present age, when, in the 'high season' some 400 aircraft fly each way across the North Atlantic in every 24-hour period, each one with about three hundred passengers aboard, and no-one gives it a second thought. Such is the magic of the accomplishments of the aviation industry.

But in early 1945 it was vastly different. At the start of war, what was known as the 'Atlantic Bridge' had been formed by the RAF in 1940, but before this there had been no direct air service across the Atlantic. Many adventurous airmen had been lost in the twenties and thirties, setting out with single-engined aeroplanes, with little or no hope of rescue should those relatively unreliable aircraft engines suddenly lose power for any reason. So Charlie and I were due for interesting and even dramatic 'flights into the unknown'.

By now, our speed in sending and receiving the Morse code had deteriorated somewhat, as the call to use it on the squadron was only spasmodic. With the wastes of the Atlantic to be conquered, knowledge of position ay all time was a prerequisite to safety of crew and aircraft and an extensive monitoring network of ground stations kept anxious tabs on all flights. These stations were situated around the rim of the Atlantic and had the most modern of equipment then available.

So it was back to the schoolroom and the buzz-buzz-buzz of the high speed Morse code, and slowly our speed re-asserted itself, with eventually, a fair standard of competence at speeds in the region of 28 words per minute. Just a few weeks ago, as I write, the final decision was made to scrap Morse code as an international means of communication. I'm not convinced of the wisdom of this. Although it hardly compares with speech for convenience, it has always provided a reliable source of contact when atmospheric and other conditions have not permitted speech contact to be established. In addition, present day communication, invariably involving the use of satellites is largely dependant on technology, using delicate equipment prone to atmospheric interference and, worse, deliberate interruption or even destruction in times of hostilities. In my opinion, the relatively primitive Morse code could still provide a 'fallback' source of communication under certain conditions.

Having reinforced one half of our 'trade qualification', radio operating, we now moved up to North Bay, Ontario, to 'gen-up' on the other half, the rather specialised navigation techniques demanded by long-distance flying. The aerodrome was half an hour or so outside the modest town of North Bay and the aircraft comprised Douglas DC3 'Dakotas' and Mosquitoes. The Dakotas were fitted out as 'aerial classrooms' with some six or seven positions for navigators to take 'shots' and compete position calculations. However, prior to being let loose in the air, we took many ground shots to improve our ability to recognise the principal stars used for astro-navigation and also to brush up on the subsequent mathematical calculations, which were done from tables.

Flying at night in the clear air of Northern Ontario with the stars shining 'fit to bust' was a fascinating and pleasant experience, greatly enhanced as our confidence grew and we realised that this old fashioned — well, it wasn't *quite* old-fashioned then — method of using those faraway and intriguing pinpoints of light could indeed guide our small and frail aeroplanes across the vast oceans of our planet. Captain Cook must have taken great pride in similar skills with early sextants that allowed him to circumnavigate the world in the late eighteenth century, when it required extraordinary spirit and courage to venture into far and unknown places.

The science of cartography — representing the 'curvaceous' surface of the earth on a flat piece of paper — was established in the middle ages. Some of the first maps have an almost childlike charm with their disproportionate land masses of the then-known world, embellishments showing angel-like figures with trumpets indicating winds and other natural phenomena or strange imaginary creatures said to lurk in far-off places and comments at points yet to be explored such as 'there be devils'. One can imagine early explorer/sailors telling tall tales to the cartographers of the day, who probably found them hard to believe and were inclined to fill in gaps with their vivid imagination.

The shortest distance between two geographical points follows the curvature of the earth, but to follow this curve would require an aircraft to fly a constantly changing compass course, which is not practical. Using a navigation chart based on the mathematical calculations of

Mercator, who lived in the sixteenth century, and splitting the north Atlantic into five sections of longitude, this curve was smoothed out into five straight lines, known as 'Rhumb Lines', which gave a compromise between the shortest distance to be traversed and allowing the aeroplane to fly over each section on a constant compass course.

This is a basic concept and we focussed our talents on getting familiar with the practical aspects of astronavigation before undertaking our first crossing, but strangely, my first crossing came before completing any of the 'airborne' astro exercises, and arose because of my dual capacity of navigator/wireless operator. For some reason, a wireless operator became unavailable for an aircraft scheduled to leave for the UK and, as I seldom let an opportunity to see Carol slip by, I immediately stuck up my hand and joined the crew.

EAST, WEST AND EAST AGAIN ACROSS THE ATLANTIC

On the 24th June 1945 in Lancaster FM 183 with Flight Lieutenant Blott as Captain, we took off from Montreal at 1255 hours. Our first stop was Goose Bay in Labrador, a large airfield and complex built up over the previous years, but in the middle of nowhere. It was one of the 'staging posts' for the Atlantic Bridge, which was built up so laboriously, under the superb organising skills of Captain Don Bennet of the pre-war Imperial Airways. He was famed for his skill and daring, shortly before the war, as the pilot of the 'upper half' of the early experiment to use a large Flying Boat as the 'Launch Vehicle' for the small four engined seaplane which separated after take-off and then flew direct across the Atlantic. His skills in every aspect of aviation—he was a qualified pilot first but added navigation, radio operating to his repertoire with seeming ease—and, I think, aeronautical engineering.

The northern route was via 'Bluie West One' in Greenland—a difficult place to get into in bad weather, being towards the end of a long gully—Rejkevik in Iceland and on to Prestwick in Scotland. Aircraft with modest endurance used this route with Goose Bay being the departure point from North America. However, all transatlantic flights were subject to the vagaries of the weather patterns, with routes being decided on the value of the normally prevailing westerly airstreams. The direct route favoured an aerodrome named 'Gander', situated in Newfoundland, but both Goose and Gander—the planners demonstrated a nice sense of humour and literary versatility—were very busy places, with a hefty contingent of the American services present.

To assist in weather forecasting over the long span of the Atlantic— how different today with world weather patterns available to all and sundry at the touch of a television button—three or four 'weather forecasting ships' were positioned permanently at regular distances across the ocean. It is probable that there were instances when aircraft were in trouble and had to ditch, they were fortuitously near to them and the crews of these ships found they had unexpected guests for dinner!

On arrival at Goose, the weather was unfavourable for the next leg and a pleasant 'night-stop', with good food and a film thrown in, nicely broke our delivery flight, and next day we flew down to Gander to position for the direct crossing.

A short time after take-off from Gander, heading East for the relatively long haul, the broken terrain gave way to the uninterrupted expanse of the Atlantic and the instant of our farewell to the land, and the broken seas on the shore, remains even today, a very clear recollection. It really was a magic moment, despite then having a fair number of flying hours over various shorelines, the difference being, perhaps, that ahead was something like 1,700 nautical miles of only sea and sky. The American song *Off We Go Into The Wide Blue Yonder* came to mind as I returned to take up my tasks on the radio.

Around the perimeter of the North Atlantic, some half a dozen radio stations kept a watchful 'eye' on all aircraft in transit. I use the word 'eye' because not only did we communicate by Morse code, but use was made of what was known as the 'Butser Group' of radio direction finding stations. These stations took bearings on the wireless transmissions of the aircraft and then passed the bearing to the aircraft to facilitate the aircraft navigator in fixing his position. A couple of such bearings, from two or more suitably placed ground stations, gave an intersecting point known as a 'fix' (as tranquillising to airmen unsure of their position as a present day 'fix') and an added finesse was that each individual bearing had a 'class' attached to it to indicate its accuracy.

After take-off and when setting course, the wireless operator transmitted the 'departure message', using the international 'Q' Code, showing time of departure, destination, expected arrival time, height relative to cloud, etc. Thereafter, for the duration of the flight, at hourly intervals, a position report was sent to base, with update of arrival time. To assist in keeping an overall appreciation of the weather patterns in the hefty expanse of the north Atlantic, and to provide the weather forecasters with actual data on which to plan ahead, an important duty of ferry crews was to compile a weather report using a standard code known as UCO.

I greatly enjoyed the progress of our flight, and the navigator and I carried out a kind of joint operation in compiling the weather and position reports, facilitated by the fact that in the Canadian built Lancasters our two positions were adjacent, with a bench type seat available.

It was a 'beaut' of trip, the navigator continually taking astro shots of the sun and I contributing with a string of radio bearings, we made our way along our intended track, following the five or so 'rhumb lines' with never a hesitation as to our exact position. The ground stations were most solicitous in their assistance to us. Every time I passed the hourly report, after signing off with the 'diddy de da de da' — 'VA' = end of transmission — the direction-finding operator would come up in a most polite way (and one can be polite when using the Morse code) with a directional bearing to help fix our position.

Aircraft then were not pressurised and flying was usually carried out at five or six thousand feet, and, with no oxygen fitted, ten thousand feet the upper limit for lengthy periods. Consequently, the sense of contact with the earth and the elements was a dominant and ever present kind of cloak of comfort, with progress, even over the sameness of the sea, readily apparent as movement towards the destination point. It is sad, in some ways, that those used only to modern jet flying, where a rapid climb is made to extreme altitude and the aircraft appears to hang in the limbo of space with never the slightest impression of forward movement, is like entering a 'never never land' similar to the impression derived from 'virtual' reality.

We were not inflicted, however, in those days, with the dreaded 'drinks trolley', with it's seemingly endless perambulations around the aisles, to provide child-like comfort for those who prefer to pretend that they have not actually left the ground and are ensconced in some kind of airborne hotel lounge bar. This routine is a severe discomfort and harassment to those who prefer to savour the significance of the technical achievements that make the whole experience possible, and consider the now standard 'in flight entertainment' of movies, television, games to play, things to buy, etc as something to be stoutly ignored.

After a flight of eight hours fifty minutes, all in daylight, we touched down at Prestwick, Ayrshire, Scotland, with a sense of achievement and one more aircraft added to the fleet set to assist in the downfall of the other enemy in the Far East. The weeks leave with Carol, in the middle of summer and the end of fighting in Europe passed quickly — at that time to traverse the Atlantic to go on leave was somewhat rare, different to today's casual wanderings — and too soon it was time to catch the 'return ferry service' from Prestwick.

I think I had assumed, by now, a bit of the air of an 'international traveller', having crossed the Atlantic a few times, and our return group gathered in the mess at Prestwick for an early dinner before take-off. Someone gave me a tip about grabbing the most comfortable spot in the aircraft, as the seating was a makeshift arrangement, and that was to jump in quickly and 'doss down' on the pile of mailbags stowed in the bomb bays in the front of the plane. It was then possible to lie out full length, far more comfortable than an indifferent, steel-framed seat.

After departure, sleep came quickly and easily, cushioned by the lumpy mail bags, but in a moment of awareness, somewhere in mid-ocean, it suddenly occurred to me that the pilot, perhaps awakening from a short doze, may have thought he was back on 'ops' with the bomb aimer shouting 'jettison bombs!' and that, before realising what he was doing, he might pull the bomb release handle, discarding us and the mail into the waiting Atlantic.

However, Liberator AL 514 of British Overseas Airways Corporation with Captain Buxton at the helm carried us safely against the prevailing westerly winds non-stop to Montreal — extra fuel tanks were fitted — with a flight time of sixteen hours, in those days a very long non-stop haul. Having breakfast next morning in a restaurant in Montreal, I did show off just a bit and flourished the English newspaper of the day before!

It has previously been mentioned that some of the Beaufighter squadrons converted to Mosquito aircraft, but my first opportunity to sample the qualities of this remarkable aeroplane came at North Bay, where there were a number of crews ex the Bomber Command Pathfinder Squadrons also engaged in ferry work. Their uniforms glistened with many decorations, testimony to the outstanding and dangerous work performed by that select bunch of airmen. Hanging around aeroplanes was a pleasant and often rewarding pastime, not everyone's cup of tea, but Charlie and I took every chance to sample what was on offer.

The outcome of this modest thirst for new experiences was a trip in a Mosquito, piloted by one of the ex-Pathfinders and it was well worth the enterprise. We took off from North Bay and sped north on a long trip, following a series of radio beacons—known as 'riding the range'—at very low level. It was incredibly exhilarating to sweep low over the timbered landscape of Northern Ontario and our most northerly turning point was a small town named Moosenee. This town is situated at the southerly end of Hudson Bay and it intrigued me to actually see the place where many of the early Arctic explorers trod their way.

Pilot and navigator sat side by side in the Mosquito, a great improvement on the Beaufighter, where the navigator languished, quite lonely, in the rear of the plane and this arrangement obviously gave a huge boost to morale. It certainly did to mine!

We lived 'high on the hog' in Montreal, with plenty of good food and entertainment, explored the numerous parks and gardens, all in smart condition and rode in the horse drawn small carriages up into the heights of Mount Royale. One weekend was spent in cottages at a river resort—the river 'Rigaud, as I recall—and we swam in its icy waters, although a later little frolic nearly had me in the clutches of the 'Grim Reaper'. The river was very wide and we rowed out to the middle, dropped anchor and 'horse-played' in the water. Unknowingly, I drifted away from the security of the boat and suddenly realised that to get back was against a fairly strong current. By the time I reached its sanctuary I was far gone with exhaustion and only aware of my desperate struggle to keep afloat. I was dragged into the boat most unceremoniously, but when recovered, I offered up a silent thanks to whoever or whatever had kept a sheltering arm around my shoulders.

The sophistication of the bilingual society, French being used with equal fluency by a large proportion of the population, gave the city a real sparkle. It also gave me an opportunity to extend my French repertoire beyond the sole expression, learned in my youth — *la plume de ma tante.* Sent to buy some milk for the flatmates, I thought 'when in Rome do as the Romans do' and before departing on my mission, learned, parrot-like, how to make my purchase in French. I recall that it went something like *'Avez vous une quatre chapin du lait'.* The startled shopkeeper played his part in the exercise and I duly staggered home proudly with the milk.

August 1945 heralded the arrival of the Atomic Age, with Hiroshima and Nagasaki taking the full might of the newly found power of the Allies. Controversy still rages about this event, with those who were not there expounding the jargon of the modern 'caring society'. The Japanese atrocities against thousands of people in the east, and the brutal mistreatment of allied prisoners of war including the beheading of shot-down airmen, appears to escape their consideration. As I remember it, a sense of massive relief was felt by all who were alive at the time. After over five years of horrific warfare, we could at long last resume normal life. It is something that remains vivid in our collective memory.

Soon I was once again 'airborne' over the Atlantic, this time in Liberator AL 603 of British Overseas Airways Corporation, with Captain Prowse at the sharp end. After a flight of thirteen hours and thirty minutes, having refuelled at Gander, we landed at Prestwick and became available for our next posting.

147 METROPOLITAN COMMUNICATION SQUADRON, CROYDON—OCTOBER 1945—JANUARY 1946

It was an honour to be posted for flying duties to this famous aerodrome—or rather 'airport'—because that was its proper designation. After the introduction of passenger-carrying services immediately after the First World War, Croydon had held pride of place as the air terminal for the city of London, with easy access to the city centre. The wide expanse of grass for landing and take-off—no surfaced runways were ever built—and the distinctive control tower were home to huge lumbering biplanes such as the Heracles and Hannibal, together with the high-winged monoplane, the Argosy and sundry other planes of that vintage. It was here that air travel 'took-off', albeit at a speed of about eighty miles per hour—with a good following wind.

One of our squadron's main tasks was to provide a daily return service to Paris for the conveyance of mail, probably largely of the diplomatic kind. The end of the war had been only some few months previously, and the reorganisation of normal routine postal and courier services was still in some state of flux.

The faithful old 'Annie'—the Avro Anson—was employed, still, alas, with a manually operated undercarriage, requiring the navigator to exercise his left arm to the tune of about one hundred and twenty turns to retract the wheels; even putting them down again before landing tended to produce a few beads of sweat, particularly if the previous night had seen a few 'ales' consumed in the revitalising city of Paris.

The aircrew were a mixed bag, emanating from all areas of the RAF, but Charlie and I were delighted to be still together. This time, however, each flight involved a different pilot, very different from my 'bonding' with Mac in 254 Squadron, with our unspoken confidence in one another and co-operation in our flying duties. There was, on each flight now, between pilot and navigator, a quick assessment of each other before settling down to the usual routine.

One Australian pilot, who I flew with on several occasions, had overcome a severe disability from a flying accident, which left him with one leg almost rigid. Sitting side by side in the Anson, it was fascinating to watch his footwork on the rudder bar, because he was obliged to manipulate and twist his whole body to achieve the control required.

Europe was still disorganised in almost every way. Displaced persons trudged from country to country, transport was spasmodic and inefficient, but above all, the lack of food and clothing overrode everything. This latter problem inevitably gave rise to a thriving 'black market' in all kinds of goods, an example of the principle that when the chips are down, the basic human instinct of self-preservation supersedes everything else. I confess to having indulged in this 'vile practice' although the limit of my 'depravity' ran to a few bars of chocolate and an odd suitcase full of bicycle inner tubes!

In this context, my first trip with the squadron, a few days after arriving, was to Jersey in the Channel Isles. The islands were, strangely, the last area of Europe to be liberated by the Allies, probably because they posed little threat by that time. The wartime conditions there had not apparently been too severe for the inhabitants, although there had been some deportations of men for 'slave labour' on the mainland.

Remarkably, my first visit on 8th October 1945 was to load up with cartons of English cigarettes! My pilot was an Australian, who was very deft with a wad of notes, which he used to buy vast quantities of cartons of cigarettes at various outlets in the town. They almost overflowed the taxi on our return to the airport for take-off, and after arrival at Croydon, almost before the Anson had touched down, he performed a speedy turn on the grass runway towards our buildings at the far side, to avoid any unnecessary interest by the Customs Officials at the main terminal.

It was obvious that this was a well-rehearsed procedure, but who the prime movers in this lovely demonstration of commercial enterprise were, I never discovered. What was in for me? As I remember, bugger all! Still, the trip to Jersey, a truly delightful place (Carol and I and the children had a refreshing holiday there in 1949, but this time by sea ferry) with a warm climate, quaint buildings and accents, all brought back to mind many years later by the exploits in the television series *Bergerac*.

Somehow or other, we had a link up with crews of another squadron who flew into Germany and—lucrative for 'loot'—Copenhagen. Their speciality was the supply of the very well made

'Telefunken' radio sets, which had strange radio valves with side-contact pins but were in performance far beyond any British product. A 'barter' system had rapidly developed, embracing many countries and types of goods, but all regarded this dubious practice as, perhaps, legitimate spoils of war.

After growing accustomed to the shortages of almost everything during the previous years, it seemed silly to deny ourselves the odd 'perk'. In any case, we were the victors! All goods had a market price relative to other goods, so, for instance, the cigarettes we brought over from the Channel Isles could be exchanged for these very desirable radio sets, and so on and so forth.

The run between Croydon and Paris took about an hour and a half each way, not very much faster than the early post-war scheduled services started after World War One. We trod the 'air-paths' of those aviators who sat high at the front in open cockpits—who had probably flown with the Royal Flying Corps, still wore goggles and, by now, badly wind-swept white scarves!

Generally, the route was over Littlehampton on the south coast and Dunkirk in France. In a previous chapter, In an earlier chapter I spoke of my 'connection' with the Airship R101, which crashed in northern France at Beauvais in 1930. When passing over this area, which is typically agricultural, the small rise where the airship pranged is clearly noticeable, evoking thoughts of the immense tragedy on that windswept, stormy night so many years before.

When the Eiffel Tower hove into view on the first trip to Paris—and what a landmark it is—it was almost possible to experience the sense of delight and excitement of this fabulous city, even though it was still going through the business of recovering from the occupation. A distinctive and rather sweet odour permeated the whole city and the air seemed remarkably different from that of, say, London. Moreover, there was a kind of exuberance and zest for life although le Bourget Airport (now almost bypassed by the present-day airports of Charles de Gaulle and Orly) was a bit of a shambles. The sprawl of this huge city, with the winding River Seine and the sights to see, such as Notre Dame, the Arc de Triumph gave us great pleasure.

On the occasions when a night stop had to be made, the Canadian Officers club was available for accommodation and opportunity taken to view the well-known nightspots. The proceeds from the disposal of the bicycle tyres more than paid for food and drink (of which there seemed to be no shortage) and a good time was had by all!

The resurgence of Paris after so many years of occupation and hardship was delightful to see, with residents of all classes and appearances from a huge variety of countries intermingling with determined enthusiasm. We managed to 'engineer' fairly frequent stopovers — usually based on a difficult-to-prove engine 'mag-drop' — an opportunity to enjoy a touch of continental living, so different from the relatively staid way of life in Britain. My time in Canada had imposed on me a thin veneer of sophistication, in that I had heard the French language used in normal living situations, but the ambience in Paris was undoubtedly the 'real thing' to me, as an original north-country boy, to whom a trip to Paris had seemed about as remote as a trip to the Moon.

Take-offs from the undulating grass airfield at Croydon were interesting in that the aircraft usually became airborne with a slight 'leap'. On one occasion, having taxied to take-off point, the port engine spluttered to a stop, with no means inside the plane to re-start it. It fell to me to get out and 'wind the thing up'. Well, not quite, but the method used was known as an 'inertial starter'. This called for turning, with ever increasing speed, a handle stuck into the engine cowling. When the force generated was suddenly let loose on the recalcitrant engine it jolted into life. The only snag, as far as the turner of the handle was concerned, was that this fairly laborious and vigorous procedure was done in such close proximity to the engine as to induce a feeling of immediate danger from the propeller. When the prop began to turn, with gusts of smoke and a hefty roar, it was far too close for comfort. Thankfully this procedure was comparatively rare!

The visual delights of the mature English countryside were markedly evident during the run from Croydon to the south coast, passing over Surrey and Sussex and the variety of attractive features along the actual coast. When flying at lower altitudes, ground details are readily recognisable, and I invariably spent enjoyable time, other than for strictly navigational purposes, picking out odd or unusual aspects of the terrain, buidings, rivers, etc. As this small area of the Earth's surface, with its inhabitants going about their daily business, unconscious of our slow overhead passage, slid beneath our plane, humanity seemed to take on a more kindly and tolerant aspect. Perhaps it was just a sense of escapism brought on by being in the air at some several thousand feet.

An eerie but delightful panorama occurred frequently when weather conditions were conducive, usually when there was that heaviness and a sense of hush in the air that happens in England at the change of season fom summer to autumn, when the field crops and fruit are mature and ripe for picking.

It is most noticeable shortly after sunrise, when a delicate mist materialises and reduces visibility, but not to the degree that prevents take-off. After surging—if one can call it that in an elderly Anson— across the bumpy airfield, through this soft mist, almost immediately after becoming airborne, visibility became almost unlimited horizontally.

The beauty, however, lay in the panoramic view of the world below, covered in a soft carpet of mist, but only to a small depth, with the result that more prominent features, like tall trees or church steeples, stood proud as though afloat in a cotton wool sea. Such magical moments make flying delightful.

Not a lot of arduous navigation was required for most of the flights between Croydon and Paris, the weather seemed to be kind to me generally, but if conditions on the return to Croydon were often less than favourable, with the cloud base at a low level. Then the usual technique of 'map-reading' along well distinguishable pinpoints introduced a significant problem when approaching Croydon airfield. Sussex had—or did have, before Dr Beeching wielded his axe and drastically reduced them—a complex network of interlinked railway lines, running mostly north and south and east and west. One very convenient north/south line, when picked up near the south coast, led the aircraft almost to the threshold of the Croydon runway, and it was usual to follow this when weather conditions were not too good.

However, it was necessary to exercise a lot of caution when following this line over the rolling Sussex Downs as, just short of a town called Redhill—aptly named as it stood on a small hill—the line entered a tunnel. With the lowering clouds ahead, the pilot had to decide, rather quickly, whether to squeeze the aircraft up over the hill in the small margin of airspace available, and subsequently hope to find a break of cloud further on to locate Croydon airfield, or do an 'about face'. Such occasions were always just a little exciting, and what is now known, rather ponderously as 'CFIT' (Controlled Flight into Terrain), nevertheless expresses a major hazard ever present to all aircraft.

On Christmas Eve 1945 a return trip to Jersey in the Channel Islands was made in order to pick up a few Christmas 'goodies' that were not available in England—rationing of many things persisted for several years after the War—and the modest network of distribution took over the disposal. Unfortunately, the Customs and Excise had being doing some homework and charges of smuggling (what a 'nice' word with its connotations of hairy seamen and tall ships) were laid against one of our colleagues. The outcome was a fine of fifty pounds—a considerable sum in those days—and he was politely requested to resign his RAF Commission.

By February 1946 I had some twenty-five return trips to Paris under my belt and it was time once again, as is the tradition in the service, to move on to pastures new. These new pastures were very alluring, as I was to be seconded to British Overseas Airways Corporation to qualify as a civilian air navigator and fly the routes to the Far East and South Africa in the converted bomber aircraft known as the Avro York and the Avro Lancastrian.

Induction to the company took place at Blackbush in Surrey, but before becoming embroiled in my new role I managed to sneak a quick trip from Blackbush up to Prestwick to spend a few days with Carol. Such opportunity to grab the odd flight was a great perk as train travel in Britain was still a tedious business and it took so long to reach such a distant destination.

SECONDED TO BOAC—FEB 1946—FEB 1947

'Far away places with strange sounding names, calling me over the sea...'
This song had a haunting melody, implying the magic and mystery of
far off places and the people there and invoked—to those 'born under
a wandering star'—a kind of restless urge to leave all behind and go and
see and explore. These days many people speak of the whole world as
though referring to their own backyard, with casual reference to places
previously associated only with the early explorers. Timbuktu,
Patagonia, Lahore, Kalgoorli, Lhasa, The Klondike, Darjeeling, etc. By
sea from England to Australia was a journey of a month, to South Africa
two weeks and to the USA four or five days. How different it all was in
1945.

With the 'jet age' now well and truly established, with about a
million passengers in the air at any given time worldwide, it is difficult
to convey a real impression of the situation only fifty years ago. The war
years had seen the incredible technical developments in aviation, with
production of aircraft reaching astronomical figures to keep up with the
terrible toll of aircraft destroyed in the hostilities. By war's end in 1945
the overall picture compared with 1939 was, to most of us, quite
unbelievable. Before the war, the era of the biplane had still not quite
expired and the emphasis was on the future use of flying boats for long
distance flights, the loss of the airship *Hindenburg* at New York in 1937
having sealed the fate of those machines for commercial purposes.

The development of commercial aviation in Britain started
properly in 1924 with the formation of Imperial Airways. Perhaps this
choice of title had the appropriate 'colonial ring' when so much of the
world map was coloured red, but it nevertheless reflected the pioneer
spirit of both management and crews that flew those fragile aeroplanes
on routes that plodded through desert and jungle to the Far East and
down though the 'Dark Continent' to South Africa.

Many of the aircrews that flew these routes provided
communication flights throughout the war in unarmed aircraft and
under dangerous conditions—the loss of one such aircraft, between
England and Lisbon in Portugal, with the actor Leslie Howard on
board, being an example. During the 1940s the title of the company
was changed to 'British Overseas Airways Corporation'—BOAC
(usually spoken as 'bow-ack') and in the immediate post-war scramble

to re-establish a world network of air routes this company had a need for both suitable aircraft and suitably qualified crews to fly them.

Consequently, it was decided to attract suitably qualified RAF airmen to obtain the necessary civilian licences to operate the hurriedly produced aeroplanes, based on wartime bombers, to get into what was an inevitable major change in world communication and transport.

At this time, demobilisation of wartime aircrews was slowly taking place, based largely on a 'first in—first out' principle, and due to the large numbers involved, frustration and concern was rife. Very few pre-war regular aircrew had survived; the vast bulk of us had entered the RAF before becoming established in a 'proper' career, so if we did not continue to fly, we were really, in effect, 'back to square one'.

Showing more than my usual initiative, I had, in September 1944, while flying on operations at North Coates, written to the Railway Air Services—who operated a small fleet of Dominie Rapide aircraft on British routes and to the continent—applying for a flying position when the war was over. I received, as I recollect, a somewhat non-committal reply; other more pressing matters engaged everyone at that moment in time.

Perhaps being lucky in having 'two strings to my bow' regarding my flying qualifications, (navigation and wireless operating) I was readily accepted for secondment to BOAC as a trainee navigating officer and started the necessary courses to obtain the all-essential Air Ministry air navigator's licence. A lot of the detail of the initial ground course training escapes my memory, but it meant several moves: from Blackbush airport in Surrey to Filton airport at Bristol and the balance of the time at Hurn airport near Bournemouth in Dorset. We were a group of about six and we all had totally different flying backgrounds in the RAF. One fellow had been a squadron leader navigation leader on pathfinder squadron, another had been on Boston aircraft with the Second Tactical Air Force (2TAF), but we all had an enthusiasm for a post-war career in aviation and an inquisitive bent as to what other parts of the world looked like.

Coincidentally, Filton Airfield at Bristol was the site of the Bristol Works where the Beaufighters had been developed and were produced, so this gave me a bit of a warm glow of 'belonging'. Nevertheless, our group of ex-RAF navigators, all bearing the seal of the King's

Commission and used to a fair level of status or kudos, felt a touch put down when using the dining facilities at this place. Separate facilities were provided for the professional engineering staff and the like, who enjoyed a dining room with service, whereas we had to lump it with the 'proles' in a type of self-service canteen. They were, of course a pretty good bunch of blokes but we, at a young and tender age in our early twenties, were still perhaps unduly conscious of our rank and dignity.

I had, at this time, acquired a motorcycle. It was a 350cc BSA—a Gold Star, to be specific—but in somewhat rough mechanical condition. A disproportionate number of ex-aircrew came to grief, shortly after the war, using this dangerous means of transport. Perhaps their survival of operational flying had induced a sense of invincibility, or maybe they were seeking to rediscover the thrills and 'adrenaline-rush' they had known on active service—who knows? While writing of my experiences in 1998, I read of the young Aussie bloke who survived a couple of tours with Pathfinder squadrons, including one 'bale-out'. He returned home to a small settlement in Western Australia, decided to go for a spin on his brother's motorcycle the day after his arrival, and, in the parlance he understood so well, 'got the chop'.

My recollection of riding this 'dangerous beast' includes surging up the steep hill in Bristol with a pilot on the pillion, in no fit or legal state to be 'in charge of a motor vehicle', and, with dodgy brakes, swerving into the opposing lane of traffic when attempting an emergency stop.

Our future role within BOAC, on gaining the necessary licence to fly and navigate with fare-paying passengers, dependant on our skills and techniques, was something to be pondered on. Three possibilities existed: Number One Line, flying converted Short Sunderlands and similar unwieldy beasts to Japan and the Far East; Number Two Line, flying Yorks and Lancastrians to the Middle East, India and South Africa; and Number Three Line, flying Boeing Constellation aircraft across the North Atlantic to the USA.

The possibility of a future posting to No. 1 Line explained our surprise, at the commencement of the course, that one subject to be tackled was 'tides'! None of us had had any experience of operating in flying boats and land aerodromes tended to remain at the same height and provide the same kind of surface regardless of weather or time of the day! This subject took many hours of study, involving the calculation of such things as high and low water at far off places that had previously been to us only names in an Atlas.

The course, nevertheless, was stimulating and interesting and we gave it our full attention. In view of our RAF qualifications we were exempted in two subjects 'Form of the Earth, Maps & Aeronautical Charts' and 'Air Navigation Instruments, Magnetism & Compasses'. One subject, 'International & United Kingdom Air Legislation' was completely new to us and took a fair bit of study to get a good grip on what was involved in the discipline of peacetime flying, something that in wartime had not been overly emphasised. It demanded knowledge of the more staid routine of civilian flying, with such things as 'rules of the road' — the circumstances under which aircraft gave way to each other — the compilation of 'flight plans', the responsibility of air carriers, and even a detailed knowledge of the precise arcs of illumination of navigation lights carried by the aircraft.

There was a complete refresher of the basics of routine air navigation, in 'dead reckoning', establishing the position of the aircraft by the various means available, etc, with emphasis that having regard to the large distances to be traversed, over comparatively isolated areas, many of the normal means of keeping to a pre-determined course would not be available.

Much importance was placed on 'climatology' — worldwide weather conditions — again in view of the fact that our routes were, literally, spread over much of the world. Coupled with this was the subject of meteorology — the detail of how weather conditions are formed and having an immediate impact on the aircraft in flight and consequently personal safety — a subject which many of us found to be a quite difficult.

I found climatology a fascinating subject, perhaps as it referred to 'far away places, etc' and we enjoyed learning the names of the different winds and other weather phenomena in those only relatively recently explored places.

We adopted the well-tried method of study that is to pair off and pound each other with the most difficult questions that we could muster. Many of these sessions took place on the beach at either Bournemouth or Christchurch, close by, but our attention was sorely tried by the more interesting young holiday-makers, who were taking advantage of the pleasant weather and the relief that there was no possibility of a sudden swoop by an FW190 pooping off his cannon. However, 'tides' gave us all a hard time, as each calculation was quite lengthy, when, for instance, our 'partner' demanded to know the precise GMT of high water at Basra in the Persian Gulf on a particular day (and how many high tides occurred during the day in question). It involved few mathematical calculations, the answer being determined by reference to various tables, but it was a tedious procedure, not to be shirked, however if the glittering prize of a civil navigators licence was to won…

The 'learning process' (today's jargon) was slow but steady, and eventually the day of the examination arrived. After the very lengthy time to train in the RAF I was well accustomed to the strain of examinations, but this one was a real challenge. Nevertheless, I felt determined to pass. We were all aware that the pass rate was about fifty percent, and even though we were in the broad stream of our activities of the past few years, the new subjects, and the more extensive knowledge required in meteorology and climatology, caused some no little anxiety.

The certificate advising candidates of the result of the examination was headed, a touch ponderously, 'Report of the Examining Board'. It was known that a failure in a subject was shown in red, so when opening the envelope, maximum impact was achieved. perhaps. Perhaps my fingers were unsteady when I opened my envelope, but no sign of the dreaded red lettering and another fairly important step in along life's pathway had been negotiated.

I received my Aircraft Navigators Licence No. 1526, dated the 12th August 1946, issued by Authority of the Minister of Civil Aviation. This gave me considerable pleasure, as throughout my boyhood years, I had seen the achievements of so many of the pioneer flyers, establishing the routes throughout the world, flying fragile machines with so few aids for their safety, and with, unfortunately so many lost in the process. To be licensed to follow, in a modest way, the footsteps of these memorable aviators was an uplifting experience.

The place names Cairo, Basra, Bandar Abbas, Johannesburg, Karachi, Kuala Lumpur, perhaps having lost a little of their old world innocence by the passing of the war, nevertheless, took on a fresh allure, and seemed now to be within the grasp of my eager, navigationally competent fingers. But not so quick, there was a couple of other important things to be dealt with, like getting 'kitted out' with the darker blue uniform of the company that I was now going to serve.

Carol, Joy and I were by this time living in flat at Wimbledon, but it was also necessary for me to obtain simple accommodation near Hurn Airport, near Bournemouth on the south coast in order to be ready to fly the aircraft up to London airport, pick up the passengers, clear customs and depart on the route. By some connection or other, I obtained 'digs' with a Jewish family of mother and son at Christchurch, and this gave rise to a couple of embarrassing moments.

The first when the 'lady of the house', on our initial meeting, enquired as to my breakfast preferences. My general knowledge was a bit sketchy and there may have been some hidden quirk, having opted to learn German before the war—I have always had a deep seated sensation that somewhere in my ancestral chain there lurks a modicum of Jewish blood—but I suggested that the normal egg and bacon would not go amiss. She politely indicated that fish would fit better with her cooking arrangements and it took a little while for me to realise that to her the thought of any freshly sizzling rashers of bacon in a pan on her stove was an anathema to her, and any Rabbi who happened along would no doubt give her a good dressing down.

The other *faux pas* was when Carol brought Joy, who was eight years old, down to Bournemouth for a days' visit. We were sitting in the house with the mother and her son, making polite conversation about nothing in particular, when a lull occurred, and Joy, addressing the son, suddenly, piped up, in her clear childish treble, 'What a big nose you have got'! There was no doubting the veracity of the observation, the aforesaid nose was, to put it as politely as possible, a remarkable example of what a 'hooter' could really develop into given free rein. The owner, the son was in his early twenties, and very pleasant as well, took what could have been interpreted as a compliment, with praiseworthy *sang froid*.

Nevertheless, the conversation quickly resumed, rather frantically, as I recall, but Joy had the bit between her teeth and was not to be deflected. 'What a big nose', she said, this time more loudly, and again the casual and non-controversial conversation was halted in it's tracks.

'It's so big, it looks just like a witch's nose!' This time there was no way that the child could be ignored, but the way out of the delicate situation was somehow achieved with good taste and no hard feelings.

ROUTE FLYING TRAINING

The possession of an Air Navigator's Licence was not, however, a *carte blanche* to jump into an aeroplane full of passengers and nip off to the other side of the world. Ability in the air had to displayed to the authorities and this entailed several 'proving flights' with assessment on return. After all, although the immediate safety of all on board was in the hands of the pilot, he needed someone to guide him through those endless and unmarked wastes of the air, and put him in a position to carry out those things that pilots do at the end of the journey.

We had completed our ground training in 'civvies' (conventional clothing) and as we were now to fly with a civilian airline, the process of kitting out in the uniform of BOAC had to be put in the hands of the local tailors accredited to the company. This seemingly innocuous process carried, remarkably, very grave implications for my well-being and once more, after the usual series of 'dicey does' in the RAF showed the randomness of whoever watches over all of us.

One training flight was a quick return trip to Karachi in a Lancastrian aircraft, achieved over a period of three days, which, for the time, was indeed rapid transit time. A roster of flying duties for several of us at Hurn had been drawn up and I found that I was marked for such a trip. It so happened that having given my personal details of measurements to the tailor—I have always been an awkward fit, having disproportionately long arms and legs—the tailor had not completed the uniform trousers, and, being Saturday. As I recall, the garment would not be ready until the following week. The outcome of this apparently trivial hiccup was that one of my colleagues was switched on the roster to fly the trip to Karachi.

The flight to Karachi was completed with no untoward incident and they departed on the return trip to Heathrow. By then they must have been fatigued—and it is to be remembered that in those days, the present very strict limits on the amount of time spent in the air in any one flight, and also between flights, had little application, the requirements of the flight taking precedence. The aircraft flew into the ground in Northern France, the only survivor being one of the stewards.

The *Findings of the Board of Enquiry* revealed some strange conclusions. Flying at about nine thousand feet in clear weather with no mechanical malfunctions and all apparently under complete control, the sole survivor, after recovering in hospital, told a strange story. He recalled that he had, even under these tranquil conditions, a sudden premonition of acute danger. He went to the toilet in the rear of the aircraft, sat on the floor and braced himself against the toilet. When he came to, he was in hospital with few injuries although temporarily blinded by the fluid from the chemical toilet.

The Board was unable to determine the actual cause of the accident, but surmised that the crew was extremely fatigued and that, perhaps, the automatic pilot had gradually allowed the aircraft to descend to the ground and into the orchard were it crashed. My navigator colleague, who was killed, had many flying hours with Bomber Command and this seemed to be a sad way to go. My memory of him and the strange coincidence involving an unfinished order to a tailor, remains vivid to this day.

Passing through Heathrow—and Gatwick, these days—is probably one of the most impressive examples of how the world has changed in my time. With four major terminals at the former, and plans for similar development at the latter, not to mention that two other London terminals, which also handle large amounts of traffic. The City Airport, in the East End of London, utilising the specially developed aircraft exhibiting 'short take off and landing' capabilities—operating within the 'sight and sound of Bow Bells' and St Paul's Cathedral—and the recently opened Airport at Stanstead in Essex, are as a planet removed from the primitive facilities through which we operated in mid 1946.

Most of the buildings then were ex-Army Nissen huts, half circular in shape and made from corrugated iron. Instead of the now moving 'walk-ways' of plush construction, it was then a walk through the dust, or, even worse, mud of inches deep. Leaving Heathrow was then a tedious business. It was a walk to the main gate, lugging whatever oriental treasures had been bargained for in the streets of Karachi, and other places, safely guided, legitimately or otherwise through the ever vigilant customs officials, a queue to get on a bus heading for Hounslow tube station and, after a wearisome flight, no holds barred to grab one of the few seats available or to hang on to one of the overhead straps.

No such difficulties these days, with every possible facility available for our creature comforts, with the need to actually walk anywhere regarded as unacceptable.

The four terminals are all closely linked, with plans for a fifth, and the latest exercise in this mass movement of human bodies, is to be whisked to the centre of London on a high-speed train service. Passenger statistics continue to spiral upwards, and the complex has taken on the aura of a cross-section of all the races and cultures in the world, with the constant hubbub of languages, dress, etc.

On 3rd July 1946, in a Dakota aircraft under the command of Captain Harvey, we took off from Aldermaston Airfield bound for Gibraltar, this being my initial route training flight. It was a plod, across the Bay of Biscay towards the north-west tip of Spain and some four years later, I was to cover the same route, this time under more turbulent conditions, aboard the *City of Durban* Union Castle liner bound for Capetown and Rhodesia.

The 'Rock' has a marked air of mystery, and history, and well deserves it's reputation as one of the Seven Wonders of the World. It just sits there and exudes an air of brooding, drawing attention to the fact that at this point, two continents are at the 'interface', as it would be expressed in modern terminology.

In the 1980s, when Carol and I lived at Hastings in East Sussex, we paid several visits to Southern Spain, the Costa del Sol towns of Marbella, Torremolinos, Malaga and, of course, the 'Rock' and Algeciras being the principal points of interest to us. Prior to leaving Hastings, on one trip, we noticed in a shop window in Hastings, a notice offering a unit for sale at el Quatro, a small village situated a few kilometres west of Algeciras. The 'price was right'—at least in relation to our then diminished income after having left the bulk of our capital in Rhodesia—and we thought a quick 'shufti' would not go amiss. The dreary weather of England was beginning to pall, so, armed with the particulars of the property we took the local bus from Algeciras to inspect what could be our new residence.

The house was disappointing in the extreme, being dark and dingy and one of a dense cluster, with a lack of privacy—and the 'patrone' had a bit of a shifty look about him and his somewhat opulent major house was choc-a-block with what seemed expensive antiques rather out of keeping with the ambience of the place. But I digress...

The real impact of the situation was the air of eerie calm and a slow but gentle kind of hush which permeated the atmosphere. It was as though time was standing still, caught in some kind of 'time -warp', with an immense weight of time and history held in abeyance. The sense of the sky and space of this pinpoint on the earths surface, with the expanse of the 'Med' spreading eastwards, and, to the west, the broad Atlantic, and beyond the Americas, resulted in a sharp intake of breath and conversation suddenly took on a whispered way, as though not to disturb whatever was so greatly affecting most of our senses. It was similar to that feeling, when, sometimes, slowly awakening from a pleasant dreamy muse, and the re-entry to the real world is resisted in order to prolong the sensuous pleasures.

The Straights of Gibraltar spread several hundred feet below, the North African coast not too far distant, and this was the 'throat' of the Mediterranean, where over centuries, from the first primitive boats, to the mighty war vessels of modern naval fleets, had made their passage, for better or worse, in storm and calm, in peace and in war. It was simple and easy to project on this narrow expanse of sea, images of such ships, particularly the 'tall ships', with full sails billowing, and to even catch a sense of the noise of their passage and the calls of the crew going about their duties.

What a superb spot this was, but with some regret, we accepted that the immediate surrounds of this cluster of units was not to our liking, in terms of privacy, etc, and we caught the bus back to Algeciras in a sombre an thoughtful mood, which lingered until dispelled with our usual 'sun-downer', the immediate cure for such matters.

But this was all in the future as we droned across the Bay of Biscay in July 1946 and I plied my Dalton 'computer' and dividers across my Mercator chart, determined to find Gibraltar and prove my worth as a civilian navigator. It was, of course, difficult to make any serious blunder, just head south and turn left at the appropriate moment and there was Gibraltar 'on the nose' after a flight of nine and a half hours.

The runway at Gib was (and still is at the time of writing) quite unusual, in that most of it's length was man-made and projected into the Bay. There have been many 'incidents' due to this, perhaps the best known being the loss of a Liberator aircraft conveying General Sykorsky of the Polish Forces, lost with all aboard due to engine failure on take-off coupled with a lack of experience on the part of the pilot.

Our evening included a visit to the famed Rock Hotel, well known to throngs of servicemen who passed through Gib in the war years. On returning to our transit quarters sometime in the small hours of the following morning revealed, when switching on the light, a most amazing infestation of cockroaches; the floor became a shimmering mass of movement as they scuttled into their nooks and crannies.

Tail winds on the return trip gave us a boost in 'ground speed' and the next trip, this time to Lisbon—Lisboa, as the natives say with a slight lisp and a 'shsh' (sounds much better)—was eagerly anticipated. Two days were spent in this delightful city. (Carol and I made a couple of visits in the 1970s and were just as charmed with not only the beauty and history of the place, but also by the natural courtesy and character of the Portuguese people, with whom we renewed our acquaintance when visiting Mozambique from Rhodesia.)

'FLYING THE LINE'

No. 2 Line, based at Hurn, Dorset, York and Lancastrian aircraft, to Cairo, Calcutta and Johannesburg.

It was nice to know, when rostered for the next trip, this time to Cairo, that I was deemed fully fledged and competent to find the way there and back. On occasions, my previous flying experiences had involved encounter with what can be described as 'inclement weather' to put it mildly, or more, aptly, on a few occasions, encounters with real 'dicey stuff'. This trip to Cairo revealed to me the dangers—and the beauty—of the massive structures of the cumulo-nimbus clouds along the coast of North Africa.

This time it was the Avro York, a four-engined hybrid of several wartime bombers, carrying 35 passengers and a crew of captain, first officer, navigating officer, flight engineer, radio officer and cabin staff of two male stewards. The latter were gentlemen recruited from a variety of sources, I think our two on this flight were ex-Merchant Navy, and sadly lacked the charm and beauty of the later recruited 'air hostesses'. However, despite the catering facilities in the aircraft, hastily put together in the same way as the aeroplane, the meals that appeared on my navigation table were not too bad, and fortunately at this time, the dreaded and ubiquitous 'drinks trolley' had not been thought up by some clever young brain.

Cruising at around two hundred knots, and with an 'all-up' take-off weight of 60,000 lbs (modern 'heavy' airliners now take-off at the incredible weight of 400,000kgs, with plans for a gross lift off weight of 650,000kgs) stretched the York to be able to fly non-stop from London to Cairo, so an intermediate stop, somewhere in the 'Med' was the usual practice.

Marignane, near Marseilles, Luqa, Malta, Castel Benito, Tripoli were used to refuel, and on occasions involved a stop over because of weather, etc. One such stop, at Castel Benito gave a sharp and unpleasant lesson in the rigours of life in the desert and an insight into the conditions encountered by the 'Desert Rats' with when in pursuit of or (in the early days) scrambling in hasty retreat from the 'Fox' — Erwin Rommel — that brave and competent commander of the German troops in the desert campaign. The evening of the stop was spent watching a film in the open air, and this resulted in bones being chilled to the marrow and unfortunately, accommodation was in short supply, which necessitated sleeping in the aircraft.

There is no way that any comfortable posture can be achieve in any aircraft and perhaps the York was a bit worse than most. The result was a most miserable night, frozen to the quick and shivering. At least it was for one night only and my sympathy went out to those who had to spend many such nights, huddled up to keep their 'core temperature' from dropping to a lethal level.

Cairo

It is hard to convey the impressions that come in quick succession when first seeing this intriguing and ancient city of early civilisation.

Flying steadily along the North African coast, usually within sight of the Mediterranean Sea, the harsh brown of the desert sands and the blue of the ocean are in marked contrast. Small settlements can be seen, but, by and large, little change takes place for most of the run. Then, suddenly, out of this monotonous vista of brown, looms up the Nile Delta, in a vivid shade of bright green with no fuzzy edge to mark the transposition but a sharp and clear dividing line between harsh desert and the verdant arable area that has sustained life in this region for so many centuries. It is quite a wondrous sight when seen from the air and even Space Shuttle crews, apparently, relish it from their 'eye in the sky'.

The north African coast is a hotbed of massive up-currents of hot and turbulent air, rising to thousands of feet and forming huge rolling banks of cumulus and cumulonimbus clouds. Aircraft are not designed to withstand the stress of sudden vertical winds of a hundred knots, or so, so great care has to be taken to weave a path through these 'canyons' in the sky.

However, after nightfall, when meteorological conditions were calm and clear, and when taking astronomical shots with the sextant for navigating, standing in the perspex dome with the sextant hooked up for steadiness, a quite overwhelming sensation manifested itself. The dome of the sky became a blaze of light with myriad pinpoints of individual stars seemingly shouting to make their presence known. This created a sensation of being uplifted into the heavens and a complete and instant severing of all connection with things earthly, as though I was totally surrounded by those distant lights and all shackles with the earth severed.

The remarkable contrast was then to gaze down vertically, through the 'drift- recorder', at the black earth below, where periodically, on the desert plain, a faint smudge of light would be discernible, indicating, perhaps, a small Bedouin settlement, or for the very faint light, the tents of a travelling camel train. The contrast between the 'up' and the 'down' view brought home, with no small impact, the puny place which we occupy in the 'great scheme of things'.

The civilian aerodrome at Cairo was Almaza, fairly close to this sprawling mass of very simple houses for the masses, with the River Nile occupying pride of place. The airport facilities were relatively simple too. The old traditional airfield, Heliopolis, was close by and this had been the one of the principal stopping points of the early record-breaking flyers to Australia and the Far East. The RAF had used Heliopolis since the early days of British rule of Egypt, and the British presence in this country was still very obvious.

The centre of Cairo was the scene of frenetic activity, the noise and the bustle quite overwhelming, particularly after a rough flight and the smells — not unpleasant — but new to our Western noses, carrying all the magic and mystery of the occidental half of the civilised world. Everywhere one went, a swarm of traders, mostly small boys anxious to clean shoes, pestered unceasingly. The latter, if thwarted in an inexperienced manner, flicked spots of shoe polish on your trousers, the act being accompanied by wild and indecipherable imprecations of dire misfortune to come. Most of us surrendered to a quick flick with the rapidly manipulated duster and honour was satisfied to a degree. Unfortunately, a short distance onwards, another swarm took over and the procedure was repeated.

A suburban network of trains existed, open carriages, with what appeared to be unfettered access to the railway line and little indication of any control of passengers or fare collection. Each coach accommodated about a hundred passengers, but the overflow, possibly another two hundred, scorned the comfort of a seat and perhaps the imposition of a fare and clung, quite precariously, to any protuberance of the coaches and covered the roof, like a swarm of bees, with no means of grasping anything, all with great abandon and very obvious enjoyment. I was impressed by the sheer exuberance and delight these unsophisticated inhabitants of this ancient city took in the making such a train journey. Many years later, in Rhodesia and its adjoining countries, I was able to see local people joy-riding in much the same way, and the pleasure they appeared to derive from it when compared to the overwhelming luxury which so many in the western civilisations gave one cause for thought.

We were accommodated at the Heliopolis Palace Hotel — always known as the 'HPH' — which had large and well-furnished rooms and a dining room of sumptuous standard. There were many large areas in the hotel which carried a constant flow of people of all races, the Arabs and their ladies being particularly noticeable for the distinctive style of their clothing, their obvious wealth and their dignified bearing. This remains a treasured memory of the standards of those bygone days, in stark contrast to the present-day 'dressing down' to casual clothes such as jeans and t-shirts and the apparent intention of so many young people to act and dress as slovenly as is possible.

A delicacy I particularly enjoyed from the extensive menu in the dining room, was a particular type of fish which I later discovered was Nile Perch, a kind of Barbel which spends its life gorging on whatever gravitates to the bottom of the River Nile. To me, it was extremely tasty, but when recounting to friends my enjoyment of this scavenging creature, I was met with looks of revulsion at my lowly epicurean standards!

A visit to the pyramids and a ride on a camel was almost obligatory for crews passing through Cairo, and I realise how lucky we were to do these things at a time when the area at Giza was totally untouched by the present dreaded wave of 'tourism'. At that time the area was very much 'rough and ready', perhaps not much different from centuries before. Nevertheless, the sight of the vast pyramids evoked a deep sense of wonder at the ability of those ancient people to conceive of and complete such a mammoth task of construction. It left me with a feeling of awe and a desire to obtain more a detailed knowledge of that wonderful and complex civilisation that existed so long ago.

Several of our crew were sitting on the veranda of the Heliopolis Palace Hotel, having a quiet beer, when glancing at the passing pedestrians, a familiar face hove into sight; it was 'Simmy', a navigator with whom I had been on the Transatlantic Ferry Group in Canada, nearly two years previously. With several other crews, he was engaged in ferrying Mosquito aircraft to New Zealand, to be part of their post-war air force. Much jollity and exchange of news ensued, well lubricated by the 'amber liquid! Simmy was quite an 'old man' by the general standards—being all of thirty—but he had the charm and persuasion of the Cockney and his spell in Canada had resulted in him taking a new and young second wife.

All crews also had access to the 'Gazira Sporting Club' near the hotel, an elite centre for well-to-do local people. It seemed to be untouched by the rigours of wartime and luxury in everything the keynote. There was a magnificent, Olympic-size swimming pool and this was utilised by many wealthy young and talented Egyptian men. They appeared to spend most of their time performing complicated and impressive dives off the topmost diving board, and did so with a very conscious awareness that those watching were suitably impressed. We certainly felt a touch envious and deflated, particularly as in those days we had been led to believe that only Europeans—and the English in particular—could exhibit sophisticated skills of this nature. This attitude had been reinforced by contact with the general population in such places as Cairo, where the use of the word 'peasant ' would not have been inaccurate, even if 'politically incorrect' by today's standards.

Interestingly, today, Americans visiting England nowadays, often express reservations about the quality of the drinking water, having ventured outside the 'cocoon' of their own country. Almost without exception, every traveller passing through Cairo succumbed to the dreaded 'gippy guts' or 'Pharaoh's revenge'. It struck with little warning and could be almost incapacitating with constant vomiting and diarrhoea. At least the return trip from Calcutta involved a 'stop-over' of couple of days, so there was a chance for the afflicted to recover. It was certainly 'not done' to desert the crew with whom one had been rostered and flying. 'Dr Browns Chlorodine', in a small bottle, was part of the equipment I carried for such flights, and sometimes, when the disease struck particularly hard, after the pre-flight preliminaries, when I had settled in the aircraft with my navigation equipment set out, this 'elixir' was tipped into the palm of the hand and licked in the hope that the trip home to England could be handled without too much discomfort.

Lydda, Israel

Number Two Line, in addition to operating through to Calcutta with York aircraft, flew part of the service to Sydney, Australia using Lancastrian aeroplanes. BOAC flew London to Lydda, then on to Karachi, where the QANTAS crews took over and flew from there to Kuala Lumpur, thence to Darwin and on to Sydney. A few of our crews were lucky enough to do the whole run through to Sydney, with the Australians coming through to England, but such trips were rare and prized.

The Lancastrian was even more uneconomical than the York, with a crew of seven but carrying only eight passengers. The latter sat sideways on what looked to be extremely basic seats, with almost no glimpse of the world outside. Many years later I learned the cost to the passenger of flying in those days. Roughly, a flight to Australia cost the equivalent of three years of the average salary. Today, the relative cost is about one or two month's salary. I have no real recollection of the passengers we carried, being preoccupied with my navigation duties, but when moving to the rear of the aircraft, in flight, to use the chemical toilet, my retained impression is that none ever looked very happy.

This was hardly surprising as we had no pressurisation and consequently flew at about nine thousand feet where for almost the whole of the time turbulence, usually quite severe, rocked and tossed the aircraft without pause. I was, fortunately, by this time, pretty inured to this problem and even derived a sense of enjoyment from the rapid tossing of the aircraft, rather like an exhilarating funfair ride.

One problem existed in carrying out my navigation, however, as it was necessary to use a pair of dividers on the navigation chart and also to draw lines. The aircraft would, just as I was poised to do such act, give either an almighty leap upwards, or downwards, with the result that the dividers stabbed the table or the required straight line took on a distinctive bend.

These were turbulent times in the yet to be established State of Israel, with acts of terrorism occurring with frightening frequency. Senior politicians of later years such as Ysak Rabin, were then leaders of the groups dedicated to 'liberating' Palestine and the British Government was hard pressed to conduct any meaningful negations because of the horror of the acts perpetrated on people innocent of any involvement in the course of events. Perhaps the most horrific terrorist act was the bombing of the King David Hotel in Tel Aviv, when almost two hundred people — mostly British servicemen — were killed.

This method of political persuasion was relatively new at the time, and methods to counteract such actions were uncertain and had to be explored. Remember, the situation in Palestine was the forerunner of the subsequent 'decolonisation' that took place in Africa, with thousands of people killed by the activities of the 'Mau Mau' and similar groups, determined to grab power at any cost of life of their fellow citizens.

A stop at Lydda meant personal movement was curtailed, any journey being undertaken in armoured vehicles. Consequently, we were unable to see much of this historic part of the world and spent most of the stop in the airport precincts. It was in this 'captive' situation that I was able to witness a significant event in that country's violent birth. The terrorist gangs attacked British troops whenever the opportunity arose and it so happened that they had taken two British Army sergeants hostage in an attempt to negotiate the release of some of their gang then in prison. It was a difficult situation as the gang leaders had set a deadline, beyond which, they had declared, they would execute the two sergeants. One of their group, one Dov Gruner, as I recall, was somehow involved in the negotiations, but had flown to New York for some reason. As our crew sat at the airport, word spread that he was on his way to Tel Aviv to enter into negotiations with the British. Regrettably and brutally the gang had by this time hanged the two sergeants in the olive groves in the vicinity and feelings were running very high at the airport. Journalists and cameramen thronged the airport as Dov Gruner disembarked from the aircraft and emotions were running at fever pitch. I had a small, simple, camera with me and utilising the flashes of dozens of press cameras, I opened my lens and snatched a shot for myself, to join the very unambitious collection in the 'family album'.

One of my most rewarding trips, from a navigational point of view, took me through Lydda, but with a chord of great sadness appearing many years later. On 10th February 1947 at 1324 GMT in aircraft Lancastrian G-AGMB with Captain Dobson, we took off from London Airport bound for Lydda, from where, with another crew the aircraft would be flown to Kuala Lumpur, then to be taken over by QANTAS. A couple of hours of daylight remained and navigation was straightforward, mostly map-reading across France, with the occasional radio bearing to help confirm position.

A phenomenon of radio bearings is that around morning and evening twilight, they become notoriously inaccurate, demanding great care when used and regarded as secondary to other navigational techniques. So out came my astronomical sextant and I had to 'shoot the stars' from then on. It was just one of those trips when everything seemed to click into place. Select three appropriate stars, take a shot of each one—the sextant had an averaging device that took the mean of sixty shots in two minutes—record the data, refer to the Air Almanac, and then the Astronomical Tables appropriate to the area of flight, complete the calculations (not very arduous), plot on the Mercator navigation chart the three position lines obtained, this whole process occupying nearly ten minutes and produced what was known as a 'cocked hat'—a small triangle on the chart that one could say, with a fair degree of confidence, that somewhere on this geometric figure, was the position of the aeroplane.

So down and across the Mediterranean we 'stooged', with me taking a series of astro shots and maintaining our pre-determined track. It was one of those rare occasions, with the weather just right, no high cloud to obscure and dim the selected star hovering in the centre of the little bubble in my sextant. The stars were nicely juxtaposed and a rock steady aircraft ensued that the aforesaid bubble did not bob and twist as was usually the case. All the necessary calculations fell into place with a satisfying smoothness—again not always the case because fatigue from engine noise always gave me a hard time and tended to result in simple addition or subtraction going slightly amiss, with the desired 'cocked hat' being large and sprawling, and throwing doubt as to the accuracy of the calculated position.

The night passed, with 'fix' after 'fix' being marked on my chart, as we headed pretty close to due east down the length of the Mediterranean. And then came that delightful moment in any flight, when the enveloping darkness suddenly gives way to a suggestion, faintly seen, that dawn is not far away. I was always very conscious of this transition from night to day, particularly when flying on operations at North Coates, it gave a sense of refreshment, even a touch awareness of survival, after the hazards of the night when mans instincts have always invoked a sense of vulnerability.

The reputation of navigators hinges on many things, some mere trifles, but when such gentlemen offer to the Captain of a ship or an aircraft, and it is usually 'put in writing', their firm opinion as to the time the vessel or aircraft will reach a predetermined point on the earth, they do so after much deliberation and assessment of all the data available, some, unfortunately, being of fleeting reliability. The Captain, not unreasonably, tends to disregard such navigator problems and keep his gaze firmly fixed on the figure given to him, as though it is engraved in stone. All aboard always have a keen, and sometimes anxious interest on the time of the forthcoming event and as it approaches, many pairs of eyes, surreptitiously flicker, more than usually, to the heading of the aircraft or ship.

A very definite, and subtle feeling becomes apparent when the time arrives and the target is not sighted. All, of course, discard from thought the problems which the navigator has in attempting to provide an accurate figure, it is his duty to get it right. Who can deny, even when sitting comfortably engrossed in a seafaring story, the surge of the spirit—and the soul—when in the olden days of exploration, such as Columbus attempting to find the Americas, the excited yell (many days after the ship's navigator had probably said "not very far now")—"Land Ahoy!"

It was not quite like this on our fight to Lydda, but to my great pleasure, after a satisfying flight, our destination airfield was 'on the nose' precisely when I said it would be. We landed after a flight of eleven hours and a half.

Some of the Captains with whom I flew were ex pre-war Imperial Airways, with many hours and remarkable experiences behind them. They were a unique breed of men, having started flying shortly after the First War and their 'patch' spread almost completely round the world. Most were formal in their duties and dignified as was in keeping with their responsibilities to their passengers. Dress standards were quite rigid and a pair of white gloves completed the image of the 'air-dog' as opposed to the sea-dog. They expected in return due deference to their status. One of the first lessons I learned, when on an early trip, was that there was a well-established manner of address and of procedures when in flight and moving around the aircraft. At the end of one leg, after landing at an intermediate point, all the crew disembarked and walked—there were no fancy high, moveable steps as of today—we merely stepped down from the plane. Unfamiliar with the firm protocol, I unwisely and brashly attempted to disembark before the Captain. He reminded me, quite unambiguously, who he was and who I was and not to do it again. Still, as a substantive Flying Officer in the

Air Force of His Majesty and shortly due to be promoted to Flight Lieutenant, the instinct was to bridle a touch, but his bearing and his ability as an airman overrode any such insubordination and I deferred to his command with alacrity.

By the time I was seconded to the airline, quite a few of the pilots were ex-RAF, either seconded like me, or having been released from the service and taken up a work contract. Some of the early joiners had been promoted to Captain rank but some were still flying as First Officers, under the command of a seasoned veteran. Some had left the service as senior officers, squadron leaders and even wing-commanders, mostly from Bomber Command where the losses were such that promotion came quickly, even to some in their very early twenties.

With such a background and bearing in mind their youthful status, to fly as 'second dickie' again must have tested their inherent sense of pride, but all seemed go smoothly nevertheless, and it was an exhilarating time for all of us, having survived the war and with a long career in aviation stretching ahead of us. Incidentally, although quite obviously all expenses were met when on the line, the basic salaries were pretty miserly, even for those times. Navigating Officer received four hundred pounds per annum, First Officer pilots eight hundred to a thousand pounds and senior Captains around fifteen hundred pounds per annum.

It was unusual to fly with the same crew members, the available grades being so different in total that rostering precluded this. Navigators were in short supply so the rest period between trips was much shorter than that for other categories. Consequently, a different atmosphere pertained on each new 'flight deck', but this soon shook down to a friendly working arrangement, as we all realised the nature and the degree of our responsibilities as now we were carrying fare-paying passengers. At least we no longer had to face up to the hazards of the dreaded 'flak'.

Strangely, it took me a long time to get over a feeling of vulnerability in the air now that I no longer had a parachute lying next to my feet. It was jokingly said that, while it would have been difficult to hurl the passengers out of the aircraft attached to parachutes, at a time of dire emergency there was no good reason why the crew should have go down with the ship!

On the Lancastrian trip mentioned just previously, this aspect of compatibility of crews took the tops with Captain Dobson as the man charge. He had the DFC—as had several other Captains—and also a DSO as I recall, but he had those subtle qualities which are part and parcel of the make-up of just a few men to whom other men respond without question. Leadership defies precise definition, but in the services it makes itself known, quite unambiguously, in almost everything that is done. It probably manifests itself in respect for the leader's judgment in whatever task is in hand, and a willingness for each subordinate to perform in a better way than he would otherwise do. So it was with Captain Dobson, and we settled down on this trip with a very comfortable atmosphere.

I was, nevertheless, a bit startled when, somewhere over the deserts of the Middle-East, he vacated his seat—the aircraft was on 'George', the automatic pilot—and told me to change seats with him. I had never had any training as a pilot, the nearest thing was, at my old skipper Mac's insistence, was to 'fly' what was known as the Link Trainer—a simple, early mechanical simulator. This indicated optimism to the 'nth' degree on the part of Mac, as the possibility of my taking over from him in a Beaufighter in flight was zero. Perhaps it was more for my morale than anything...

'Dobbie' pointed out that he was keen to qualify as an aircraft navigator, possibly influenced by the fact that Air Vice Marshall Don Bennett, head of the Pathfinder Force was qualified in every category of flying duties, including engineering and wireless operating. On a more practical level, as a pilot of Lancasters he had likely given all his crew a chance to get their hands on the 'wheel', not only to create a healthy crew spirit but also, should he have been injured, at least a modest chance that other crew member could have a stab at handling the aeroplane.

With 'George' disengaged, I must say it was thrilling to wrestle with this massive beast, trying to keep on course, and feel the sense of power from its four Rolls Royce Merlin engines; quite overwhelming really. It was totally unlike the usual position for a navigator, standing behind the pilot, although this was satisfying in itself, it was the superior position and view of the whole forward aspect that gripped the feelings.

Even more satisfying was the feel of the control column, with its steady vibration running up the wrists and into the body and the senses.

I had quite a long spell at the controls and Dobbie did his thing at my navigation table with quite a flourish and it was evident that he made a regular practice of this novel—an unthinkable procedure by any of the pre-war skippers—and it was just part and parcel of his generosity of spirit.

The return trip to Karachi in the Lancastrian took about three days. Although the outward bound leg down the Mediterranean had been a 'milk run', the long arm of the 'Grim Reaper' nearly grasped us on the return trip. As is often the case in such instances, the onset of this gentleman's attentions was so swift and unexpected that the odds of escaping him were formidable; well beyond, I would guess, those that any decent 'bookie' would be prepared to offer bets on.

The main runway at Luqa, ran, I think, east to west, with most take-offs to the west. It had to be used by any big aircraft, heavy with fuel, even when there was a high increment of crosswind, as was the case for this flight. Malta is a mass of low stone walls, in fact the whole Island has a kind of craggy appearance, and the sprawl of these walls had not been greatly interrupted when the runway was established. Malta had been the scene of heavy bombing during the war, with the Luftwaffe doing its damnedest to subdue the island. In the very early days, the Air Defence aircraft included three old biplane fighters—Gladiators (appropriate in the circumstances) nicknamed Faith, Hope and Charity. These names were also appropriate because despite all odds, the island weathered the onslaught and was subsequently awarded the George Cross for valour, a singular and unique accolade.

Sometime after my 'spell at the controls'—for which I was very grateful to Captain Dobson—we landed at Malta to refuel in order to cope with the prevailing west winds on the way to London. The Lancaster was perhaps the most loved aircraft of the war, as all who had the privilege of crewing them agree to a man. The power and sound of its four Merlin engines had a sweetness that permeated the mind and exhilarated the blood, and this was the situation as we lined up on the runway to take-off for London.

All crew members usually size up the general situation prior to the pilot opening the throttles, and, with few exceptions, all pulses tend to quicken just a 'tad'. Flying, over a period of time, one develops a kind of innate sense of awareness of all the factors pertaining at any given moment, and a subtle sense of hidden dangers which may lead to an unpleasant incident. How this works from psychological point of view I do not know, but it is very real and the degree of its development in an individual perhaps explains why some aviators plod on accumulating hour after hour, and seem to be quite invincible.

I stood in the well, just behind the two pilots and Dobbie opened the throttles for take-off with a heavy load of fuel and a factor of crosswind for him to contend with. With the surge of power and the lifting of the tail, however, it quickly became apparent that the aircraft was affected by the crosswind and it started to drift across the runway despite the efforts of Dobbie to restrain it. He had made, when flying with Bomber Command, many such take-offs, with delicate parameters, but this, I think, taxed him just a bit. However, experience counts so much in flying and he rose to the occasion with verve and confidence.

As we gathered speed, slowly—well, quite quickly really—and slid across the runway towards its rough edge, flying sped had still not been attained. Nevertheless, all was not lost and recourse was made to a device fitted to the throttles. The levers move in a kind of slot, pushing forward to open the throttles for more power (unlike French aircraft where the reverse is the case) but movement beyond the power level the engines will normally produce for standard take-offs is limited by a barrier of copper wire. In emergences the pilot can thrust the throttles forward and break the wire to obtain extra power from the engines. As I recall this was known as 'going though the gate'.

And that is what Dobbie did, in a remarkably cool manner, as befitting a man of his experience and composure under stress. I know I was sweating rather profusely as the undercarriage was raised just a split second before the plane arrived at a series of low (but high enough) stone walls that would have 'tripped us up' without a doubt.

Captain Dobson continued to fly with the Company, later re-named British Airways, but to my greats sadness I read of his demise in a most unusual aircraft accident that even all his professional expertise and vast experience could overcome. Nineteen years after our 'near miss' at Luqa, when the Gods had unexpectedly smiled on us, fortune was less forgiving. In 1965 he was flying a Boeing 707 on a flight from Tokyo to London. Shortly after take-off from Tokyo, a minor diversion was made to show the passengers a closer view of Mount Fuji, a normal kind of event on such flights. In 1965, scientific knowledge of weather, involving gross and unexpected turbulence of upper winds was still a bit sketchy, but sadly, so often aviation learns its lessons the hard way.

As Dobbie circled closer to the mountain, a remarkable combination of local weather patterns caused a high velocity vertical wind to develop, although there was no visual indication and nothing in the aircraft instruments warned of its presence. As the 707 became grossly overstressed it started to disintegrate; failure of the rudder was the trigger for total destruction. There were no survivors.

In summary, it may be said that such aviation accidents hinge on what frequently appear to be small and not overly significant circumstances — 'for want of a nail the horse was lost', etc etc.

These factors are probably always in constant ebb and flow, normally supplementing and then cancelling each other, with the end result being a 'non-event'. But perhaps some hidden and incomprehensible force, holding sway over this cancelling effect, suddenly either loses control or, even with malevolence, influences numerous 'imponderable factors' on it's course to precipitate a devastating climax.

With the build up of flying time, all airmen are prey to the unpredictability of such factors, despite the developing confidence and professionalism. All experience the suddenness of the onset of a situation which demands extra vigilance, and which, when, overcome, leaves behind a sense of narrow escape. Such was the later feeling as we safely became airborne at Luqa in 1947 but sadly this was not to be the lot of my greatly respected fellow airman, Dobbie, all those years later.

Basra, Iraq

The Routes were planned using sectors of about four or five hours flying time for the York (but longer for the Lancastrian) and more in keeping with the with the service through to Australia. After Cairo, the next leg for the Calcutta service had to be arranged to avoid flying over Saudi Arabia, consequently, the course immediately after taking off from Cairo was north-east, passing over Israel and the Dead Sea, Jordan to a point in what was soon desert terrain, with almost no possibility of obtaining a visual fix from anything on the ground.

After a couple of hours or so in this wilderness one hoped to locate a 'way-point' (modern parlance) known as 'LG3'. A place called Rutbah was close by—I have no confirmation of its history, but assume that it was one of the early staging points in the twenties and thirties. Called 'Landing Ground No. 3' it was at a convenient distance for the limited range of the aircraft in those days. It certainly had a feeling of remoteness about it, but was sighted with great relief in the early days when airmen often perished in the desert from thirst after a forced landing.

This sector was not overly interesting but after turning over LG3, the run down to Basra was a south-easterly course and gradually the scenery changed. The overall feeling in this part of the Middle East is a subtle sense of history and this became more evident from our altitude of some nine thousand feet, in very bumpy weather, as we soon sighted the change in the appearance of the ground. Slowly, it became apparent that the previous harshness was giving way to a more gentle and soft terrain with the appearance of water gradually becoming more widespread. This is the beginning of the Euphrates River, probably the cradle of civilisation, and somewhere in the vicinity was the ancient city of Ur of the Chaldees. The river merged further down towards the Persian Gulf with the River Tigris in a massive confluence.

At this point in the journey, the mystic east beckoned ever more strongly and it is to be remembered that at this time, almost all the way ahead the map was still coloured red, denoting colonies of the British Empire, with still only a hint the air that all would soon be changing. Basra was probably one of the easiest places to navigate to, the plumes of fire from the oil refineries at Abadan hove in view from many miles distant, and the aerodrome was alongside the river, —known as *Shat-el-Arab*—which had facilities for the landing and take-off of the flying boats that operated the BOAC service through to Tokyo. A similar 'water-borne' service went down through Africa to Durban—both journeys taking lengthy period of time to complete. The legs flown were short and mostly in daylight, with night stops being made in quite luxurious hotels, with the accommodation in-flight styled on a hotel lounge.

Two friends from South Africa made the trip to England in the late 1940s and were enchanted by every aspect of the arrangements, with time to explore such places as Entebbe, Khartoum, Cairo Valletta and Malta after a short days flying. How different to the present day, with no room to stretch the legs, loss of all contact with 'Mother Earth' the hassle of the departure lounge, the anxious watch of the carousel looking for luggage and, worst of all, the in-flight tedium of the drinks trolley and the constant invitations to do some 'duty-free' shopping.

Re-fuelling at Basra took about an hour, and we had to visit the Operations Office to check weather, etc and file a flight plan for the next sector. Here the navigating officer had a bit of a disadvantage as his duties took up a lot of the time on the ground, whereas the other members could relax for a spell. By the time we all re-boarded the aeroplane, however, the merciless sun had heated the interior of the plane to an almost unbearable temperature and it was only when we had climbed to about six thousand feet did it become bearable again.

One of my duties was to record the time it took for the aircraft to take-off—that is, from beginning to roll to the wheels leaving the runway. This was useful information for the engineers as take-off time was related to the maximum permitted load for each and every sector. The higher the temperature, the longer the take-off took and consequently, the lower maximum weight. Basra, as I recall was usually about fifty five seconds, performed with stately grace by the old Yorks and little indication of the power of the thrust of the engines when full load was taken. I stood up in the astrodome on take-off and watched the top of the plane, and after the tail lifted up and the plane slowly gathered speed it was fascinating to observe the wing tips gradually lift up as the wing took the weight from the undercarriage.

The amount of this movement was probably of significant interest and I think the modern airliner, such as the Boeing 747 is designed to allow a wing deflection in turbulence of about twelve feet! It is also not generally known that modern jets are so designed with a 'shear pin' attaching the engines to the wings so that in extreme circumstances, the engine will drop off rather than the wing collapse. One of the pleasures of a flight in present day aircraft is the wonderful feeling of acceleration on take-off, being thrust against the back of the seat, and the high angle at which one is hurled upwards towards the high heavens; its all good stuff!

There was only one runway at Basra and I recall it never seemed to be too long for a take-off and somewhat claustrophobic in the bargain, in that it was lined on both sides by avenues of tall palm trees. Basra was not a place conducive to lingering or to find that a night stop was required, it was merely a place to top up the fuel tanks and it was a sense of relief when the undercarriage came up and the next sector, to Karachi was in front of us.

This part of the flight was probably the most interesting, the long haul down the Persian Gulf, surmounting the long arm of the Oman Peninsular, and skirting the coastline along the mountainous Persia, Balucistan and then Pakistan. This part of the world had an intensity of age about it, perhaps because it was the primitive sea route from the Middle to the Far East. Marco Polo took the inland route—the 'high road'—in his journeys of exploration, and arduous it must have been, traversing the Gobi Desert, through a great range of weather and temperature. Cruising along comfortably in the York, with the aircraft position always easily to hand, thoughts drifted to what it must have been like all those centuries ago and what the Arab seafarers in their dhows would have made of our 'wing-ed monster' hurtling across the sky!

But the Persian Gulf has seen much tension and activity in recent years, with the build up of large fleets of the USA, the loss of an Iranian airliner, with all on board, and a number of shipping losses of both sides. A new airport at Abu Dhabi is a major stopping point for flights between Europe and the East, although improved aircraft with extended range now over-fly the Gulf. On a recent flight from Singapore to London the night was very clear and suddenly the darkness was broken by a vast expanse of light from the oil wells which proliferate in this area, probably Bahrain. The amount of oil consumed by the world in one twenty four hour period staggers the imagination.

The finger of the Oman Peninsular projects northwards towards Bander Abbas, with the Straits of Hormuz intervening. On the peninsular is one of the oldest aerodromes of the RAF, Sharjah, where some of the pre-war long serving airmen that taught us descriptive and very rude Air Force songs at North Coates spent their time in the thirties 'getting their knees brown'. In such faraway places, ladies, even of the most disreputable variety, were in drastically short supply. Loneliness was a fertile field for the rough but witty humour that provided light relief from the sterile and celibate life these young and lusty airmen in their prime must have had to contend with.

For some reason or other, I always considered crossing the Peninsular as a kind of 'gateway' to the Far East and used the time it took to cross from one side to the other a useful benchmark for checking the ground speed of the aircraft. With Bandar Abbas to the left, it was a pleasant and easy run, parallel with the coast. The navigational procedure was to take 'running fixes' using recognised points on the coast, this information always being useful to recalculate the always welcomed ETA at the next significant landmark.

It was standard practice not to cross the coastline into the territory of Baluchistan, home to probably some of the most precipitous cliffs and crags in the world, where in places the mountains soar to 8,000 feet, not far below the operational height of our aeroplane, but on one occasion, massive clouds made such a detour necessary. It was remote and unspoilt and had a great impact on the senses. Looking down at its rugged, natural beauty one seemed to be looking back in time.

Along this part of the coast were two 'landing grounds' that had no doubt very welcome to early aviators in these parts: Jask, in Iraq and Giwani in Baluchistan (which is part of Pakistan). One scheduled service to Karachi was such that this area was flown at night, with a dawn arrival at that city. The night was very black, when flying east, but the interval between night and day in these latitudes is very short and the transition almost abrupt, although not abrupt enough to miss the discernible small glow of light dead ahead followed by the burst of the rays of sunlight which transformed the environment and lifted the spirits.

In addition, there ahead was the river Indus and the sprawling 'minareted' city of Karachi, as we approached to land at Karachi civil airport. I was reminded of my tenuous boyhood link with the Airship R101 by the sight of the huge hangar that had been built in 1930 to house this 'ship of the air' on its expected triumphal arrival (it's still there today). Perhaps the Italian lyric *'Que sera sera'* sums up one's feelings when viewing this sad relic of man's constant quest for progress.

Outward bound, Karachi was the first place to take two days rest – 'slip', as it was known—so it was a welcome break from the vibration and noise of the four Merlin engines that were so close to my navigation table. The round trip to Calcutta, including another slip at Cairo on the way home took about ten days. Karachi was more pleasant and our transit quarters situated in a fairly quiet suburb, just a short ride in a *gharry*—a horse-drawn cab. These were the days before all such places were inundated with tourists: from young drop-outs seeking the culture of the East and a personal Guru, to retirees wishing to vicariously experience 'alternative lifestyles'. Simply to watch the local inhabitants going about their traditional way of life was to us a new and exciting experience.

One mercenary practice in which the crews indulged, however, was 'carpet buying'. Rationing of almost everything still existed in Britain, foodstuffs, clothes, household equipment, etc. and the back street vendors in Karachi had cottoned onto the fact that there was beginning to be a regular flow of prospective buyers passing through their city. It was possible to order a gentleman's suit there on the way to Calcutta and pick up the finished article on the way back to the UK the following day. And the same with a pair of custom made shoes! The quality of the material and the workmanship was good and this was a popular means of getting such items 'off the ration'.

The buying of Indian carpets was quite a humorous and interesting way of spending a couple of hours of our 'slip time' and took a kind of ritualised form. The back streets where this took place were congested with little attempt at presentation of the goods, with carpets piled up in random fashion and all taking place with the accompaniment of a cacophony of shouts, imprecations, oriental music, constant accosting by street beggars and, above all, the aromas of the Orient. The latter were, strangely, not at all unpleasant, merely the tang of everyday living of these poor but energetic people so far removed from the village of Spondon in Derbyshire where I had grown up. Whilst strolling in these congested streets one would sometimes encounter a totally naked, and frightfully hirsute 'holy man', who would pass by, oblivious to everything but his constantly repeated mumble of prayer. If such an occurrence had happened in Spondon it would have certainly raised the hackles of the local police constable!

I found the whole place highly interesting and later, in Africa, saw the same basic unsophisticated way of life that, tough as it is, seemed closer to man's heart than the complex and stressful ways of the West.

Prospective customers for carpets were seated on a dais, plied with tea and soft drinks, and with a wild flurry of activity, the parade of carpets began. One after the other, they were thrown down, into what became a massive pile, with wild and exaggerated claims as to their quality, colour, durability etc, and, even thrown in, the benefit of the good luck that would accompany this purchase of this beautiful item of floor covering. It was all done with frantic gestures indicating the hardships of the extended family that had to be supported by each valued sale, driven home by repetition, in that distinctive form of 'pidgin' English that oriental peoples manage to learn, and which, quite unkindly we westerners tend to find amusing.

Unable to resist such blandishments and not averse to the high praises heaped on me, indicating that I was a 'fine gentleman' I committed myself to a delightful plain Indian carpet, some twelve by nine feet, which would be sent to my home in England, with all the necessary documentation, shipping arrangements completed by the vendor. Remarkably, and a tribute to the inherent honesty of these struggling sellers, it arrived in Wimbledon, England, in fairly quick time and subsequently gave us good service in Rhodesia, although by this time the odd threadbare patch had become evident.

Another excursion most of us took during our stay in Karachi was to visit a small resort nearby, where we 'partook of tea' and, to my latter day horror, swam in some part of the wide estuary of the Indus River. The river, I later learned, had by this point in its journey, already served the communities for many hundreds of miles of upstream as a sewer and much else besides. I close my mind as to what kind of 'close encounters' I may have had whilst enjoying a leisurely swim in what appeared at that time to be quite an attractive venue and an excellent way to escape the heat of the city!

Delhi, India

The two day break at Karachi was a very welcome relief as I found the loud noise of the four Rolls Royce Merlin engines seemed to echo and reverberate around my navigator's position and induce much fatigue. Wearing headphones was uncomfortable and clumsy and I generally discarded them in favour of a wad of cotton wool. The flight deck crew could only converse by shouting and this added to the stress. Constant heat at the intermediate stops was also oppressive and tiring and this, coupled with the engine noise in my ears, which persisted for many hours after landing, generally left me 'a bit lackadaisical' when there was a chance of some recreational activity.

My digestive system also took a bit of a beating, with sleep being taken at varying times, day and night, and meals in flight had to be 'scoffed on the run', so to speak. On occasions, on some schedules, a lapse of thirty hours or more would occur between waking for duty and the eventual time of flopping down to sleep. How very different now, with absolutely rigid controls of the length of time aircrew can be on duty and with the same restrictive measures on obtaining adequate rest immediately prior to the trip and between trips.

There is something unique about being part of a flight deck crew. On most flights, all members soon settle down to their respective duties and an air of quiet confidence permeates the somewhat narrow confines 'up front'. Each goes about the task in hand all this individual expertise slots together smoothly, resulting in the objective of flying from A to B efficiently and safely. The tasks of each crew member being equally important, mutual confidence is essential for an air of satisfaction and well-being to exist. The aircraft itself, seems to assume a lively role in creating this atmosphere, and when the weather is particularly favourable, the sense of pleasure to all as the miles slip by is tangible, but largely unspoken, but manifesting itself in the sense of fellowship, camaraderie, whatever, that forms a solid base for recall in later years.

Landings and take-offs are always special. After the hustle and bustle of preparing for the trip, the run to the airport, the pre-flight briefing, etc, settling down to positions in the plane, the 'line up' on the end of the runway always seemed to be a special moment in all flights. The run-up of the engines to full power, with the accompanying vibration of the airframe, and then back to the quiet of the idle, followed by the confident thrust of the throttles by the Captain, never failed to gave a real sense of excitement. With landings, the generally relaxed *en route* atmosphere dissipates as the destination airport comes into view. This point in the flight has great significance for the navigator, as there is always a sense of achievement at having completed the task in hand, more so when the final course and time of arrival given to the pilot back along the track is close to the calculations.

All pilots adopt some personal variation in what is basically a standard technique for landing an aircraft, in the broad approach to the runway, the attitude of the plane, the degree of turn to the final approach and the manner in which the plane alights on the runway. Indeed, some pilots exhibit a touch of flamboyance in this regard and become 'characters' easily recognised by other crews when their techniques are discreetly mentioned. However, that moment when the wheels actually touch the ground—and stay there—is for crew and passengers alike, a significant moment, despite the thrill of flying, signifying a safe return to our natural environment.

The run from Karachi to Delhi's Palam Airport took nearly four hours—longer than it takes Concorde to fly from London to New York—with places from the history books of this turbulent country, slowly coming into view, from our viewpoint at about nine thousand feet before disappearing beneath our wings. A couple of centuries ago, some had been the scene of war and violence, with dreadful atrocities, with no quarter given to the vanquished of either side. Skirting the fertile plain of the Indus River, and after overflying Hyderabad, the landscape changed to the barrenness of the Indian Desert, which provided few landmarks for navigation. It was, nevertheless, in its bleakness, another interesting variation in the range of geographical features that a trip from England to the East could offer to any traveller, and I took my usual delight in focussing down through the Drift Recorder on the passing countryside, for no other reason that I found it enjoyable.

Refuelling at Delhi took about an hour and although the cockpit was covered temporary with shade cloth, on re-entering the aircraft, the heat was like a blast furnace, with relief arriving only when reaching a higher altitude. The next leg to Calcutta also took about four hours and this time, running close to the course of the River Ganges—the most densely populated area of India—became starkly apparent, with village after village merging with the next. Even today, with the eye of television probing and reporting over most of the world, few Westerners have any grasp of the density of the population or the way of life for so many millions of people, eking out a meagre existence from overworked agricultural lands.

The south-east course of the aircraft was over such places as Lucknow, Allahabad, Benares, Patna, crossing and re-crossing the river Ganges, in which river the faithful put their implicit trust, by bathing and washing daily. Some present-day professional photographers have done well to catch the humanity of these scenes, with the rising or setting sun providing a backdrop of inspiring beauty.

A most beautiful sight on this leg, and completely contrasting with the rough and tumble of man's affairs down below, was the glory of the Himalayan Mountains. The range was about two hundred miles distant, but even from our flying height of nine thousand feet, the snow capped peaks loomed majestically into the clear, cold air. This occasion always drew the rapt attention of our passengers, and I found it interesting to note their reactions. The awesome sight of the Himalayas invoked quiet introspection amongst most, perhaps because to behold such awesome natural beauty inevitably brings about a sense of our own puny significance in the natural order of things.

The sprawling, high-density houses—I avoid the use of the word 'slums'—extended far out from the city of Calcutta. Our destination Airport was Dum Dum, a name now best known for the 'dum dum bullet'—a metal-cased bullet with a soft core exposed at the tip that expands on impact and inflicts gross injury on human flesh—a particularly nasty development in projectiles that was first manufactured at an armoury on the outskirts of Dum Dum.

At this time the whole of India was in turmoil, with 'freedom' the rallying call, but the precise terms and arrangements to implement this, far from clear. During the war there had been recruitment of disenchanted Indians by the Japanese, resulting in several regiments fighting on their side, and the whole country was under great tension.

After arrival at Dum Dum, as a safety precaution, we were ferried into Calcutta in armed vehicles. The route took us through the narrow and congested streets, affording us a good view of everyday life there as we wound our way along. The squalor and degradation was unbelievable; it hardly seemed possible that any reasonable kind of life could exist in such cramped conditions. But in the midst of all this, the human spirit refused to capitulate and the city's inhabitants went about life with a determination and energy that would put to shame those in more favourable circumstances who often appear not to appreciate their good fortune.

One vivid memory of this small moment in my travels still stands out. As we made our way through the streets, peering through the safety grids welded onto the sides of the vehicle that carried us, the mass of people ebbed and flowed constantly. Suddenly, out of this mass of humanity, a lone figure caught my attention. It was a Holy Man, I think, marked not by his style of clothing, which differed little from the normal simple and untailored wrap, but by his dignity and bearing. He strode along through the squalor and filth, part of the throng and yet not of the throng. He had an aura of goodness and, possibly, righteousness. His features were impressive, reflecting character, strength and simplicity. I have never forgotten this lone figure.

Sadly, slaughter on a massive scale was just around the corner from my visit in 1946. Lord Mountbatten had the unenviable task of implementing the decision to 'free India' — *Jai Hind*, I think was the term in the native language — but bloodshed, terror, torture and genocide took over without respite for a seemingly interminable period. It was estimated that between two and three million of these unfortunate people lost their lives during the period of 'partition', trying to flee between the two major enclaves of population, the Hindus and the Muslims. Atrocities almost beyond belief took place before the final establishment of the two new countries, India and Pakistan, the latter then to be subdivided into East and West Pakistan, with East Pakistan later being renamed Bangladesh. The inherent and apparently irreconcilable differences between the followers of these two historic religions is still very much evident today, and the recent acquisition by India and Pakistan of nuclear weapons — with every indication that their use will only demand modest provocation — is a matter for great concern.

Did that lone figure I observed in the desolate slums of Calcutta in 1946 survive the horrendous slaughter that overcame his way of life? It has always been my fervent hope that fate was kind to him.

One night only was spent at the end of our eastern service, and the flight schedule gave little or no time to sample the delights of this bustling and overpopulated city. The heat, even in the rather luxurious hotel in which we spent the night, was almost intolerable, with some relief in the dining room where 'punka louvres' were kept swinging by young Indian servants — *punka-wallahs'*. It still very much 'The Raj' and would no doubt have horrified the present crop of 'bleeding hearts' who see nothing good in those days of colonial power. In India, and as I later found out, in Africa, post colonial times were marked by plummeting economic status and development and the consequent difficulty of the population to find work of any nature. Any job, no matter how menial or lowly paid, was eagerly sought and held onto.

The stop, nevertheless gave an opportunity to visit the Bazaars, where it all came together in a seething mass of humanity, crammed into narrow lanes between the innumerable individual traders, each with his own speciality, and announcing in loud tones the quality of his wares. The din was terrific, but it was almost impossible to resist the blandishments for long, the outcome being the procurement of an example of 'Benares Ware' in the form of a cocktail shaker to adorn a shelf at home.

Then it was time to 'about face', as the Americans say — or *pinduka* in African terms — and the long haul back to London was started the next morning. In those days, due to the speed and range of the aircraft, schedules were based largely on flights by daylight, as airport facilities were not, as today, available over twenty four hours. By this time, the irregular meals, the heat, noise, etc, was beginning to have an effect on my stamina, exacerbated by inevitable bouts of 'Gippy guts' and 'Delhi belly'. Although the art of navigation demands little in the way of muscular strength, a certain amount of 'teeth gritting' took place if a supply of Dr Browns Chlorodine was not readily available!

Johannesburg, South Africa

In conjunction with South African Airways, BOAC also operated a regular service to Johannesburg, via Cairo and down through the centre of Africa. I looked forward to completing one of these trips as it would entail visiting totally new territory, which was a constant theme in my mind in those days. Over the years, I have been thankful that, for some obscure reason, the seed of 'wanderlust'—and it has still not expired—was set deep into my mind.

London to Johannesburg was a three-day trip, with some rest periods in Cairo and Johannesburg. I looked forward particularly to being rostered for a flight to the 'dark continent' because, as previously mentioned, in 1942 I had missed out on a trip to South Africa with the Empire Air Training Scheme and had gone to Canada instead.

Only four years later, I and my family 'upped-sticks' and migrated to that wonderful, pristine, magnificent—no adjective can possibly describe it—delight that was Rhodesia in 1950.

The run from Hurn, England to Cairo, Egypt, from take-off to landing, took 19 hours of constant flying duties, plus a couple of hours before the flight. I mention this as an example of the regulations then existing which permitted such onerous demands on flight crews. It is difficult to compare the physical demands of those days to the somewhat different stresses of operating high-speed jet aircraft, with their less forgiving characteristics, at thirty to forty thousand feet. However, the ambience of the environment in a modern aircraft, with efficient air-conditioning, less noise and vibration and comfortable working conditions on the flight deck, together with far better cuisine than that provided by the makeshift catering in those early days, lends me to conclude that present crews have it pretty good!

Nevertheless, I wouldn't have missed the experiences that came my way for the world.

The run from Cairo to Johannesburg took 20 hours flying time in a York, then a 'state of the art' passenger aircraft. Heading more or less due south from Cairo, I had a feeling of pleasant anticipation of seeing central Africa for the first time, and the prospect of crossing the equator was an event of major significance in my quest for world travel.

The first scheduled stop was Khartoum, Sudan—Wadi Seidna Airport—and the course roughly followed the Nile, over-flying such places as Thebes (Luxor) where the green that immediately fringed the river was in stark contrast to the undulating brown of the desert. Hanging in the hot African air at nine thousand feet, a strange timelessness seemed to seep into the mind as the surroundings of the aircraft cockpit faded into a vague background. Africa is different; it induces something like lethargy, but also promotes a sense of identification with the more fundamental aspects of life. It is far removed from the synthetic, highly developed, technologised and trivial way of life of the European continent, and once experienced, is never forgotten. Our subsequent thirty years in Africa were wonderful—a deep-rooted experience, remembered with pride and gratitude. Africa seems to strike further into one's being—perhaps because it is the birthplace of mankind—and touch one's inner senses as no other place can.

The route was circuitous to avoid territorial boundaries, but different legs were designed to over-fly Juba in Sudan, Kampala and Entebbe in Uganda, with Nairobi in Kenya as the first refuelling and rest stop. Crossing the equator for the first time, I made a specific point of noting the occasion in my logbook. It was at 1000 hours GMT on 19th September 1946, over the middle of Lake Victoria. Unfortunately (or perhaps fortunately) there was no aviation equivalent of the seaboard ceremony of 'crossing the line', with Neptune and his minions doing all kinds of things—some not too pleasant—to the first-time 'over the liners'. Knowing that water runs down the plug-hole in an anti-clockwise direction in the northern hemisphere, and the other way round in the south, can one presume that at the equator it simply drops down vertically? Or does it hesitate and make up its mind at the last moment?

The crew rest was taken in Nairobi, at the 'New Stanley Hotel'—a previous one must have been burnt down—a delightful colonial-type place, with, I think, a thatched roof, formed into a kind of quadrangle and only the usual single storey building. This stopover was memorable due to the incredible number of choices from the lengthy dining room menu, and the sights, sound and heady primitive smell of Africa.

Strangely, many of my strong recollections of my extensive travels in various continents, focus on smell in recalling a particular place, in equal strength to the visual memories of a location. Canada had its own pungency, with the crisp coldness and the summer heat in the Lakes of Ontario; Paris, a sweet and heady scented atmosphere, with the Metro exuding a kind of metallic and unique aroma; India had a spicy and earthy tang.

The departure, early the next morning, bound for Salisbury, Rhodesia, had a slight but interesting deviation from the normal procedure of take-off and climb to cruising altitude. Mount Kenya, some eighteen thousand feet high, is fairly close to the city of Nairobi, and such an obstacle never fails to focus the attention of pilots, and the other members of a crew, who do not have direct control over the movement of the aircraft, perhaps display an even greater interest in such immovable projections into the sky! With visibility quite restricted at the time of our departure, it was necessary, owing to the direction of the runway to be used, that the aircraft be flown blind in a direct line towards this mountain for a certain length of time. Needless to say, the passage of this was carefully and surreptitiously monitored by all on the flight deck.

This leg was quite long, almost six hours, and passed over Tanzania and Northern Rhodesia, and although I am unable to recall the turning points, the vastness of the territory, rolling and varied in appearance, caught my imagination, with the crossing of the mighty Zambezi River a very notable moment. Rhodesia was then largely undeveloped and although host to many thousands of trainee airmen under the 'Empire Air Training Scheme', the main airport at Salisbury, called Belvedere, still had only grass landing areas. The climate, social conditions, etc, greatly favoured Southern Rhodesia as a colony for the training of aircrew, although only pilots were involved. Over the years since then, it was amazing how often, in casual meetings, in many different countries and circumstances, one would hear pilot's say "Ah, yes, I did my Elementary and Service Flying training at so-and-so airfield."

Thornhill near Gwelo, Heany and Induna near Bulawayo, Mt Hampden near Salisbury were all pilot training stations. Two other stories are always connected and recounted with the experiences of those days. The 'intake centre' at Bulawayo was, for convenience and perhaps lack of other appropriate facilities, at the Bulawayo Show-grounds—an Annual Show, as in most colonies, an event of much importance for the 'settlers' to get together and display their activities and results in livestock breeding agricultural developments, etc. Permanent facilities existed for the housing of livestock over the period of the show, including pigs, swine, call them what you will, and these consisted of brickbuilt pens.

The rapid influx of young trainees, however, overtook the ability of the authorities to construct hut-type accommodation and a bit of 'lateral thinking', perhaps by a Station Warrant Officer disinclined to pamper his flock of young gentlemen, resulted in the pig pens being hosed down and touched up a bit to provide sleeping quarters for the trainees. When chance meetings recall the early years of air force careers begun in Rhodesia, the story of the pig pens is invariable recounted, without rancour but as a humorous interlude. The 'pig pens' were still in existence in the Fifties when we attended the agricultural shows, and are perhaps still there to this day, having perhaps been declared 'listed buildings', as is the wont these days!

Bulawayo, at the beginning of the war, was a small and unsophisticated city with a small European population, but around the city, in what were known as 'townships', lived a large population of the local people. The social system, whereby the whites and Africans lived in harmony but with little personal contact other than in the 'workplace', had been established over many years and had well served all the inhabitants. Inter-racial marriage was rare and personal contact of the lustful type not approved of by either whites or blacks. The establishment of an RAF training camp, however, heralded the arrival of many thousands of young men at probably the peak of their virility—for want of a better description—their numbers far exceeding the availability of suitable companions of their own racial type.

The story I am about to recount requires the above somewhat lengthy background, and goes as follows:

Two indigenous ladies, with perhaps slightly soiled reputations met in Bulawayo, with one of them very obviously far gone in pregnancy. After the usual excited salutations, with much laughter and good humour, Lady A asked, 'Ini lo?' (meaning, in the local patois, "What is this?" or "What have we here?").

Lady B, with a suddenly subdued expression, replied, "Ikona Heany lo" (indicating that her unborn child was the product of a liaison with one of the 'boys in blue' at the nearby Training Camp). Airmen have always been noted for their initiative when circumstances do not provide for their creature comforts, almost on a par with the renowned achievements of the US forces in wartime Britain, who, within a few hours of arriving on our shores had surrounded themselves with all the essentials in life—food, entertainment and feminine company—and to a high standard of luxury. Unlike birds, which do not fly at night, airmen soar to some of their best performances during the hours of darkness!

The short refuelling stop at Salisbury in 1946 had no major significance at the time, the thought of migrating from England was not yet so much as a twinkle in my eye, but somehow the 'feel' of the place, the air, or some other indefinable thing, made its impact, despite the usual fatigue experienced on these tiring and noisy flight legs. However, this brief glimpse of 'Gods own country' must have left its mark deep down somewhere, as, with Carol, Joy and Nicholas we arrived on a permanent basis about four years later, and the brief flight path in 1946, to and from Johannesburg was but a taster to the endless travels over thousands of miles that was my later good fortune when with Rhodesia Railways.

An hour later, after refuelling, the final stage in this long haul was started, with a planned three hour flight to Johannesburg, the 'city of gold'. Now superseded by the sophisticated Jan Smuts International Airport, our destination was a more modest terminal called Palmeit-fontein. The easiest form of aircraft navigation is under what is known to the pilot as VFR—Visual Flight Rules. In other words, the visibility is such that he can see where he is going by looking at the ground and recognising where he is in real terms. Large rivers are clearly distinguishable, by their general meandering gait and are always welcomed by flyers as the bends stand out in a very unmistakable way.

Having utilised the Nile in the north, the Zambezi when crossing into Rhodesia, the next river to follow was the 'Great, Green, Greasy Limpopo' as we crossed the border into South Africa from Mozambique. Green and greasy indeed it looked from our usual vantage point of nine thousand feet, though beyond viewing height for the fearsome crocodiles that infested its waters, feared greatly by the Africans and which took a terrible toll of lives.

A landmark, shortly after crossing into South Africa, is the Zoutspan range of mountains, where, about ten years later, our family spent a night-stop on the way down to Durban, our first of many trips to the lovely and happy land of such a mixture of races and cultures. Accommodation was in the well known style of small Rondevals and the hospitality the unvarying kind, a sincere welcome and kind and thoughtful attention. But it was icy cold, being in the mountains and it was with relief that we departed the next morning for the southern parts and the warm and welcoming waters of the Indian Ocean at Durban.

There was little difficulty, during the long approach to Johannes-burg, to distinguish the city from the rolling veldt of the Northern Transvaal. The 'spoil' from many years of mining the rich gold bearing ores, stood high, but untidy, around the mines close to the city limits. Six and a half thousand feet above sea level, the mine shafts penetrate over twelve thousand feet, the bottom of the shaft consequently being six thousand feet below sea level! From London to Johannesburg had required a total of 33 flying hours over three days, compared with today's non-stop flights of ten or eleven hours; my, how the world has shrunk.

The end of every journey was, as usual, a welcome relief. It had been a long haul from London, so we had a few days rest to explore the attractions of the city, from our hotel accommodation in central Johannesburg, — I think it was in Eloff Street, the main thoroughfare. Now 'darkest Africa' would be ours to explore for a short while. As on all my lengthy trips, however, my physical recovery time was fairly long, and strangely, with no previous history of this, I suffered attacks of 'nose bleeding' of a fairly copious kind.

I am unable to recall my personal impressions of seeing, first hand, the mixed population of Europeans, both English speaking and Afrikaans, the Bantu, the Indians and the remarkable variety of what were officially known as 'Cape coloured'. The latter ranged in hue from almost indistinguishable from white — another official racial classification — to those almost indistinguishable from African. Everywhere there was an atmosphere of liveliness and zest for life, whatever category was involved. This visit was, of course, before the official implementation of what became known, and misunderstood, as 'apartheid' at the tail-end of many hundreds of years of colonial rule.

Fifty years on, the present Johannesburg is almost unrecognisable from that immediate post-war visit, with freeways lacing over and around the central part and skyscrapers of immense height. One of the changes in human attitudes over this period is in the treatment of wild animals. All members of our crew, unfamiliar with Africa, held that deeply-rooted notion that, perhaps it would not be too unlikely that the odd wild animal, perhaps even a lion or elephant, would be unexpectedly encountered.

A visit to the well-known Zoo in the outskirts of the City was obviously a priority, so off we went. By today's standards, however, the official in charge would probably face a maximum jail term, as the zoo contained many beautiful and intriguing African animals, but most were housed in concrete boxes, totally devoid of any objects or facilities related to their natural habitat. These poor caged creatures constantly turned and paced over the few feet available for them to move and it seemed so ironic that this should be their fate in the land of their origin with the vast areas of untouched bush and veldt so close but yet so far away.

Now, of course, the National Parks of South Africa provide the absolute zenith in wildlife facilities and management, but that visit to those unfortunate animals in 1946, still lingers in my mind.

The sluggishness, on takeoff, of the York aeroplane has been mentioned, as I usually noted the time from 'roll' to 'lift off', when at the rated 'all-up weight'. A considerable adjustment to this weight was necessary when operating through many of the airports in Africa, which were located at heights of over five thousand feet. The reluctance of the plane to leave the security and comfort of Mother Earth was very noticeable, particularly as the extremely long runways of the present day were still in the future. But the plane served us well, and was very conveniently designed for the Navigator to carry out his duties in relative comfort and with the speed that is frequently of importance under certain conditions.

A topic which arises when airmen meet and 'open the hangar doors' is invariably that of 'loosing an engine'. Understandably, for pilots, this event often suddenly tests their skill in rapid response in no uncertain terms, and with any engine out of commission, the approach and landing demands that little extra touch of style. During my fairly short time with BOAC I only experienced the loss of an engine on one occasion. Flying with Captain Veasey, an old hand from pre-war Imperial Airways, we had refuelled at Wadi Seidna, near Khartoum on our way back to Cairo, with an estimated flight time of just over five hours, when about thirty minutes into the flight, the starboard outer engine gave up the ghost.

The Captain, naturally completely unfazed by the event, simply trimmed the aircraft to handle the asymmetric conditions before considering his options. The choice was to either return to the nearby security of our departure point or to press on to Cairo, still about five hours away. The option to return would have meant great inconvenience, as the facilities to effect repairs were limited and if it meant a change of engine, the delays would have been more serious. With what I thought great aplomb, he chose the latter option and we continued on our way north towards Cairo, with a significant reduction in speed but certainly no lack of confidence in our trustworthy steed. Due to the slew of the plane, however, the heading indicated on the aircraft compasses was out of kilter, but with clear visibility of the Nile and adjoining tributaries, it was not difficult to maintain our intended track. Approaching Almaza Airport on arrival at Cairo after some five hours on three engines, the ungainliness of the aircraft became more apparent, but Captain Veasey, like the good trooper he was, soared in like a bird and 'greased' the York onto the runway without a bump.

Mac and I flew together in Beaufighters for well over a year and never had an engine give even the slightest flinch of misbehaving. Despite the fabulous reputation of the 'Beau', however, it was a bit dodgy with an engine out, demanding much physical strength to maintain control. The other hazards were quite sufficient for both of us, anyway.

Recently released figures show some startling comparisons with flying then and flying now. In 1947 more people died in aircraft accidents than in 1997. This despite the one thousand or so percentage increase in the number air travellers. The cost of air travel, over the same interval, has decreased by about thirty fold. The compiler of these statistics asserted that, for any individual, it would be necessary to embark on a flight every day for twenty six thousand years before becoming a casualty in an aircraft crash!

Such odds and such amazing safety is a fine tribute to the industry as a whole, with crash investigators showing high dedication and professionalism. In such a remarkable industry, with technological change so intense and rapid, many fortunes were won and lost. The failure of the Concorde concept and the consequent loss of leadership by the British aviation industry, nevertheless opened the way for the American Boeing company to leap forward and create the present superb varieties of their product. Just stop and consider, for instance, the design and performance of the Boeing 747 aircraft, which came into service in 1975; it is surely one of the wonders of the twentieth century, yet it is normally taken completely for granted.

Not by those of my generation, however, as I look back to my boyhood in Spondon, at the time of record-breakers such as Amy Johnson, who dazzled us with their daring and enterprise, setting off in such flimsy craft to fly to places almost beyond our awareness. I complain not about the era in which I grew up, for few people in human history have had the good fortune to see the remarkable changes that have taken place within my lifetime.

SOME OBSERVATIONS AND THOUGHTS REGARDING 'FLYING THE ROUTES'

All professional airmen have their own individual attitude towards the dangers of their job. For most it can be assumed that the philosophy of competency and continuing dedication to achieving the highest possible standard of performance will mitigate or perhaps even eliminate the odds of coming to grief. The attitude of *'que sera sera'* is unusual; pilots are unwilling to relinquish their inherent trait of exercising command or control of their actions and also their destiny.

Unfortunately, the fates can conspire to produce situations whereby control is of no avail, even when the ultimate degree of competency is to hand. It is said that most flying, certainly on regular schedules, is "ninety nine percent sheer boredom and one percent sheer terror". Perhaps terror is overstating it. It would certainly not be the first reaction of fully trained flight crews as the instinctive reaction has been programmed into them by many hours of repetitive exercises in the flight simulator. Only when all possible remedial actions had been taken and it is concluded that nothing further can be done and defeat is acknowledged might these well trained professionals give way to such a thing as terror.

There is little discussion by crews, of such matters, and, as with wartime operational flying, a blasé attitude seems the most suitable cover for one's personal feelings.

On one occasion, returning from a trip to Calcutta, I recall, that as we cruised in our usual way, somewhere over the sands of the Middle East, I seemed to drop into a kind of reverie. Coming to with bit of a jolt, my first coherent thought was of the day and time. It was, I think, Thursday afternoon and it was three o'clock. My next thought, was one of disembodiment, along the lines of 'What on earth am I doing here, plodding along in an aeroplane, and for what strange purpose?' An odd moment, but quickly overcome by the demands of my navigational duties.

Relative to this aspect of safety in the air, I had, in the interests of making myself available to meet the roster of flight schedules, rented a room in a small and genteel guest house in Christchurch, fairly close to Hurn Airport, our base. It was occupied almost entirely by ladies of mature years, mostly in black dresses and lace and dignified in mien. On the rare occasions when we happened to meet in the sitting room, I was either going on a trip or returning, and was in the uniform of BOAC. The uniform probably triggered memories of the First World War, when they were undoubtedly in their prime, and they regarded me with some interest, although their natural courtesy hampered their curiosity as to who I was and what was my calling. About this time, there had unfortunately been several disastrous aircraft accidents, with many casualties and the maximum publicity in the newspapers— thankfully, in those days, the probing cameras of the television 'ghouls' had not yet reached the stage of today, when they seem to be 'on site' at any major catastrophe almost before the emergency services.

One of these elderly ladies plucked up sufficient courage to comment to me on this spate of 'prangs' and realising my involvement in flying, ventured an opinion on the matter. Perhaps her knowledge of aviation had ceased with the end of the First War, because having expressed her horror at the loss of so many lives in the recent accidents, she suggested that surely fewer lives would have been lost if, at the time of the impending crash, the occupants had jumped out immediately before the aeroplane hit the ground! Her concern, her sweetness for expressing it, and her unworldliness remain a sweet memory.

The general facilities for carrying out navigation tasks in Yorks and Lancastrians were quite good but I found 'flying the routes' very tiring, with the noise and vibration in the aircraft probably the most significant reason. The post-flight buzzing in my ears left me with a sense of vagueness for well into the following day. The long and irregular hours of duty, commencing and finishing at any time of day or night, the heat, the strange foods—perhaps 'un-English' puts it better—and the meals in the aircraft taken only at intervals which slotted in with flying requirements, tended to plague the digestive system 'something cruel'. I had to resort as mentioned previously, to the soothing syrup produced by the good Dr Brown, but considering that it was based on Chlorodine, it would now probably be a 'banned substance'—it certainly was not 'performance-enhancing' as along with its gut-soothing effect it also induced a touch of lethargy, a dangerous by-product at nine thousand feet!

'Jet Lag' had not been 'invented' in 1947, but its pernicious effects were there, even without name. A lot of the flying was east to west and vice versa, over far longer time-spans than today, and although most modern aircraft are pressurised to provide an atmosphere equivalent to about seven thousand feet, we usually cruised at about nine thousand feet owing to the design of the planes of the time prohibiting this luxury. These factors imposed a greater load on bodily stamina, as did the significant changes in temperature from the small variations in UK to the sweltering heat of the Middle and Far East. An hour or so spent at some intermediate stopover for refuelling, often meant climbing into an aircraft that had stood in the blazing sunlight for this period, with the interior temperature probably at the upper limit of human tolerance (Calcutta being one of our destinations, probably not far removed from that in the infamous 'Hole of Calcutta'!) If this observation raises the thought of exaggeration, my recollection of these conditions is vivid and correct.

I had been granted what was known as 'extended service commission' by the RAF and was on secondment to British Overseas Airways Corporation, but there was some pressure to relinquish my RAF commission and join the company on a permanent basis. As a flight lieutenant, I recall my salary was about a thousand pounds a year, with some family allowances, generous by comparison with the terms offered by the company, which were four hundred pounds a year, plus all living expenses when on line duty. These figures seem incredible by today's standards, but they need to be put in perspective by remembering that a wage of five pounds a week was the lot of the average working man in those days.

'Decision time' now reared its head, with the important considerations being income—when isn't *that* important?—whether the role of Aircraft Navigator remained attractive to me, and also my long-term career prospects. There were also the long and frequent absences from Carol and Joy, this being the most unsatisfactory aspect of what superficially appeared to be an occupation of some 'glamour'. (Although, I must confess to experiencing a certain ego boost when dressed in airline uniform with the odd 'gong' displayed, and on occasions perambulating through the passengers when in flight to pass on titbits of 'flight crew wisdom'!). The final question was: 'What to do otherwise?' as I had little or no really useful attributes or qualifications with which to tempt any prospective employer. By this time, the majority of ex-servicemen had been absorbed into employment and the available work opportunities had shrunk to not very attractive offers.

The long-term future for Aircraft Navigating Officers was problematic. A new Airline, British South American Airlines had come into being, using the newly introduced aircraft, the Avro Tudor, which embodied the 'state of the art' in design and also some comfort, and, as I recall, using the term 'Starliner' for their services. Some very senior RAF officers were involved—I think financially as well—and the route to the South American countries offered promise of perhaps a lucrative and expanding market. But disaster quickly struck and two flights were lost without trace on what was a very long haul across the Atlantic with little latitude for alternate destinations if strong headwinds or navigational problems were encountered. In fact one of the RAF

Officers, Air Vice Marshal Broadbent, was lost, after an illustrious wartime career, on one these flights.

It is my recollection that for the first time, three qualified pilots were carried on the flight deck, with the junior pilot carrying out the task of navigation. I hasten to state that this implies no doubts about the policy or the ability of the unfortunate crews involved—such a policy was sensible crew utilisation in the long-term.

Combined with this, rapid developments in radio communication meant that a contact could be maintained over longer distances, with speech contact being available both to pilots and also for navigational purposes.

Qantas Airline, due to its lengthy routes over water and vast isolated areas, was perhaps the last company to retain Navigators, who were finally made redundant in the mid 1950s. The goal of operating with minimum crew has now reached amazing new economies. Most new large aircraft now fly with just two pilots, even the Flight Engineer has become redundant, and with present airliner speeds close to Mach I, it is a reasonable stint of duty for one crew to handle any major long distance leg in the schedule. This reduction in the number of components in the industry has seen even the number of engines in modern planes reduced, with the reliability of engine units being so great that ETOPS—extended twin operations—are allowed with even two-engined aircraft being permitted to travel over water, provided that the aircraft can fly to an alternative landing ground in a time of three hours or less if the pilot has to close down one of the engines. Further, to utilise crew to best advantage, aircraft now have appropriate accommodation next to the flight deck for spare crew to be on hand for the next duty and so avoid long layovers at places on the route.

Nevertheless, looking at the policy of crew rationalisation, it is hard, and even demeaning, as a fully licensed aircraft navigating officer, to be aware that your direct replacement is a small black box, a little larger than a cigarette packet! By day and by night, in all kinds of weathers, over the whole of the surface of the globe, it will state the precise position, height above ground—something a Navigator could never do—give the course, distance and time of arrival at the next required position, and all on what is probably a one and a half volt battery! The final blow to our 'self-esteem' is that such devices are now available over the counter of most electronic retailers for just a few hundred dollars.

Further economies in numbers of trained personnel have been made possible by the introduction of the 'glass cockpit' and modern computers with their ability to take an active part in the operation of any aircraft. These pieces of equipment are now of such remarkable capacity and flexibility that they seem to be a crew member in their own right, although there is much controversy, among pilots and researchers as to the relationship between the 'organic and non-organic occupants of the sharp end'.

Two conflicting views presently prevail, firstly that the computer is there to fly and control the aircraft in almost all phases of flight, the pilot's job being merely to monitor the actions to ensure conformity to the proper parameters. The opposing view is that the pilots should have absolute control over the plane and merely utilise the facilities of the computer to relieve them of some of the tedium of the more routine parts of their duties.

Regrettably there have been instances where the computer has either overridden the actions of the pilot, which were correct in terms of the aircraft situation, resulting in a major disaster, or misled the crew into a situation not of their making, again with extreme results. It would seem that air transport of passengers, under total and complete automation, is still a long way down the track, with doubts that it will ever to become fully acceptable.

In February 1947, as post war reconstruction was gathering momentum, winter conditions of unique severity struck with a vengeance. Snow and ice coated the entire country, with temperatures at the bottom of the thermometer, and a national disaster was promulgated. Almost all activities came to a halt, with the wholesale closure of factories and other facilities. The country literally froze to a halt. Returning from Calcutta, with its aforementioned heat, our crew deplaned at Heathrow, with its Nissen-type terminal buildings and faced the Arctic blasts of this terrible English winter. With no surplus body fat, perhaps I suffered more than most, but this episode was instrumental in determining my next 'career move' as it has now been 'jargonised'.

The icy wastes that greeted us on our return to England, put the whole future in a better perspective for me. Having considered the matters mentioned above, with not a little regret, I decided that the future of our family—Nicholas was now in the offing—would be better served by my pursuing a more stable and less physically demanding occupation. A return to the RAF appeared to be the next logical step to wait and see what the fickle finger of fate had in store for us.

RAF METROPOLITAN COMMUNICATION SQUADRON HENDON, NORTH LONDON FEB 1947–FEB 1948.

Postings—movements from one place to another—in the services, either happen instantly, or involve highly protracted complications. It was very much a case ofthe latter when I decided to 'return to the fold' of the RAF. Altogether, it took from February to June to complete the transaction, but it was, in fact, no hardship. Carol, Joy and I were now comfortably set up in a flat in Wimbledon, very convenient to the centre of London—nine minutes to Waterloo station, with trains every few minutes—and I found this time a welcome relief from flying activities. Since my first 'airborne experience' on Friday November 13th 1942—'lucky for some'—I had been continuously engaged in some type of aerial activity and it was a pleasure to sleep when man is designed to sleep and eat at established mealtimes with normal intervals in between.

After the cruel conditions of February, spring finally arrived and we were able to get about and see some of the attractions near where we lived and also in and about London proper. Meanwhile, I paid many visits to RAF Transport Command Headquarters at Uxbridge, North West London, in an attempt to finalise my return to the service that had 'owned' me for the past few years. Strangely, although it appeared to me to be a fairly straightforward matter, affairs seemed to drag on with no discernible progress towards my return. Perhaps, at this time, discussions were taking place at government level as to the future role and manning of the post-war RAF and it was not prudent to make commitments to any aircrew still remaining 'on the books' as in my case.

The posting that finally came my way was just about as good as it could get. Joining the Metropolitan Communication Squadron—the 'Met Com Squadron'—at Hendon meant that it would be permissible for me to 'live out' at Wimbledon and more often than not, report daily for flying duties. Another attraction was that it would be back to flying the good old Avro Anson aircraft—all who had known this venerable old lady held her in high regard—and the flying would certainly not involve routine hauls over the same and sometimes tediously repetitive sections.

Hendon, perhaps next to Cranwell, in Lincolnshire, is the name that springs to mind when reference is made to flying. The Hendon Air Displays, starting in the 1920s had international status as a 'showcase' of developments in aircraft construction and for the style and daring of the flying that took place there—usually at 'nought feet'– most of it with serious intentions but some intended for comic effect. Huge crowds were always attracted, the aerodrome being close to London. To be based there stirred my enthusiasm and sense of pride, and was an appropriate successor to my previous base at Croydon, another 'historic' home of early aviation.

Located next to the aerodrome was the Metropolitan Police College, where training of senior officers took place. This also housed what was known as the 'Black Museum' which displayed artefacts and exhibits of the many murders that had made the British public gasp in horror as details were promulgated in the press with titillating effect that did wonders for newspaper distribution figures.

There were no tarmac runways, just a not particularity large grass area, with the east end of this bordered by the main railway line to the north. This line was on a high embankment and when coming in to land towards the west, the pilot had to surmount this embankment with a bit of a tug on the control column. The aerodrome was closely surrounded by housing, which left little room for any pilot to manoeuvre should trouble arise.

The Officers Mess facilities were excellent, but living out I had little course to use them, except on the very infrequent times when I was required to perform the duties of 'Officer of the Day'. However, it was a long and tedious journey from Wimbledon to Hendon—fifty minutes or so by bus and tube followed by a short walk to the station main gate.

It was good to get flying again after quite a long layoff and also to fall into the friendly and comforting arms of the RAF, to which I had become accustomed and somewhat reliant. The change back into RAF uniform did not go amiss either. So it was that on 27th June 1947, with pilot Flt/Lt Sparkes, I made a return trip to Wroughton, home of the main hospital of the RAF. This put me firmly 'back into circulation' and was the first of many enjoyable excursions from this pleasant station in the reliable and comfortable Anson, which by this time had undergone some metamorphosis into the Mark 19, with greatly enhanced comfort and appearance. Furthermore, and to the relief of all navigators, the 'wind-up undercarriage'—that had hitherto required one hundred and twenty gruelling turns of the handle—had been updated by being connected to the aircraft hydraulic supply and now required, thankfully, only the flick of a switch.

Only a few miles north of London, Hendon was ideally situated near to the Air Ministry in central London and also the Headquarters of the other services. Its prime role, as the name Metropolitan Communication Squadron indicates—in actual fact, No. 147 Squadron—was to provide terminal facilities and aircraft for the benefit of the staff of these establishments in their travel requirements around the British Isles and the continent. Hendon was also the base for same requirements of the American Airforce, based across the other side of the aerodrome and flying their own aircraft.

I was soon to discover that Hendon also operated in another role. All pilots need to keep their hand in, in actual flying, being required to fly so many hours per annum, in order not to loose their touch. Perhaps there exists a regulation that should they not maintain this quota, then a full refresher course may have been obligatory. This situation had a direct result in my participation of the activities of the squadron, in a kind of oblique way.

The Air Ministry housed a large number of pilots and other aircrew, who had established fairly deep roots therein, no doubt climbed a few rungs on the ladder of promotion, and were, in many cases, past the first flush of youth and its attendant quick reaction speed. Being a navigator, I always, naturally, took a keen interest in the overall physical appearance of the pilot to whom I was to put my faith, trust, confidence, etc, his general personality, and above all, his facility with the controls of an aircraft, this being the ultimate criterion.

Most of the pilots were 'tour expired', from many and varied Commands and Squadrons and had flown a wide variety of aircraft, from fighters to heavy four engined types. They also ranged from those of my own rank, Flight Lieutenant to very senior ranks. Many had not flown for a considerable length of time and very few had flown the Avro Anson, which was, by any comparison, a basic and simple plane. 147 Squadron had it's complement of pilots and navigators, but owing to the nature and variety of the individual 'sorties', we were not 'crewed' but flew with a different partner on most trips. 'No probs', as we say here in Australia.

However, the problem, insofar as we Navigators were concerned, was when one of the aforesaid gentlemen from the Air Ministry, short in hours and a touch long in the tooth, felt an urge to take to the skies, for legitimate and justified reasons or otherwise. Pilot and Navigator sat side by side in the Anson, I had a small navigation table in front of me with the radio equipment to my rear, a full view ahead and also a very close view of the activities of my partner.

Some trips took several days, and, needless to say, compatibility and confidence was a prime requisite to the successful operation of the exercise. On not a few occasions, when we took up our positions on the 'flight deck', my careful scrutiny of my guiding hand for the next few days was discreet but decidedly thorough. Fortunately, old instincts die hard, like never forgetting to know how to ride a bicycle, but it was somewhat disconcerting to me to observe my mate for the next trip carefully exploring, after boarding the plane, the relative simplicity of the controls and instruments, with an air of unfamiliarity—even bewilderment. Being incapable of active participation, having had no pilot training, and two or three steps down the ladder of rank, I had to tolerate 'Sir's' quick re-familiarisation with the basic ingredients and kept my muttered brief call on my guardian angel limited to a whisper!

Only one occasion gave me real cause for concern, when visiting several RAF stations in Germany. Taking-off from one place, the runway was more than adequate for the Anson and my 'skipper'—who had previously given me a touch of anxiety—opened up with confidence and, as usual, the tail of the plane rose quickly as flying speed was nearly reached. This is always a critical moment, but at this precise time, a lorry, presumably engaged on runway maintenance, was driven onto the runway some distance ahead of our aircraft, which was now feeling the wind under it's wings and desperate to soar into the 'wide blue yonder'. The situation left two possibilities, either stop or go, the latter less desirable as it was the doubtful whether we had sufficient flying speed to surmount the offending lorry.

Leaving a long plume of smoke behind us, as the pilot stood—and I mean stood—on the brakes, the aircraft swerved and swung around in the attempt to avoid a catastrophic meeting with the lorry. Raising the undercarriage was the final additional option, but all came well as we screeched to a halt uncomfortably close to a 'prang'. The Wing Commander, after we returned to the UK, went back to his office in the Air Ministry no doubt to savour the comfort and safety of his cushy number and I continued to scrutinise even more carefully the credentials of my flying partners!

During the eight months that I served with the squadron, the UK—and to a lesser degree Europe—was my 'oyster', and in this time I visited some sixty different aerodromes, of various Commands, some still functioning as flying bases and others at minimum strength and activity owing to the post-war economies. This type of life, to be bound for destinations not anticipated and usually only known a short time before take-off, suited me admirably. The thrill of the unknown, at brief notice, has always stirred my interest and enthusiasm and was a welcome change from the arduous flights with BOAC.

It also provided another unexpected bonus. Having been in the RAF since 1941, and having progressed through almost all ranks, I was still very aware of difference in rank and retained the required attitude of respect and deference. It had become deeply ingrained, even though I was a 'general duties officer', which, strangely, was the term for aircrew. Flying duties made most of us less inclined towards undue formality (on occasions we were even a bit flippant). It had no component of servility, it was, simply, that it was a code of conduct, in the best interests of the individual and the service generally. Each individual knew his exact place in the hierarchy and personal contact was conducted accordingly.

The system has much to recommend it and regrettably, it has given way in present times to a laxity and confusion, contributing nothing to either party or the social systems generally. The universal use of Christian names by all and sundry, at first contact, has the result of awkwardness and inefficiency, and, as a 'senior citizen' it jars somewhat to be addressed by one's Christian name by even toddlers in nappies!

The experience of 'rubbing shoulders' with very senior officers of the services gave me a new insight into a much broader spectrum of social life and with no exceptions, I found them to be delightful, considerate and helpful in many different ways. The more senior, the more apparent were these qualities, and they portrayed the essential leadership that had steered us safely through the previous years of war, when at so many times defeat had seemed more likely than victory.

Most were products of the pre-war services and all had that indefinable bearing that was reflected in the public school system. The circuit in which I now found myself was a long call from my early days in Spondon, where education ceased at fourteen and there was no time for niceties beyond the need to make a modest living to survive. I felt that I was fortunate to have achieved a role in this situation, and it was again thanks to whatever star had been kind to me.

In July, 1947, I logged a trip to Holland and Germany, with stops at Eindhoven, Buckeburg, Hamburg (Fuhlsbuttel) and Berlin (Gatow). Many strong impressions remain of my war experiences, but paramount is the memory of my first sight of the city of Hamburg. We flew around the city at about a couple of thousand feet, and the sight of the incredible devastation was almost overwhelming. The efforts of RAF Bomber Command had been publicised, of course, as spur to victory and I think all had become inured, to some degree, to the havoc that was being wrought on the cities of Germany, but to see the actual result of mass bombing, immediately below the aircraft was shattering.

There was nothing but square miles of rubble, with just a few walls standing stark and isolated, through which paths had been bulldozed for access. One could not help imagining the horror and terror experienced by the inhabitants when the city literally caught fire and the infamous 'firestorm' developed that resulted in the streets melting, with the smoke and smell of the burning city rising to the crews of the bomber force at twenty thousand feet. Much has been argued about the policy of this method of war, but my view is that it was the only real way open to our forces to achieve any tangible progress towards victory for all of humanity. Anyway... they started it!

The night stops in Germany evoked a strange feeling of unreality. From 1939, our avowed enemy had been Germany and its people and to be in the country, in transit accommodation, in close proximity to them was, I suppose, a kind of anticlimax. To see them in the flesh, going about their daily lives, contrasted starkly to the images that had been built up over the years that they were somehow 'not like us', and prone to perpetrating horrors of the worst kind, left an overwhelming feeling of anticlimax, tinged, nevertheless with a fear that some of them might prove hostile and attempt to retaliate on a personal basis.

At one stay, our accommodation was provided within the airport, and, as I recall, large numbers of German servicemen — or perhaps ex-servicemen — were billeted close by. They appeared not greatly different from us, stemming from the same ancestors and possessing the same characteristics of individual self-reliance and preferring a life along ordered lines. They did not seem to be overly humbled by 'coming second' in the war, but they did seem to emanate an air of loss and confusion.

Of the memories still in my mind of these early visits to Germany, perhaps the most poignant is of an elderly couple. It had become my habit, when abroad with BOAC, to buy a token bunch of flowers and a bottle of wine or liqueur for Carol as a present. I would put the blossoms in the rear of the fuselage of the plane, beyond the passenger area, where it was cool, and Carol always welcomed these gifts from a 'far away place', as they certainly were in those early days before international jet travel became commonplace. The bottle of whatever, consumed in the warmth of our flat in Wimbledon was a most enjoyable to celebrate my return to home and family.

A night stop, in either Berlin or Hamburg, as I recall, was made in transit accommodation in a suburban area, and as it was a pleasant warm summer's evening I decided to take a stroll in the close vicinity. Most of the small residential houses had escaped bomb damage, and as I walked along this quiet street, which was quite untidy, with the small area in front of each house, unkempt, which was not surprising under the circumstances, I came to one that was bright and alive with magnificent rose blooms. My 'flower boy' routine immediately sprang to mind, and a quick assessment of my resources, financial and of bartering value, was made. It had been necessary for the Authorities to establish strict control of money in Germany to defeat the 'black market' and the currency had a special name, which I cannot recall. But I did have some chocolate and cigarettes, which were equally welcomed in any transaction.

I had seen only few civilians in the street and the house appeared to be quiet with no one in evidence. Being keen, however, I approached, knocked on the door and waited. Nothing happened and another knock was made. After a lengthy pause, the door was opened a crack, and an elderly face appeared. I was, of course, in RAF uniform, and immediately attempted to explain my intentions. With little or no German, other than a few trite phrases, it was not easy, but I tried to convey, by my expressions and bearing, that I wanted to establish contact with the householder. The door opened further, and another face appeared, and it was evident that they were an elderly couple, very elderly in fact, but to my concern they displayed such fear and anxiety that I hesitated as to my next course of action. Having lived in fear for so long, it was obvious that to be suddenly confronted at their door by a man in uniform was just about as bad as it could get.

It took some time to put them at ease, but when I moved to the roses and made my congratulations on their handiwork obvious, the breakthrough came and they insisted that they present me with a bunch. I took from my pocket all the cigarettes and chocolate I had with me and offered them to the couple, but they strongly declined to accept, until I made it clear that this was the only way I would take my present for Carol. They were quite overwhelmed by the luxury of these simple items and profuse in thanking me as I said goodbye. This small incident reminded me that I had negotiated the war in relative comfort and that over the past few years millions of people all over Europe had suffered greatly, from hunger and danger, with survival always doubtful. Those two elderly, frightened faces in that doorway in Hamburg are still a very vivid memory and represent, to me, completely, the essence of those times.

At one transit accommodation centre, I think it was Buckeburg, an RAF sergeant seemed to be in charge. He had set up within the area, an elaborate centre for the barter exchange of various household items, bric-a-brac, etc. All these goodies were on display, as in a shop, and although some of the 'funny money ' was used to buy, the established currency of the day was, again, chocolate and cigarettes. (Bicycle tyres were more commonly used in France). Such a procedure, by today's standards, that the local German people should part with their personal and perhaps treasured possessions, for a few piffling goods, seems unfair and immoral, but times were cruel, and necessity drives a hard bargain. We still have a wine decanter and several glasses, exquisite in design, acquired under these dubious circumstances, and although I refrain from describing the set as 'war loot', they are, in all honesty, just that.

One of the squadron's aircraft was fitted out as an ambulance, requiring only simple adjustment to put it into this mode. The side of the aircraft was hinged to allow a stretcher to be slid in and secured in position. It came my way to undertake a couple of trips carrying patients, who were accompanied by a WAAF medical orderly, to the principle RAF hospital at Wroughton in Derbyshire.

One trip, the only time I flew by night from Hendon, was to Aldergrove in Northern Ireland, to collect a Wing Commander and take him to Wroughton hospital for urgent medical attention. Perhaps his injuries could have been described as 'self-inflicted' because he had become rather 'sloshed' in the mess, late at night, had fallen into the fireplace and had become quite badly burnt. So, with a night sky now unfamiliar to me and not a lot of real aids to navigation, I had to navigate across the Irish Sea and back again to rescue this unfortunate victim of 'demon drink'.

The other trip was a sad journey for a young airman. He had been in Wrougton Hospital for some time and there was little hope for his recovery from a serious illness. It was decided that he should be taken home to his parents in Inverness, Scotland, for his final days and we flew to the hospital to transport him there. The WAAF medical orderly seemed to me to be very young, but she was skilled and attentive and very thorough in looking after the patient. The flight to Inverness was quite a long one for the Anson, but we were pleased to see the young man safely home to his family and our crew felt that this flight was a very worthy one.

It was necessary to spend the night at Inverness, and although the next day was a long trip, it was pleasant to travel down the length of Britain, with the rolling hills of the Penines below us. Sometime during this journey home to Hendon I glanced back into the passenger area of the plane and saw the young lady orderly was asleep in her seat, with her arm supporting her head. She had been personally concerned about her charge and now seemed quite exhausted. When people, and animals, sleep they take on an appearance of total submission and innocence, and this seems even more evident, somehow, when people are asleep in an aircraft, perhaps because the upper air has an inbuilt sense of tranquillity. She epitomised the beauty of youth and dedication to her nursing calling and this quick glance at her, fast asleep, as we flew along at a couple of thousand feet, remains vivid in my memory of my flying days.

Shepherding Air Force 'VIPs' around their 'patch' brought many perks. In the late summer of 1947, before the construction of the 'Berlin Wall' and when the cleavage between east and west was taking on a more sinister note, the service chiefs decided that as the use of airborne forces had already proved its worth, and as future military actions would more than likely use this method of getting at the enemy, much could be learned from a major exercise of the combined forces. The exercise was given the operational tag of 'Longstop'. We took a group down to Salisbury Plain — I think we landed at Netheravon, a First World War flying ground — and had a ringside seat for the show. And what an impressive occasion it turned out to be. The sky was full of Dakotas, each dropping about forty paratroopers, with all their gear hanging below on ropes. As they streamed out of the planes, in what appeared to be terrible confusion, there seemed scarcely enough room for each man to avoid becoming entangled with his fellow parachutists. Nevertheless, they all floated down safely in great style.

Next it was the Airborne Forces Glider Regiment who showed their stuff and out of this congested sky, having just cast off from the tow, came the Horsas and Hanibals — I am not sure of the precise types — to add to this awe inspiring display of men performing at their most aggressive. It was Arnhem and Njmagen rolled into one and it became easy to imagine the consternation of the German Forces when such an 'air armada' appeared in the sky above them. What a lovely word 'Armada' is; it somehow captures the spirit of men at war—defending their territory against invaders and their womenfolk from a 'fate worse than death'. With an atmosphere full of adrenalin, this display seemed to demonstrate what life in the Armed Forces is all about, and the excitement of all—including our somewhat stoic VIPs—at this glorious display, gave us a sense of pride in our commitment to the services.

The paratroopers, who were dropped from the standard height of about 600 feet with their heavy burdens, landed very quickly. Touchdown being a most vulnerable time for them, their training emphasises quick recovery and assembly as fighting groups. We were impressed by how quickly they regrouped and were ready for action. Over one thousand men arrived by parachute and, as I recall, the most serious injury was one sprained ankle. A pretty good effort that augured well should it be necessary to deploy these troops in any future 'real' situation.

Perhaps the stirring sight of these 'men from the sky' became part of our family folklore and I repeated it on so many occasions that it became embedded in the young mind of our son Nicholas, with the result that he decided, when old enough, to give it a go. One Monday morning, when at the office, I was surprised when he phoned me from the town where he was then living. Quite casually he dropped into the conversation that he had made his first parachute jump the previous day and what a surge of pride this old Dad felt in such an accomplishment by his 'number one son'!

At that time, 'hobby' parachutists used parachutes of the most basic type, the most popular and inexpensive being the Irvin type used by American paratroopers, which had a very limited degree of manoeuvrability by the user. The Reserve Chute had a simple canopy and was of the type used by Royal Air Force aircrew. With a relatively small diameter canopy, it brought the user to earth with a solid bang. The modern 'flying wing' chute, that allows the operator to perform quite remarkable aerial manoeuvres, was not then even on the drawing board.

Subsequently, it gave Carol and me much pleasure, and strangely, little concern, to attend our son's jumping occasions. It was invariably possible to distinguish Nicholas from his fellow jumpers, in the time of their 'free-fall', not only be his general physique but also by our strong parental bond. He closed his 'log book' after about seven hundred jumps (when marriage loomed) but he never sustained any injury of significance.

I recall that a rough calculation of all his jumps, showed that, during the 'free-fall' time before opening the chute, a total of nearly four hours of flight with 'no visible means of support' had elapsed. So the response, when asked, perhaps in general conversation, 'how much flying time', a quirky answer would be, simply, 'four hours', prompting, perhaps, a smile of condolence. 'Yes', could be the retort, 'but I did it without wings'!

Gradually, aviation was becoming more sophisticated, in aircraft design, systems carried in the aircraft, and facilities on the ground for navigation, and also through air traffic control, which was having to deal with a rapidly increasing number of flights. In September 1947, a trans-Atlantic flight of major significance was made, and by coincidence, we flew a group of senior officers to Brize Norton station where the aircraft had landed. The purpose of the flight had been to test the efficiency of combining the two most important requirements of aircraft operating: the actual physical control of the plane and the system to navigate it to a predetermined flight path and landing at it's destination.

'George', the automatic pilot that kept the plane in a stable position had its origins in the early thirties when the record-breakers were attempting extremely long solo flights, and was used in many wartime planes. It had also become possible for aircraft to be set to fly towards radio beams transmitted from ground stations, and over the North Atlantic, other more sophisticated aids to navigation had been developed. But probably more important, in view of the fact that landing an aircraft is the most accident prone phase of the flight, exacerbated by the notoriously bad weather which so frequently covers the eastern seaboard of Europe, this aircraft—a Liberator I think—was fitted with a reliable automatic system which could land the plane, almost 'hands-off', in adverse conditions.

In 1947, a Landing Aid was in vogue, called GCA—Ground Controlled Approach. The main principle was that radar equipment on the approach to the runway put the pilot in a position to make the long final approach, where more sensitive equipment at the end of the runway gave him guidance for the actual touchdown. A ground controller in the tower was able to see, on a cathode ray tube, the actual position of the aircraft in relation to the runway, the angle of approach, etc. By maintaining conversation with the pilot, the plane would be told to veer left or right, whether the height and speed was correct, etc. until according to the plot on the operator's screen, the plane was correct to touch- down. It had a good reputation but was not totally satisfactory for a completely 'blind landing' — it was always necessary for the pilot to be able to see the runway at the moment of touchdown.

On one occasion we were required to fly to Lyneham in Wiltshire, which was the main flying base of RAF Transport Command. Many types of aircraft flew from there, to all parts of the world and it had preference in being equipped with the GCA system. It seemed to be a good opportunity for use to try out this 'new-fangled' aid to landing and we set out with this in mind. Approaching Lyneham, we called for the service of GCA, despite the fact that the weather was 'CAVU' (ceiling and visibility unlimited). It turned out that it was a good thing that we had such ideal weather conditions…

After calling the operator and requesting the use of the aid, the pilot quickly slipped into the patter of the procedure, responding to the directions given, such as 'slightly left', 'a little too high', etc. This started some distance from the aerodrome, several miles or so, and we watched with keen interest how the instructions related to our actual position in relation to the aerodrome and the runway in particular. Our approach speed was relatively slow and we gradually made our way to Lyneham, but it became clear that something was amiss, as the instructions received on the radio appeared not to conform with what we observed outside the aircraft.

As we became closer and lower, to the point when the controller indicated that touchdown was imminent, my Skipper and I saw clearly, thanks to the good weather conditions, that this would have meant a landing far short of even the aerodrome boundary. The aircraft was under full control of my colleague and with no further ado, he rectified the situation and brought the aeroplane in for a satisfactory approach and landing. What gave rise to this anomalous situation was not pursued; it could have been some fleeting aberration in the performance of the equipment, a freak meteorological variation in atmospheric air pressure, or something yet to be researched and compensated for. One of the distinctive advantages of the Anson, like the De Haviland Mosquito, was that the navigator sat side by side with the pilot, unlike in the Beaufighter, where the he was in the rear of the plane, with a less clear view of what lay dead ahead, and playing only a passive part in the manoeuvring of the aeroplane. Landings, in particular, always raised more than a passing interest of the pilot's finesse. This afforded me the opportunity of witnessing the above incident at Lyneham, and confirming that the approaching ground was 'not quite where it should have been' for myself.

Whatever the causes were for the 'aberration' on this 'dry run' they did nothing to improve our confidence in this particular system.

Many years later a phenomenon know as 'wind shear' was fully understood and concluded as the prime cause of several fatal landing accidents. Many of the principle airports now have sophisticated equipment to detect this event, which is, basically, rapidly changing wind speed and direction over a very short distance and which makes it almost impossible for the pilot to have absolute control of the aircraft at the critical point of touch- down.

The immediate post-war period was a difficult time for Britain, as her old established colonies started to express a wish to 'cast off the shackles of colonial oppression'. This, sadly, was to lead to uncontrolled slaughter on an almost unbelievable scale accompanied by sadistic brutality that beggars belief.

The RAF seemed a pale shadow of its former self. With the disappearance of its overriding *raison d'etre* — to win and survive — there seemed a lack of purpose in many of the duties carried out and the close personal friendships that had previously done much to maintain morale amongst aircrew became quite fleeting, as almost every flight was carried out with different men. It was always a pleasant surprise to discover that a trip was to be with someone known from a previous occasion.

Many changes were taking place, and it was a time when the skills of each category of aircrew were honed by undertaking specialised courses to bring them up to speed with the latest developments in their particular field. Consequently, I found myself spending a couple of weeks at a training establishment in Nottinghamshire to learn about 'Night Vision'. There was no airfield, and to my amazement, I found the Station Commanding Officer was an air gunner, with proof of his ability in this field evident in his row of 'gongs'. He was obviously the type with the appropriates background and skills, but at that time, for an air gunner to become a squadron leader was limited to wartime Bomber Command Operational Squadrons and then, as I recall, only on an 'acting' basis.

This said, I must confess that it sounds rather pompous; air gunners, and particularly the rear gunner in a four-engined aircraft, isolated from the rest of the crew, had perhaps the most uncomfortable and dangerous task of all aircrew. It just happens to be unique in my experience of the RAF, however, the officer concerned ran the station with pride and efficiency. Nowadays, command of a squadron and above is not limited only to pilots, as it once was; navigators have been appointed to command fighter squadrons and aircrew of other than pilots have attained Air Rank.

I was due for another remarkable surprise. The Course had been carefully put together, with classroom lectures and a large variety of rooms containing an impressive amount of equipment to demonstrate the vagaries and hidden aspects of human vision and how the eye performs its functions. Mac and I had flown many hours at night and prior to crewing together, much of the navigational training had been night flying, so initially it was not clear what benefit the course could impart.

After the introductory lectures, etc, most of the time was spent in the simulators which instantly proved to all of us that we really knew very little of the way to use our eyes to best advantage at night. I think it occurred to most of us that we had, perhaps, been lucky to survive those occasions of near misses with other aircraft when a quick word of warning to our pilot was necessary. Towards the end of our tour, Mac and I had a very near miss when landing at North Coates after returning from a sortie, with the 'offending' aircraft sitting just above us at touchdown. Briefly, we were shown the necessity to adapt to the night by shading the eyes for a minimum period to allow them to modify their performance and how, when entering a room which appears to be in total darkness, as the eyes adapt, objects become visible to a clear degree.

Most impressive was the deliberate manipulation of ones eyes to achieve a greatly improved vision in the dark by being aware of the two different 'viewing' areas of the eyes, known as the 'rods' and the 'cones'—which are which I fail to remember. By averting the gaze to a small degree to one side of the target, it becomes instantly within sight. On some basis or other, a mark was awarded at the end of the course, and mine was twenty nine out of thirty; what this implied I never discovered but it sounded OK. Now, when driving at night, approaching headlights and lack of marking at the nearside of the road sharply jog my memory that some 'wear and tear' has set in the since those youthful days.

After two weeks absence from my family, I was pleased to return to the comforts of home. Living in single quarters and spending evenings—well some, at least—in the officers mess and bar, had quickly palled.

In early August, Carol was getting a bit heavy as Nicholas began to develop rapidly—with his 'ETA' early in October—and we all felt in need of a holiday. The weather was exceptionally warm, but travel was still a bit of a problem in post-war Britain and funds were not too good into the bargain. After considering a few options, we decided to go to North Devon, to a small village called Coombe Martin. This had a touch of nostalgia for me as at the age of fifteen or sixteen, feeling the urge to head for far horizons—it certainly appeared far away from Spondon—I used my free travel facility with the railways to spend a week in a small boarding house. The week gave us much pleasure, being our first holiday as a family, I taught Joy how to swim in the decidedly cool waters of the Bristol Channel and as the village was on hills and cliffs, gave Carol a push from behind when the upgrades became too difficult.

Many of the trips from Hendon entailed a series of visits to several aerodromes, either in one day or several days. On occasions, five or six calls were made in one day, but everywhere I visited, I found it interesting and even exciting, whether in Britain or the Continent. England had virtually become one big airfield by the time the war was over, and I was familiar not with all their names but the vast majority, together with the type of operations carried out and the type of aircraft used. With the disappearance of the previous ever-present hazard of being suddenly confronted by enemy fighters—the Beaufighter despite its super performance was easy meat for any self-respecting Luftwaffe pilot—an air of easy calm took over and all the excursions were carried out in leisure and a sense of anticipation as what the next visit would bring forth.

With my inherent 'wanderlust' adequately catered for and being comfortable in our flat at Wimbledon, we awaited the arrival of our second child—after our holiday at Coombe Martin we had more or less decided that if it was a boy he would be called Martin—this period was tranquil and rewarding.

Life was not easy for many ex-servicemen; by now the sight of men in uniform was becoming quite rare. Travelling to and from Hendon by bus and train I was conscious of my uniformed appearance, often getting envious glances from some who were having difficulty in rehabilitating to civilian life. My display of the standard 'gongs'— representing service in particular areas of operations—usually drew attention, as the reputation of the services was still high. However, many civilians seemed to have an air of depression and defeat and this, unfortunately, rubbed off a bit on me. Coupled with the claustrophobic conditions of travel by Underground, my journey became something of an ordeal to be tolerated for the sake of the privileges and other benefits. I still find that travelling in Underground trains lowers my general spirits and brings a feeling of claustrophobia.

The time for the arrival of Nicholas drew near and the usual arrangements were made with the Doctor and Maternity Home close by, near Wimbledon Hill. I was excused flying duties for ten or so days before the event was due to happen but the arrival became overdue.

On the ninth of October, I flew to Brough, near Hull, with F/L McMeekan—a 'privilege' trip to take his wife to her home for some reason or other; I will refer to this later.

On the morning of 10th October, when Carol was showing no signs of activity, I departed to Hendon as usual and found that I was rostered to fly to Honington in Lincolnshire and return with Wing Commander Langlois. Shortly after I left home, needless to say, Murphy's Law took over and Carol felt the first pangs of labour. Packing a small suitcase of necessities, she walked to the bus stop and caught the next bus to the Nursing Home and settled in to await the birth — somewhat different to procedures these days, when giving birth demands care and attention of quite incredible complexity.

My pilot and I spent the day at Honington and in the early afternoon took off the return to Hendon. I was later able to confirm that at the time of Nicholas's actual birth, we were still airborne on the way back. Perhaps a small and not dramatically important fact of life but it somehow gave me quite a kick that my 'first born' arrived whilst I was drifting along at a couple of thousand feet in the environment in which by now I was familiar and comfortable. Could there be any connection with this fact and that Nicholas took to the air as a skydiver, with enjoyment and confidence when 'jumping out of parachutes' (sic) was regarded as a crazy sport of much danger. Who knows?

Twenty-five years on, the next limb of the tree, my grandson Jonathan, decided on a career involving the upper atmosphere. Is there some mysterious link? Whatever the reason, I find this thought not unduly fanciful, and I feel I have reached an age when I should be given some tolerance in mentioning such coincidental aspects of life! With no drama intended, the odds of those lucky enough to have flown on an operational squadron and survived, can but feel that there is more to luck and fate than meets the eye.

Recently — as I write in November 1998 — the English *Weekly Telegraph*, noted for its responsible journalism, gave excellent, sensitive and extensive coverage of the various Armistice Day ceremonies carried out in Britain. It was touching to see photographs that caught the full emotion of this traditional event. The aged, but proud and upright veterans of the First World War particularly jolted my innermost feelings with the realisation that these few survivors had known the horror of trench warfare and massive slaughter, and yet the fickleness of fate had decreed their survival to over one hundred years of life. Particularly gratifying, and uplifting was the dedication of the public in honouring this occasion. It reflected a remarkable change from the cynicism and coarsening which has seemingly taken a firm grip on the attitude of so many, both 'celebrities' and the general population at large. The event brought a kind of hush over the whole country, and the 'two minute silence' was observed with great solemnity throughout the land, by businesses, transport systems—even Heathrow Airport suspended operations—and remarkably (my cynicism is deeply rooted) even the tills at some supermarket checkouts were stilled.

Perhaps the present uncertainties in world affairs may have prompted this seriousness, because over the past decades, it has been the vogue to also discard so many of the centuries old ceremonies and rituals that have given Britain its unique place in history and world affairs. Be that as it may, the emotion, even when read after the event was palpable and encouraging for the future and the politicians should note well this resurgence of respect for those who gave their whole for their country and fellowmen.

This lengthy digression is regretted, but the ceremony brought to mind Armistice Day in 1947, when I found myself taking part in the very large commemorative parade at RAF Hendon, still a very important focus of RAF activities. Living out, with my family at Wimbledon, it was only very infrequently that I found myself 'orderly officer of the day'. Like most 'general duties officers'—the strange designation for aircrew—I was not overly familiar with the practicalities of performing, for 24 hours, the mundane, tedious, but apparently essential task of visiting various parts of the complex to ensure all was 'in order'. In fact, I was largely unaware of what precisely was supposed to be happening in the various nooks and crannies of the aerodrome and relied heavily on the 'duty sergeant' who accompanied me to brief me before my unfamiliarity showed through my facade of competence. Regular RAF sergeants have a remarkable technique of guiding officers in such matters whilst still allowing them to believe that they are 'in charge' and are punctilious in maintaining the correct relationship between different ranks, never stepping into the area of familiarity.

Part of the routine, for instance, was to enter the Airmen's Mess at a meal time, when the accompanying sergeant would bellow, "Attention, Orderly Officer!" then pause before asking "Any Complaints?" I don't think I ever discovered what I was supposed to do should any recalcitrant airman have the temerity to stand up and say "Yes, I have a complaint." Would I be called upon to taste the offending dish? Cook him another egg? Chastise the cook? Of course, for every contingency in the service there was a well tried precedent which regular and more experienced officers knew and could use as a 'fall-back' response. Perhaps Air Force food, by now, was so palatable that no complaint was called for. When a lowly airman myself, and having the same opportunity to object, my memory is that I considered the 'scoff' to be 'fair enough'.

The Armistice Day Parade in 1947 was close enough to the end of the war to merit full ceremonial treatment and the station was put into a high state of activity and excitement as it became apparent that many senior officers of all the services would be invited to attend. I was detailed off to be the officer who would control the party in charge of the actual handling of the flag and so determine the end of the 'two minutes silence'. Despite the feeling of honour and responsibility in doing this, I was concerned that all should go well and that I would be able to mark the end of the period directly, but I was unsure exactly how this would be achieved. The use of a wrist watch, or stop watch was obviously not in keeping with the dignity of the occasion and as I recall, it was left to me to mentally calculate the period of time and then give an almost imperceptible inclination of my head, whereupon the airmen handling the flag rope would lower and raise the Union Jack.

The occasion is one which I treasure and although thoughts of old friends come to mind unprompted at quite random times, this particular ceremony somehow gave me the opportunity to physically participate and so better express my respect for fallen comrades.

I have mentioned that some trips involved quite a few 'ports of call' and in early December, with not too pleasant weather for flying or personal comfort, Flt/Lt Nicholls and I took off with a party of the 'upper echelon' on a tour of aerodromes, this to last a whole week. First we visited Llanbedr, in Wales and hence to Wigtown, in Scotland for a night stop. The next day we went to Kinloss, Dyce, Edzell, Arbroath and spent the night at Turnhouse near Glasgow. From there we visited Abbotsinch and Port Ellen, also in Scotland, and then across the Irish Sea to Aldergrove in Northern Ireland. Finally, next day, we dropped in at Bovingdon, before returning to Hendon. All these aerodromes were of significance during the war years and the probable purpose of the visits by our passengers involved making important decisions regarding their new status in peacetime Britain.

It was on this trip, that, at one of the 'dromes in Scotland, I saw a vast congregation of discarded Lancaster Bombers, standing forlornly around the aerodrome perimeter. This totally unexpected sight literally 'hit me in the guts' and I was so moved and affected that I felt obliged to put pen to paper to record my innermost feelings. The piece I wrote is provided as an Appendix to these memoirs and I make no apology for expressing the deeply felt emotions that I felt at the time.

It is not easy to convey the relationship which wartime aircrews established with their 'steeds of the air', it had to be experienced to understand it, but this relationship became ever more close as it was usual to be repeatedly allocated a specific aircraft, known by an initial letter. Mac and I invariably flew 'P' for Peter and to climb into this particular aircraft preparatory to a trip, induced a sense of trust and comfort that all, would go well. A totally different atmosphere permeated the aircraft and affected our performance if for some reason we were not given 'our own' aircraft.

With regard to 'P' for Peter, I was due to get another gut-wrenching experience. Visiting one aerodrome, when flying from Hendon, we landed and taxied towards the control buildings. As usual at most places, aeroplanes stand around seemingly in no particular place or order, clear, obviously, of the runway area. As we proceeded along the taxi path, I happened to glance out and saw what I instantly recognised as a Beaufighter. However, it was a Beaufighter in desperate straits; it had obviously used for fire-fighting practice and was in its last throes before finally expiring. Still visible on the fire-scarred fuselage was the code letter 'P' for Peter. As Ned Kelly, the notorious Australian Bushranger said, just before being hanged in 1878, 'Such is life...'

When Carol and I were living in Scotland—Girvan on the West coast near Ayre—in 1944/5, we acquired an affection for the Scots, their sense of humour and zest for life that is quite different from the English, who have an inherent 'stodginess'. We attended dances and parties, during which many inhibitions were shed in the course of performing wild and vigorous activities like 'The Gay Gordons', 'Strip the Willow', (not the 'widow'!) etc—usually carried out in premises of small space resulting in hot and heavily perspiring bodies gyrating at high speed with seemingly an unlimited supply of energy.

So it was with some disappointment that we were not together for 'Hogmanay' of December 31st 1947. The day previously, I had flown up to an aerodrome called Bircham Newton, in the north of Norfolk in order to undertake yet another course, this time in 'Blind Landings'. "Drat and a pox on the RAF!" was my first response, but duty knows no refusal. However, it turned out to be very interesting and the system was again a forerunner of the elaborate and highly efficient and reliable procedures of the present day.

Anson and Airspeed Oxford aircraft were used, and my pilot, also from Hendon, was Flt/Lt Nicholls. The object of the exercise was for us to attain co-ordination in receiving radio signals from the ground transmitters in order to be able to land in comfort and safety in quite adverse weather conditions. The equipment to hopefully achieve this desirable situation was known as 'Rebecca/Babs'—the latter meaning 'Blind Approach Beacons System' although the meaning of the former escapes my memory. Via this airborne equipment we were able to home to the aerodrome, always the first essential, and thereafter, the course of the plane could be seen on a cathode ray tube—read TV screen—by the navigator, who would then respond to the picture by directing the pilot—left—right—up—down, etc with the distance to touchdown also relayed.

I think I operated under some kind of hood or perhaps my seat was turned around in order to stop me looking out of the plane and 'cheating'. I recall that, having paid proper attention to the sound of blips and the trace displayed on the screen, it was possible for me to direct the pilot to such a degree of accuracy that I could put him exactly at the centre of the runway.

Together, we did just over a dozen trips, in some ten hours of flying and felt satisfied and competent with our achievement. In order to reinforce my navigator's awareness of a pilot's skills, I was also able to carry out five hours of training in the 'Link Trainer'—a very elementary flight simulator which calls for the operator to use controls similar to those in an aircraft and guide or steer a small object called the 'crab' along a required path on a large table. This sounds a simple and easy thing to do, but this little 'crab', as it made its way across the table, left behind a tell-tale line of ink, which the instructor would closely observe and pass critical comments. Present day systems provide almost virtual reality and can simulate every possible situation to test the pilot's skills. Although they probably cost as much as a large jet aeroplane, they provide enormous savings in the cost of flight training and add greatly to aircraft safety. A session in such a trainer with a skilled instructor, can leave even experienced crews totally exhausted, but at the same time knowledgeable of dangerous situations that might only arise once, and then perhaps with horrible finality, in the lifetime of a pilot.

Returning home after just over a week, Carol and I enjoyed our belated Hogmanay celebration, but we missed the good companionship and wild exhilaration of our friends in Scotland, the 'First Footing Ceremony' and the exhortation 'lang may your lum reek' — spoken with the appropriate burr — after the gift of a piece of coal, was much in our minds. England seemed tame by comparison.

EPILOGUE

During January and early February 1948, my log book reflects only a couple of trips, perhaps I took leave to be at home with Carol and Joy and, perhaps, get my hand in as a new and inexperienced father, by changing nappies and preparing feeds for young Nicholas. Life in the flat—12 Alwynne Mansions, Wimbledon—was reasonably comfortable, with trains every few minutes to Waterloo, taking about nine minutes.

Ours was the top flat of three, all the others being occupied by elderly retired people. Our arrival, with Joy as the 'first child on the block' and then the arrival of Nicholas, must have jolted the previous tranquillity of the surroundings, but they responded with kindness and understanding and Joy quickly made friends with the elderly ladies. One flat was occupied by a Mr and Mrs Douglas Belcher. Douglas had been a Sergeant in the Army in 1915 and had won the Victoria Cross for bravery for a single-handedly tackling a German machine gun nest. He was still a very big and powerful man, impressive in bearing and presence. I regarded him with great respect—it is not every day that one meets a holder of the VC—and it was indeed a privilege to be his neighbour.

It appeared, as the future shape of the RAF was beginning to emerge, that I would not be part of it, because I received my 'de-mob' papers, with instructions to report to Warton, near Blackpool on the 22nd February. That date rang the bell of coincidence—I was born on 22-2-22—but I fail to recall my reaction to the fact that my services were being dispensed with. It was the 'push', the 'ogre of redundancy', but certainly not a 'golden handshake'. Some time later, when I collected my 'gratuity', it came to the magnificent amount of one hundred and ten pounds, after seven years service!

Dressed in 'civvies', I collected this huge sum from a bank, all in small notes to inflate its apparent munificence and had to walk some few hundred yards to a Post Office where I wished to deposit it for convenience of access—which, considering the state of our finances, I knew would be necessary sooner rather than later. This loot was tucked into an innermost pocket for security and although mugging was pretty unlikely in those days, I recall treading my way over this short distance with a beating heart in case anyone should snatch from me the fruits of my quite long and faithful service to King and Country.

I had enjoyed serving in almost all the lower ranks, from Aircraftsman Second Class, ditto First Class (this a quite rare one), Leading Aircraftsman, Sergeant, Fight Sergeant, Pilot Officer, Flying Officer, and the peak of my particular ladder, Flight Lieutenant.

Going through the routine of the 'de-mob' process invoked a strong sense of loss and depression. The civilian clothing that was collected from a series of counters, rather like the queues for self-service food, looked drab and had little or no style or cut and had obviously come off a hastily assembled factory production line in order to cope with the huge number of servicemen returning to 'civvy street'. Having disproportionately long arms and legs, I had to take what was on offer, resulting, when I did regretfully shed my well worn but 'self-esteem invoking' Aircrew officer's togs, not only in a dreadfully uncomfortable ensemble but also in a picture not pretty to a casual observer!

The *pièce de resistance* was the greatcoat. It certainly conformed to its name as it was huge, with massively wide shoulders, extremely large lapels and it swept the floor as I walked. It was made of some thick material, had solid bulk and was not easy to put on; in fact it almost required an assistant to hold it during this process. It was a bit chequered in colour and would have collected little notice if worn on the Steppes in Russia in mid winter, deflecting snow, ice and permafrost with ease. We took it with us when we emigrated to Africa and carted it around many, many, house moves, usually in temperatures of the high thirties. It was never worn, but for some reason I was loath to part with it. I think it was finally abandoned, probably to be eaten by termites, when we left Africa to move back to England in 1980. It deserved to be placed in a military museum, but I didn't think of it at the time!

After my last flight in the RAF on 22nd February 1948, it was sixteen years before I became 'airborne' again when a flight of just a few minutes gave me a bigger fright than probably all my airforce trips. By then, as a fairly junior officer with the Rhodesia Railways, I was involved in sales and advertising. A project was developed which involved the use of a helicopter to fly at low level around one of our trains running in the countryside, circling to take photographs from different angles. The 'chopper' was a very basic Bell 47G model, with seating designed for the pilot and one passenger, but involved in the project was a young lady required for the action in the studio, who occupied the available seat to enjoy the action in the air. It so happened that the chopper had to make a short flight to the main airport, and without thinking too much about the flimsiness of the machine, I blurted out that I would like to join the flight. Anyway, the young lady sat in the middle and I was obliged to perch myself on the outside, held in place by a very narrow strap that would hardly have been sufficient to hold a suitcase together. Oh, and yes, the door next to me had been removed to facilitate the photography on the previous flight, leaving a large and menacing hole over which my left buttock dangled in space.

It was sixteen years since my feet had been 'off the deck', and with some trepidation I clutched the back of the seat as the pilot wound up the revs prior to take-off. I had never been up vertically in an aircraft before and I exaggerate not when I say that I was petrified. At least it stopped me reminiscing about my aeronautical exploits for a while — well, for a couple of weeks or so!

From that first flight on 13th November 1941 to the last flight on 22nd February 1948, I had accumulated a total of 1420 flying hours. Not a lot really, compared with the amazing flying hours of pilots who spent a career in civil aviation on the 'long haul' routes. Over twenty thousand hours was commonplace, with one extraordinary achievement of thirty thousand hours spent in the air.

This equates to approximately six months, day and night, aloft in the company of the winds and clouds, and with, say, an average flight time of six hours, five thousand individual take-offs and landings. It is not possible to comprehend, even with the proven reliability of modern aeroplanes, the countless opportunities for some catastrophic mechanical failure to arise during this period. Also to be noted is the incredible skill and reliability of the pilot to have been able to safely handle the countless situations, when the weather, and the multitude of other problems that can suddenly arise even in what appears to be a routine and uneventful flight.

It is said that 'there are old pilots and there are bold pilots, but there are no old, bold pilots'. How true. The facial characteristics of pilots with these amazing flight times are intriguing, their eyes reflecting their many hours of flight. This subtle indication of their experiences is difficult to define in everyday terms, but to me it suggests a kind of calmness, even a remoteness, not a weariness, but reflecting an empathy with the elements on high in the sky. There is no 'cockiness' or arrogance, and their general demeanour seems to indicate that although not an area for great introspection, they are not totally unaware of the kindness of fate that has served them so well.

Looking back to my early days in Spondon, with my poor physique, not a lot on offer towards other than a fairly mundane career in a basic, repetitive type occupation, I frequently give my thanks to whatever it was that guided me to aviation and provided me with so many exciting times. And that is not all, as in retirement, my enthusiasm for aviation, modern and vintage persists and provides endless interest and entertainment, through the modern periodicals and through association with old friends of similar background. My pride knew no bounds when Nicholas became a skydiver and with Jonathan now well into his career as a commercial pilot, further thanks have been given to that mysterious power that we call 'Fate'.

In my 'pre-war memories', I mentioned a cycle ride to Hucknall aerodrome near Nottingham to see the aircraft of those days, such as the Hawker Fury, Hart, Demon and others. Biplanes not far removed from the First World War, it was beyond my wildest dreams that one day I would have the privilege of experiencing flight in some not dissimilar and others more 'state of the art', developed rapidly through the pressure of a new war—the types of planes I recorded in my Flying Log Book: Whitley, Dominie, Proctor, Anson, Oxford, Beaufort, Walrus (Flying Boat), Dakota, Beaufighter, Mosquito, Lancaster, Lancastrian, York, Liberator.

A POST-WAR CAREER

Suddenly it was all over and new dawns were breaking, strangely without the sounds of aircraft engines. The kit bag was put away with a sigh of regret along with the special folding bags that crews used to keep uniform jackets uncreased — invented for aircrews of the American Airforces — also stacked in the wardrobe. The small and battered holdall for 'night stops', bearing many labels of 'far away places with strange sounding names' and, perhaps with a touch of swagger, a creased and dog-eared label, 'BOAC Crew', was optimistically put not quite so far into the cupboard as if, by some strange quirk, it would be handy for a quick getaway should the phone ring with the requirement for my urgent attendance for a trip to some old familiar place over that still tempting horizon.

My wings definitely felt clipped! Despite everything otherwise nice, there was a hollow feeling not to be easily dismissed, a feeling that the end of a road had been reached and that the restraints of a more civilised and orderly life were closing in with remorseless power, with 'never more to roam' the game-plan for the future. The shedding of uniform, in itself, had a feeling not of 're-birth' but of entry into uncharted waters, and which waters contained unfamiliar ebbs and flows which indicated that life's progress would not be under the personal control that seven years service life had eventually produced.

The standard 'de-mob' clothes of very modest quality and hurried mass-production, reflected nothing in the way of sartorial elegance. In fact, we looked not dissimilar to those poor unfortunates lucky to have survived the concentration camps of Europe, who had been re-suited shortly after rescue.

But perhaps — and this is only human nature — the biggest impact was the loss of visible status. Suddenly we were one of the throng, part of the run of the mill, the hurly burly of humanity, any old Tom, Dick or even Harry. We had no 'datum points' to establish where we stood in relation to others. Not like in the service where the tiers of rank gave order and cohesion to every relationship and were instinctively assessed and adhered to without conscious thought.

Maybe our lives had been run on elitist principles, but it had produced admirable results, with the self-respect and discipline from achieving acceptance in ones own group, and the use of these same qualities to easily associate with those of higher or lower rank. These qualities, this view of life in general, clearly distinguishes those who had the good fortune of knowing service life and shines through even in civilian life. It is a rock of solid foundation, built up from early days of warfare—the Roman Legionaries were attuned to the same basic philosophy—but all servicemen feel a sense of uncertainty and disorientation when thrust into 'civvy street'. Fortunately, these problems of 'integration'—perhaps even 'rehabilitation'—can be overcome, because service life has also produced the attitude that firm resolution will surmount all difficulties.

So it was a case of—as the terminology went in those days—'press on regardless'! But to where? And how to 'press on'?

I had been given a year and a half extension of my RAF Commission—otherwise I would have been eligible for demobilisation about mid 1946—so by the time of my own demobilisation, most of the servicemen who had left in the normal way had already been absorbed into civilian life, commerce and industry was slowly gathering way. However, this activity was not great enough to offer latecomers like me much of a choice and I realised that it was not going to be easy to find something to my liking.

In any case, what did I have much to offer to any prospective employer. Like most ex-aircrew I had little or no pre-war managerial or supervisory experience and service life had called only for me to manage my own affairs, unlike senior NCOs who had spent many years organising manpower to the best ability of the task in hand. Returning to the railways did not grab my enthusiasm as the long-term prospects were very poor. By this time, there had been established a kind of employment agency or service, near Victoria in London. It was solely for ex-officers from all the services and much sympathetic assistance was given by the mature staff. Large noticeboards displayed a brief description of job vacancies that employers wished to fill, and after perusing said board, one made enquiries and an interview with the prospective employer was arranged. There was one snag. Almost all the jobs were humdrum to the point of absolute boredom, certainly after perambulating to far off places for so long, in the clear and unfettered 'blue yonder'.

These filled me with an air of gloom and despondency, the like of which I never felt in the Air Force, even during dark and dismal days when flying was cancelled or we were mourning losses of comrades on the previous sortie. Choice items like:

'Wardens wanted for the British Museum,
uniforms provided, etc, etc,
Five pounds per week'

It was sad to see Army gentlemen exuding that unmistakable air of junior officer rank, pausing embarrassed, and hopefully unobserved, to quickly note down the details of such gems of future careers in the new England that had emerged after the ruinous war.

I had several uninspiring interviews with employers and I'm sure that they regarded me without enthusiasm as my morale was beginning to take a downward plunge and I was well aware that I cut no pretty picture of being 'bright eyed and bushy tailed'. I recall that in this regard, I had my tail between my legs for most of the time.

Redeeming features of this period, however, were the pleasures of family life at the flat in Wimbledon. Joy was enjoying school on Wimbledon Common and young Nicholas gaining strength and the darling of the several elderly couples who lived in the adjoining flats. The arrival of baby Nicholas in this previous enclave for the elderly must have caused them some initial concern but they were so very pleasant and helpful to us all, despite the disturbance of the early morning feed and Carol's vigorous poking of the coal stove to clean and re-light the fire and generate some warmth.

My pre-war enthusiasm for amateur radio had been sharpened by qualifying as an RAF Observer I had the ability to send and receive the Morse code at fairly high speed, together with a greatly increased knowledge of radio theory and also the skill to handle the communication equipment.

The Post Office authorities in England, together with the organisation for amateur radio had come to a very sensible arrangement whereby many with the radio operating and technical skills could obtain a licence to become a 'ham' without the need to pass the previous stringent tests which pertained before the war.

I received my licence at the end of 1947 and almost immediately went 'on the air' using Morse code and this gave me a welcome outlet to continue my 'earthly wanderings' without leaving my home. Putting together the various items of equipment also gave me much pleasure, albeit that it was done on the floor of the dining room, which doubled as a bedroom for Nicholas, and I was ably assisted by one Ted Pearson who lived very close by and had spent many years in the Merchant Navy as a Marconi company radio operator.

(Appendix 000 is a short article I wrote for a ham radio magazine which describes this venture into the world of amateur radio, a lifelong interest that has given me many hours of friendly conversations with contacts all over the world.)

With little real enthusiasm, I persevered with the quest to find some kind of work that fired my interest, but it was hard going. Interviews with employers, in themselves vastly different from the forceful and direct senior RAF officers who had won my respect and admiration, with discussions often taking place with the background of industrial noise of machinery churning out some kind of objects or appliances, left me depressed and disillusioned with post war England.

One particular enquiry through the officer's bureau was more depressing than most. I spotted on the noticeboard a vacancy for a clerk—in those days almost every other person was a 'clerk'—but I think that there was a rider to this vacancy that it would involve 'training in management' and as it was at a Hospital in South London, which was convenient to Wimbledon, my spirits rose an almost imperceptible degree. I decided that little would be lost by further enquiry so an interview at the hospital was organised. So off I went to the hospital to present myself in best bib and tucker with a vague expectation that this could be the day when I would step onto the bottom rung of a new ladder leading to who knew where.

There was a dramatic anti-climax when, on approaching the hospital, I found that it was for the treatment of what we, in those days, perhaps a touch unkindly, called 'mental defectives'. My early RAF training on the parade ground, however, stood me in good stead, and with a audible 'about turn' I 'scarpered' in a quite undignified way back from whence I had come, with a determination that whatever happened as far as a future career was concerned this was not to be it!

But something had to done, as finances were becoming a bit of a problem and so, with a sense of capitulation, I approached the London Midland and Scottish Railways — my pre-war employers — to see what was on offer. I was, technically 'still on their books' and merely absent in the armed services, so I was sure that I could be re-absorbed into their bosom if I should so decide. A tentative approach to their head office in London resulted in an interview at St Pancras Station.

Coincidence plays a remarkable part in human activity, and so it was when I went to meet my 'interviewer' at St Pancras, when, not far into the interview, quite unexpectedly, the subject of radio communication came up, probably from a reference to my wartime qualifications. George Walton, the gentlemen conducting the interview, mentioned, with an evident touch of pride, that he had recently qualified as a radio amateur. I almost blurted out "Well, blow me down!" but the gravity of the situation stopped me, but when I confirmed that I too was an amateur radio enthusiast, my future with the LMS Railway Company was in the bag.

George was a fairly senior officer — railways for a very long time retained the early tradition of 'officers and men' — and had served in the First World War. He was then approaching sixty years of age, was of modest education but had laboured long and hard to achieve the required standard of technical knowledge and the speed in Morse code to obtain his licence to operate. I thought it was a sterling effort and enhanced my opinion of him, as in addition, he discreetly understood and sympathised with my generation, who after several exciting and adventurous years, had been literally 'brought down to earth' and were trying to come to terms with what a more mundane future held in store for us. He was an excellent supervisor and we became firm friends.

I took up my duties as a 'train controller' at St Pancras railway station, with the area of operation extending over a wide part of the system, but more importantly, my decision to do so, had quite unbelievable long term ramifications.

It was, although I was not even remotely aware of it at the time, one of those moments in life that 'if taken at the flood, leads on to better things'—or words to that effect. It was a defining moment that put me and my family on course, a couple of years later, to enter another and exciting phase, the like of which we had no previous experience, namely, in 1950, our 'passage to Rhodesia' and my subsequently wonderful, varied and rewarding career with Rhodesia Railways. This, in turn, gave way to an equally remarkable and satisfying later life in retirement, when in 1989 it was time for our 'passage to Australia'.

As I write this today, I again offer silent thanks to those mysterious forces which control such critical events; they have been kind to me beyond any measure which words could adequately express.

But what of old Mates from flying days? How did they fare in the lottery of life?

THE FORTUNES OF OLD COLLEAGUES

Jeff McCarrison

Stepping from our Beaufighter, after the last trip of our operational tour on March 9th 1945, Jeff McCarrison –always Mac to his friends—and I bade farewell to each other, with Mac heading back to New Zealand. The plunge into post-war life took us on totally remote and unconnected paths. Careers and responsibilities took priority and it was not until our maturing years that the close bond of friendship we established as an 'aircrew' prompted the desire to re-establish contact.

The details of the way this was achieved escapes me, but the strong impression is that I wrote to some ex-service organisation in New Zealand that published such requests to meet old comrades, and we started to correspond. Mac had married Audrey, they had three children and Mac, with his father, had constructed two massive greenhouses for the commercial production of tomatoes. He was also engaged in rural road transport in the Auckland area. It was very apparent that life was good. As described in a previous chapter, we eventually met in 1988 when Carol and I were travelling to Australia to see whether we wanted to migrate there.

At that first meeting, a few small 'fibs' were exchanged regarding our immunity to the passing years, but it was a great and emotional reunion. We sat late into the night, with recall honed to a razor's edge, reliving some of the more dramatic incidents encountered during our tour, so much so that I became quite frightened—perhaps more so than the first time round, when youth's protective arm of almost unquestioned immortality shielded me from the true reality of the situation! Strangely, Mac and I tended to remember more vividly quite different aspects as the details came swinging back to mind.

How strange is the human memory, with its ability to sift and reshuffle those intricate events that occur as we travel, willy-nilly along life's highway.

Carol and I had the pleasure in about 1995 of a visit from Mac and Audrey, who spent a week with us, and we still keep in touch on a regular basis. Great mates, great memories.

Lawrence Granville Brown

I have referred frequently in these memoirs to my good friend 'Charlie' Brown, more formally, Laurence Granville. We came together on the same course, as newly qualified Observers at East Fortune Operational Training Unit in November 1943 and I have made many references to him in these writings. We both came from a modest, rural background, had the same type of humour and, as so often happens in service life, hit it off so well that we virtually became inseparable. With our wives, we continued to meet after the war was over, but when Carol and I left for Rhodesia in 1950, exchanges of correspondence became spasmodic — living in the Rhodesian bush with no postal facilities was not conducive to putting pen to paper — and we soon lost touch with each other.

Carol and I returned to live in England, at Hastings East Sussex in 1980 and shortly after this, despite the quite involved and stressful situation that was our lot, stemming from the political changes that had occurred in Rhodesia, my thoughts often turned to my good friend Charlie and what hand he had been dealt in the post-war years. As it turned out, it was not a good hand; in fact it was unbelievably sad.

How to get in touch was the first problem. I knew that he came from a small village near Chelmsford in Essex, called Great Dunmow, and as a 'flyer' I wrote to the postmaster there explaining my mission. His reply, as he had been there pre-war and was familiar with the residents, was almost immediate, indicating that he had passed on my address to Charlie's sister. I have included, at Appendix XXX the letter I received from Charlie, in facsimile form, in order to retain the poignancy of the message which it contained. Incredibly, he lived only a matter of twenty minutes drive from where Carol and I lived in Hastings, East Sussex.

Charlie had become, in 1964, seventeen years previously, a victim of that dreaded disease, multiple sclerosis, which had affected his well-being to the point that, by then, he was confined to a wheelchair.

Remarkably, his speech was little affected when we met shortly after regaining contact, but the movement of his legs and arms was limited to only minor control in one arm. His son Mervyn, born shortly after war's end and who had been engaged as an apprentice in the boat-building industry on the south coast, had also been struck down by this dread disease and was, by 1981, most severely physically handicapped, with constant uncontrolled movements of his limbs and his speech so spasmodic and distorted as to be virtually incomprehensible.

They both lived at home, with Doris having the almost super-human task of looking after both of them. The house was fitted with electric hoists to assist in their movements, but it was necessary for Doris to provide almost constant physical assistance both day and night.

The joy and pleasure of our re-union after so many years and with so many shared experiences of happy, youthful times was offset by the almost unbearable agony of seeing my close Air Force companion in such dire straights. Charlie and Mervyn — named after Charlie's RNZAF pilot — were in a state of fairly rapid deterioration by now, with the prognosis for the future offering little hope. The situation was, frankly, more than I could bear, having so optimistically anticipated meeting once again to recount our times together and how we fared after we left the service.

I was totally unable to control my emotions and every visit left me worse than ever, and despite the fortitude of Charlie and Mervyn — and the incredible dedication of Doris — I found, to my shame, that my visits became less frequent. It was a situation that overwhelmed my self control and induced a sense of rage that Charlie, having survived so many close encounters, had been so let down by fate. It was grotesque in the extreme. My feelings were exacerbated, quite illogically, by the attitude of both Charlie and Mervyn, who appeared to tolerate their misfortune with an inner fortitude and even a wry sense of humour. They both felt the power of my distress and, amazingly, our roles became reversed, with them offering *me* comfort, instead of the visitor arriving to comfort the sick!

But the course of the disease was unrelenting and one day I received a call from Doris to say that Charlie was in hospital at Eastbourne. The hospital was extremely old, in sad need of main-tenance, the decor being the traditional green and brown. It had probably remained unchanged since it handled the sick and wounded from the First World War, or even, likely, from the Boer War of the turn of the century.

It was not a place for those in dire straits and when I visited Charlie, needless to say, and not only because of his medical condition, he was very low in spirits. Having been in a wheelchair for so many long years, the circulation to his legs was starting to fail and Charlie and Doris were confronted with a decision regarding the amputation of his limbs. It was not really a question of a decision; the situation demanded immediate action by the surgeons. Sadly, but perhaps mercifully, Charlie died during the operation a few days later.

He was given a military funeral service, followed by cremation and a funeral wake. It was my first experience of a wake, this ceremony going back into the mists of time, perhaps connected with Irish folklore, and despite my sorrow of the occasion, it was impossible not to accept that human nature, being a strange commodity, employs devious practices to allow acceptance of the death of dear friends and relatives. The affair developed into quite a boisterous affair, with singing and joking, stories of earlier days of those in attendance and consumption of a very large amount of alcohol. It was just the tonic that most of us needed—I certainly did—and it cemented so many happy memories of past times that Charlie and I had enjoyed.

The expression, 'now at peace' was never more appropriate as in the passing of Laurence Granville Brown. He was—as we say here in Australia—a Bloody Good Bloke.

Jimmie Rodgers

Jimmie and I first met at Air Navigation School, Mount Hope, Ontario in January 1943 and together with several others—as one always tended to form cliques in the service—we became close friends. We enjoyed the same sense of humour and the constant ribaldry and ribbing of friends that is such an integral factor of service life, no doubt now known, in politically correct language, as the 'bonding process'. So when we were given a mid-term break, our small group took advantage of the fact that the city of Detroit was only a reasonable distance away by train, and the lure of the 'good ol' USA' drew us irresistibly.

Much alcohol was consumed, and on arrival at Detroit, a bit bemused to be in America, we somehow located the friendly facilities that assisted American servicemen in overnight accommodation. They also put us on track for the United Services Organisation — the USO as it was known in many parts of the world — with extensive comforts for men away from home. It was almost entirely manned by volunteers, of all ages, probably providing comfort of only a totally innocent or innocuous type, although 'you know what sailors are'. Anyway, our visit was to be short and, as I recall, principally to revel in a spot of freedom and to catch a glimpse of what was then to all of us, the magical USA.

Our RAF uniforms drew instant attention, and we were plied with drinks and good natured chat. The average American drips with social bonhomie and the evening went with a great swing. It was, of course, early in the war, when the European Theatre of Operations seemed to most of our hosts to be a place of great danger. They knew that the Battle of Britain had been fought and won by 'The Few' and our RAF uniforms seemed to indicate to most of our hosts that they were in the presence of some of those 'heroes of the hour'. By then, of course, the 'London Blitz', with its heavy bombings, was fresh in their minds and their admiration and gratitude that we were from a country that was heroically resisting the rapid advances of the forces of darkness in the shape of the Nazis, prompted them to spoil us to an embarrassing degree.

Strangely, speaking of embarrassment, a simple and humorous 'trick' lingers in my memories of that visit. Drinking beer generally results in men making frequent visits to the 'gentlemen's convenience'. In this facility there stood a model of an attractive lady, modestly dressed — there was much modesty in those days, as against the present — but her dress was short and flared out at the hem. Men rapidly lose natural inhibitions, even after a small intake of the 'devils brew' and also have an insatiable curiosity as to the female form. The temptation to lift the dress to see what it discreetly kept from view was irresistible and, ahem, ahem, so I was told later, revealed nothing that was immodest. But the cunning proprietor had ingeniously wired the dress to some device so that when an inquisitive male took the bait, a loud bell rang in the general drinking area with the result that, as the miscreant emerged he was, to his astonishment and embarrassment, loudly clapped and cheered!

Jimmie and I laboured our way through the navigation school, graduated as sergeant observers, competed a general reconnaissance course at Prince Edward Island, and returned to England a board the ship *Aquitania* along with nearly fifteen hundred US servicemen. Our paths then separated and we joined different squadrons at different stations, Jimmie going to No. 235 and me to No. 254.

In Autumn 1944, Jimmie and his pilot were detached to an aerodrome in Devon to carry out strikes against shipping and coastal defences in the Bay of Biscay, particularly in the area of the estuary of the Gironde river. They met with heavy opposition, both from ground defences and also Luftwaffe fighters, such as JU88s and the dreaded FW190s and ME109s. I think it was the 'press-on spirit' of Jimmie and his mate during these operations that resulted in a well deserved award of the DFC—Distinguished Flying Cross—to them both. The pilots of Beaufighters, being in control of the aircraft, obviously determined the aggressiveness and, with luck, the outcome of any attack, and were therefore more often favoured with such an award. It is to Jimmy's credit that his part in ensuring the success of the missions, by his performance and behaviour, as an observer, resulted in him also being honoured.

Shortly after this, Jimmie and his pilot converted from Beaufighters to Mosquitoes and operated from a base in Scotland, undertaking Strike Wing actions off the coast of Norway. I envied the flying he was able to experience in the Mosquito—my two short trips from North Bay in Canada at the end of the war gave me a taste of the exhilaration of low level flight in the 'front seat'. He completed his tour just before war's end.

It was about 1995 that we re-established contact, and I was delighted find that Jimmie had prospered, in all respects, having taken up dentistry after the war and had reached a very senior position in his profession. Married and with several children and grandchildren, we had a stirring re-union at his home in Esher, Surrey, in 1996, after making telephone arrangements to meet in nearby Kingston.

There was, of course, the usual problem of recognising old friends—in this case, extremely old,—in a public place, but at a range of fifty yards, recognition was instant and resulted in both of us taking off in a shambling style suitable to elderly gentlemen, to a very effusive greeting. Jimmie had become involved in governmental policy and teaching regarding dentistry and had been awarded several Governorships in this field. We now correspond on a regular basis.

Through Jimmie, I learned of another instance of the randomness of survival in war. One of our colleagues at Navigation School had been 'Johnny' Walker. I held him in great respect as he had a deformity of one arm that, if not for his determination, and I gather, the influence of his father who was a senior Naval officer, would have certainly meant his disqualification from flying duties. At an aerodrome in Scotland, he and his pilot had taxied out for take off and were awaiting the arrival of another plane, before turning onto the end of the runway to go. However, the incoming aircraft, also a Mosquito, was not correctly lined up and as it came in to land, its undercarriage struck the cockpit of Walker's plane, killing both the crew instantly. A most unfortunate and totally unpredictable accident.

THE 'BEAUFIGHTER SPIRIT' LIVES ON

I have briefly mentioned above, those with whom I had personal contact and friendship beyond the very strong bonds that we all of us who knew and flew that 'magnificent machine' experienced on a daily basis and who are also frequently recalled to memory, even with the slightest trigger.

To enhance these memories, in a practical way, and provide for opportunity to meet old comrades for recreation and reminiscences, several organisations exist, through the dedicated efforts of just a few individuals.

North Coates Strike Wing Re-Union Group

Squadron Leader Pat Fry, served with distinction with 236 Squadron, North Coates, followed a career in civil aviation after the war and retired to live near Brighton in England. With commendable dedication, he established the above association, produces newsletters and arranges periodic meetings and visits. One of the prime and most dangerous targets of the Wing was the Dutch Port of Den Helder, and some eight attacks were carried out against this heavily defended centre of enemy shipping. Pat participated in six of these sorties and had the most amazing luck to survive unscathed and has been dedicated to perpetuating the memory of those lost on these, and occasions concerning other targets.

Unfortunately, owing to the re-unions taking place in Europe, I have been unable to attend, but it evident from the informative newsletters Pat produces, there still exists a strong sense of camaraderie of the surviving members of 254, 236 and 143 Squadrons. Several major projects have seen the establishment of commemorative plaques to lost crew members and as the majority of the Wing's operations took place along the Dutch coast, the hospitality and warmth of the Dutch people has been a factor on achieving this.

The Beaufighter Club of Western Australia

With the memory of the strong bond between all crews who flew Beaufighters and knowing that many of them had come from the colonies and other countries, it occurred to me shortly after Carol and I arrived in Australia, that some kind of association in the Perth area might provide the opportunity for old crews to meet.

The outcome of enquiries revealed that quite a number of ex-Beaufighter men lived in the area, and 'The Beaufighter Club of Western Australia' was duly formed, initially with about sixty members.

The majority of members flew with the Royal Australian Air Force Squadrons 30 and 31, operating in the area immediately to the north of Australia, but several individuals were active in Burma, with some four or five operating with the Strike Wings in Western Europe. The principal figure in the organisation is retired Air Commodore Sam Dallywater, who commanded No 30 Squadron RAAF, and through his good offices and service connections, all members are favoured in many ways by lively contacts with serving air force members and facilities.

The type of operations of the Beaufighter Squadrons in the Pacific Area were fundamentally similar to operations in Europe, but important differences were the general climate and living conditions and the large distances to be flown over the sea and areas held by the enemy. In Europe, survival and treatment of those shot down and captured were in the terms of the Geneva Convention but such humanity did not hold sway in the Pacific, with several gross incidents of captured crews being beheaded by the Japanese.

The formation of our group initiated the wish to provide some tangible evidence of the achievements of not only the crews but also of the Beaufighter aircraft itself. Those of us who survived, feel that some greater hand than ours had been kind to us—that sounds a rather grand statement, but it is nonetheless an honest admission—but our deep feelings for our lost comrades of those days drives the instinct to not let them be forgotten.

The outcome of these wishes was the establishment, at the entrance to the Royal Australian Air Force Museum at Bullcreek, Perth, of a plaque commemorating the qualities of the Beaufighter, in all theatres of operation and by all squadrons. The unveiling was a moving ceremony and was attended by many dignitaries, with Air Commodore Sam Dallywater officiating.

The second project was to provide, in the general body of the museum—which, incidentally has accumulated a large and remarkable diversity of historical aviation items—a suitable exhibit devoted to Beaufighters, again in worldwide operations. A widespread request for suitable items resulted in an enthusiastic response, with members and others digging deep into their personal treasures with a commendable degree of generosity and the outcome is an impressive and interesting free-standing exhibit, topped by a large model of a Beaufighter aeroplane kindly provided by the Aeromodellers of Perth.

This model is finished in the colours of the late Wing Commander Jack Sandford, DSO, DFC, RAAF, who, with great verve and leadership, flew many Beaufighter operations in the Pacific Theatre, and provides an immediate focal point for all visitors.

There are, of course numerous groups, worldwide, similar to the two described above and, with the advent of 'information technology', web pages on the Internet, designed to provide information and answer queries regarding the Beaufighter.

One aspect of commemoration of those flying days still irks every member or interested person. About eight thousand Beaufighters were produced, and possibly six or so still exist as static exhibits in various museums. There is, however, not one of these planes, in an 'airworthy condition', capable of once again emitting that roar and surge of power at 'take-off' and sweeping into the blue sky above.

But all is not lost and we take heart that here, in Australia, there is a muted rumour that this gap in history and in our own personal memories, may be remedied in the not too distant future.

It is our fervent wish that once again, a pair of mighty Hercules engines will thunder across the sky and make all our hearts beat faster as in times of old.

'Whispering Death', will ye no come back again?

Additional Material

The Beaufighter Aeroplane

General background

In Britain, in the mid thirties, it became apparent that there was urgent necessity to rearm all the Services, with Air Power the first priority. Many of the "front line fighters" had showed little change from the aeroplanes extant at the end of the First World War, being mostly biplanes, and sadly lacking in the rapid technological improvements that the designers in Germany, Holland and other countries had been able to achieve. The civil war in Spain, starting in 1936, proved the prowess of these new designs and the large reservoir of trained pilots in Germany were able to hone their skills in aerial combat to a standard far exceeding the resources and abilities of Britain.

The Bristol Aircraft Company was one of the pioneer manufacturers of aeroplanes, being formed in 1910 and had produced many different types of aircraft which gave excellent service in the First World War, and when the call came in 1935, for urgent up date and production of planes to meet the growing challenge, responded with alacrity. The major step, in design, was from the previous, flimsy biplanes to the then revolutionary all metal, twin-engined monoplane, with great improvement in operating and maximum speeds. It was called the 'Blenheim', could serve in the role of fighter, bomber, reconnaissance, etc and came into service in 1936.

However, the performance of the Blenheim needed to be improved and shortly afterwards, Bristol's new concept, the 'Beaufort' appeared on the scene, similar in design and appearance but faster, and capable of carrying a torpedo. However, the power-plants, two Bristol 'Taurus' engines, of about one thousand horsepower, were not capable of allowing the aircraft to achieve the high speeds that were necessary to respond to the three hundred mile per hour speeds of the fighters being produced in Germany. Consequently, another rethink was necessary — perhaps back to the drawing board! — and suddenly, very likely through the manufacture of the Bristol 'Hercules' engine of over sixteen hundred horse power, the word 'Beaufighter' joined the English vocabulary.

It is difficult to define the breakthrough point in most activities but the advent of the Beaufighter, even in it's emergent design, was a most significant step in producing an aircraft with so many capabilities and potential for multi purpose roles highly conducive to the progress of war.

This fledgling, embodying the genes of an honourable line of aircraft, back to 1910, and also many of the structures and components of the Blenheim and Beaufort, became a firm favourite with all who knew her — ships and planes are always female — and served us well and faithfully. It was often described, most aptly, as "two engines closely followed by a fuselage"!

The Beaufighter served, as stated, in many roles, but I will restrict the following details to those appropriate to the aircraft that operate with the anti- shipping Strike Wings.

Bristol Beaufighter TF X (torpedo-fighter)

Wing span	57 ft. 10 inches
Height	15 ft. 10inches
Wing area	510 sq. feet
Weight	Max take-off 25,400 lbs.
Power Plants	Two Bristol "Hercules" V1 or XV1 engines, with 14 cylinders. Two row, air cooled, sleeve radial engines, with two speed superchargers rated at 1615 hp for take-off, 1675 hp at 4,500 feet and 1.445 hp at 12,000 feet. Three bladed Rotal fully feathering constant speed propellers of 12 ft. diameter.
Fuel capacity	624 imp gals in six wing tanks if wing guns not fitted, 550 imp gals in four tanks if guns installed.
Performance	Max speed 325 mph at 8,500 ft, 333 mph at 15,600 ft. Max cruise 276 mph at 15000 ft.
Service ceiling	26,500 ft
Range	With 550 imp gals 1,480 miles at 243 mph
	With 624 imp gals at 15,000 feet 1.810 miles

Armaments	Four twenty millimetre Oerlikon cannon mounted in the fuselage,"cocked" by the Navigator and fired by the pilot. A single .303 Browning machine gun mounted in the rear of the Navigator's cupola. A single 18 inch torpedo carried below the fuselage and released by the pilot.
or alternatively	Six (three under each wing) 60 lb rockets.
	Two 500lb bombs carried under the fuselage and a 250 bomb under each wing. These were only carried for specific targets such as German "E Boats" around the time of "D" Day.

Navigation, Radio and Pilot Aids

Radio Altimeter	Could be pre-set to allow the pilot to fly at extremely low altitude over the sea (usually at 50 ft).
Ranging Device	(for Torpedo Squadrons) which the pilot set to the optimum range for attack—1000 yards—and which provided a visual and audible indication at that point ASV Set (Air to Surface Vessels). Operated by the Navigator to search and detect possible targets at max range of 90 miles
Drift Recorder	Operated by the Navigator for navigation purposes, largely to maintain required track as a routine procedure.
VHF Radio Set	For relatively short range communication between aircraft, aerodrome control etc. operated by the pilot and a great friend when it was necessary to obtain "a course to steer" (a QDM) in order to find the home airfield.
M/F-H/F	Radio Telegraphy Set operated by the Navigator and used, when on reconnaissance duties, to report of the movement of enemy shipping, etc. also to obtain a "QDM" when rather further away from home!
"GEE"	Radar Navigation Set operated by the Navigator and designed to give a very accurate fix over somewhat limited distance owing to the low level at which the Strike Wings operated. Used with great success by Bomber Command.
"I.F.F." Set	(Identification, Friend or Foe) How appropriately named! When switched on gave a "blip" on a screen at a ground control station to avoid our crews being subject to "friendly fire". Regrettably, it was learned that the fighters of the Luftwaffe were able to home onto an aircraft displaying his "blip" and many were shot down before this was detected. A good example of a a "no win situation"!

Note: Most of the above listed Aids were standard equipment in all aircraft, essential for the normal flying and navigational requirements. Other of the Aids were installed at different times to meet differing operational needs and also, I would imagine, to test the efficiency of new technical developments that came on stream as the war progressed.

"Beaufighter aircraft have again attacked enemy shipping in the North Sea..."

(BBC Radio News Broadcast)

The 'Buzz' or 'there's a flap on.'

The opening of the speaker switch on the Aerodrome Tannoy System always produced a sudden hum and instantly halted conversation and activity from one end of the aerodrome to the other, in offices, Messes, servicing areas, etc, so that in the second or so before the actual message was transmitted, ears were alert and ready.

Everyone was involved, in their own particular capacity, in the prime function of the stations, that being to get Beaufighters into the air in order to strike the enemy, at any time, and wherever he may be located.

So, the crisp and unambiguous message "All crews to the Ops Room," jolted the adrenalin into a quick spurt and a hasty grab for the "tools of the trade"—the navigation bag of equipment, flying gear, etc. (Parachutes, that true friend of the airman, were drawn after the briefing but there was some optimism in so doing, as flight was at sea level, with exit from the plane extremely difficult in an emergency.)

The 'call to arms' however, could also come in a more subtle and stealthy way, in the darkness of the night, with deep sleep suddenly and dreamily broken by a shake of the shoulder and a glimmer of a flashlight held by the duty sergeant, with the instant comprehension that duty called and it would be a long day ahead, with all kinds of intriguing possibilities to be faced and, hopefully, overcome with dedication and no lack of courage.

With only two members per crew, the flow of bodies from the various quarters, so responding to the call, was no very large throng, but the movement carried with it a sense of purpose and an almost intangible sense of closeness of spirit and affection that results from young men having trained together in achieving competence in the delicate business of taking—in a quite personal way—war to the enemy in the not overly friendly environment of the air.

This stage of the proceedings was dominated by curiosity rather than apprehension about the nature of the operation about to be mounted. The wide variety of the forces of the enemy, the extensive area over which we had operational responsibility and the day by day change in the 'battle line' between friend and foe, meant that discovering the specific task to be accomplished was uppermost in all minds.

The Preliminaries

Gathering in the briefing room, much chatter and 'joshing' ensued, as the arrival of the various Briefing Officers was awaited. The senior officer was greeted with due deference, by all standing—on the usual "Atten-shun!" by the Orderly Sergeant—and the plan was revealed in detail, to be greeted by a variety of responses from the crews.

Each crew member, depending on his previous encounters with the enemy and his own personal fears and anxieties, reacted differently and quietly muttered "oohs" and "ahs" did not go amiss, with also the odd more ribald exclamation from the more forthright 'colonials'! Particularly notorious and dangerous targets naturally tended to instil a "bit of a hush" but there was nevertheless less a quickening of the pulse of all those present who were about to meet the foe; a meeting that would be virtually face to face.

So what gave rise to this gathering of hustle and bustle and young blood surging? Where had the buzz come from that the enemy had exposed his flank and that the time was ripe to give him a touch of British steel?

From various sources actually, perhaps a reconnaissance aircraft on a lonely mission had come across, quite unexpectedly, the give-away wakes of ships, either lumbering along or at high speed, trying to reach the safety of a friendly port before being detected. Or, as ships must at sometime enter and leave port, they may have been spotted by members of the 'underground' who, by complicated chains of passing information, and always at great personal danger, had 'did-did-de-dah-ed' the shipping activities to their mentor sitting somewhere in England. Intelligence information may also have arrived thanks to the efforts of the Royal Navy, with their fast reconnaissance torpedo boats or other RAF Commands, whose aircraft may have spotted something of interest in the course of their actions over the seas and shores of the 'Fortress Europe'.

Alternatively, should there be a lull in well-defined targets presenting themselves, a 'sweep' would be carried out, when we would be 'looking for a target of opportunity'. The senior officers seemed to be able to read the morale of the crews with an amazing facility and such operations were largely carried out to stimulate the will to win — not that I recall that at any time was there any lapse of what was known as 'the on-on spirit'.

Targets were in two main areas, the southern tip of Norway — about at the limit of prudent range — or the Dutch Frisian Islands, extending along to the German Islands and the heavily defended island of Heligoland. Immediately prior to and after the 'D'-Day landings on 6th June 1944 our squadrons were also deployed to operate in the eastern end of the English Channel, searching for the German 'E' Boats, but this was not normally our designated role.

The initial description of the task ahead was followed by a briefing from the Meteorological Officer, who provided us with details of general weather conditions and wind speeds and directions over the area, to enable Navigators to complete their all-important Flight Plans. The Intelligence Officer followed, divulging what was known of the current hazards of enemy 'flak' positions and fighter activity. His report was greeted with an apparent air of nonchalance by most, but in the private knowledge that our planes were no match for ME 109s or FW 190s should we be caught in the open.

The Station Commander, Group Captain Braithwaite, an elderly, by comparison with the aircrews, pre-war officer of dignified and impressive carriage, frequently addressed us and we all knew that we carried his blessing and also, though it was discreetly suppressed, his evident wish that he could accompany us on the mission. Leisurely scanning an English newspaper several years after the war, I was distressed to read of an RAF aircraft accident in southern England and that this respected 'Station Master' had met his death in an Avro Anson — one of the safest plane in the Service.

The moment of completion of the briefing formalities, induced several strange emotions. There was that kind of 'end of term' sense of exhilaration, but also a very strong sense of commitment to whatever the next few hours would bring. Remarkably, there was little or no sense of foreboding, anxiety or the more trivial kinds of worry. There was a "for better or worse — the die is cast — come what may" kind of atmosphere, with a sense of camaraderie overriding everything else. It was now just a matter of getting on with the job in hand.

Before emplaning, if time permitted, another matter, by this time a tradition of the Air Force, almost a solemn ritual before combat, brought us all together, regardless of rank, into a dining room for our pre-flight meal. Eggs and bacon was the invariable meal, eaten with gusto amid animated conversation. Upon our safe return to base we would be provided with the same gourmet luxury, so we frequently indulged in stress-reducing exchanges such as "Can I have your egg if you get the chop / go for a Burton / the Grim Reaper gets you" — and similar well-used and comforting euphemisms.

To the 'sturdy mounts'

Briefing had determined the times for transport to the aircraft, standing at the various dispersal points, start-up times for engines and take-off time for each section or flight. It was some distance to travel to the planes and, encumbered with our equipment, we boarded jeeps and other small vehicles, mostly driven by young ladies of the Women's Auxiliary Air Force. Whether or not the decision that these driving duties should be carried out by young ladies was deliberate and based on some psychological concept I don't know, but the memory of those journeys to the aircraft remains firmly fixed in my mind.

It is almost impossible to express the effect that this touch of warmth and femininity had on our innermost feelings, at a moment when masculine and aggressive attitudes were coming to the fore in our unconscious knowledge that we were shortly to enter a hostile domain, with survival far from certain. The young ladies, all of whom seemed to be of more than usual sensitivity, invariably knew many of the crew members on a personal basis through activities on the Station. This contact with them at the time their departure for a fate unknown, and perhaps, as in so many instances, for the last time, must have been stressful in the extreme. However, they always bore the strain of their duties with fortitude and good humour and sent us on our way somehow comforted and confident.

All of us who experienced this quite intimate contact owe those wonderful young women a heartfelt 'thank you' wherever they may be. Every trip, every briefing, every target, had its own set of memorable circumstances, some more firmly embedded in the complex mass of neurons and infinitely small electrical charges that make up or brain. Writing this now, I am suddenly and swiftly 'time-warped' to an amazing tranquil English summer evening.

Each crew was dropped off from the motor transport, at their allocated plane—Mac and I regarded 'P' for Peter as more or less our regular 'mount'—and owing to the distance kept between all the aircraft at 'dispersal', we were then on our own, to await the scheduled time to proceed. On this particular evening, we arrived at 'P' for Peter somewhat early, and about ten minutes had to elapse before we needed to get in the plane for Mac to start the engines preparatory to take-off. After the noise and clamour of the previous briefing and subsequent activities, there was a now a remarkable stillness, with some muted sounds in the distance and a tang in the air of the scents of the English countryside.

Everything took on a kind of hush, as though in suspension, but not as a preliminary to perhaps some hard and furious action in the offing. It seemed to be some kind of pause and very welcome it was too. Being unaccustomed to thinking of the war in other than immediately personal terms—patriotism, nationalism, love of country, etc being matters to be pondered not too deeply and certainly to be avoided in discussion, I was surprised to find myself quite overwhelmed, in this silence, by a sudden surge of affection for all that was England.

This unusual air of sweet and calm emotion was rippled by the start up of a distant engine, followed, one by one, by others until some sixty Bristol Hercules engines, each of sixteen hundred horsepower, rose to a crescendo and shook the air with their potent power. In our turn, we taxied along to take-off point and set off to do what duty called us to do.

Airborne

In Appendix B, entitled 'The Runway' I include a description of a procedure for take-off when a large number of aircraft were involved in one operation. For ease of reading, this is included below:

"One UK Beaufighter Station had one runway east/west, with the east end almost on the sea, and also a wide expanse of grass to permit take off and landing north and south. With a large force of aircraft, say 40 or 50 or so, setting out on a planned 'strike' or seeking a target of opportunity, a special, and somewhat spectacular procedure for takeoff evolved. This entailed, after briefing and start up, careful taxiing and positioning for take-off in alternative pairs. When airborne, low altitude and a lengthy run away from the aerodrome was made, with aircraft subsequently taking off and turning in towards the long gaggle and forming up in loose formation.

The procedure was so organised, with precise timing, that when the whole Strike Wing swept back across the aerodrome at about 75 feet and with an almighty roar, the formation had tightened up in more orderly fashion. For the crews, on such a 'fly-past', the sight of the aerodrome staff, out in their numbers by the control tower, to wave and cheer us on our way, was most exhilarating, encouraging and quite unforgettable. This procedure, viewed in retrospect, was one of those aspects of service leadership and morale, planned with little pomp or fuss, that enabled the aircrews to express their appreciation of the dedication of all ranks and trades who contributed, in whatever capacity, and in hard weather conditions, to put in the air such a potent attack force.

To experience the sight from the ground, when not taking a flying part, was also most moving, with the overpowering roar of those sturdy and reliable Hercules 1650 horsepower engines gradually becoming faint in the distance and the airfield overtaken by a solemn and tangible silence. Time seemed to stand still, until gradually the onlookers dispersed to carry out their many duties.

Everyone was aware of the approximate time that the aircraft were due to return and a gentle wave of anticipation became apparent, a kind of ripple of hope that all would return unscathed to be counted.

Sadly, only too often, not all would return to be counted, but hope always lingered and was extended until no further extension of time was feasible. Sometimes a buzz of excitement, long after this extension had lapsed, occurred, with news that someone had lobbed into another 'drome, condition unknown, casualty not stated. Anxiety once more took over, until the identity of the crew filtered through, with either the great sense of relief that a close colleague had 'made it'."

The Plan of Action

The basic intent of the Strike Wing was to sink or damage ships, and where there was opportunity, attack coastal military installations and any other facility that contributed material aid to the enemy. The technique to achieve this objective, using naval torpedoes, had started during the first World War, using lumbering planes of the day, with not a lot of success and very heavy loss of aircraft and crews. During the early course of the war, the Royal Navy was equipped with Fairey Swordfish aircraft, which became involved in several disastrous encounters with German naval vessels, when the attacking aircraft were virtually annihilated. Not surprising, when you consider that the speed for the drop of the torpedo was some eighty knots, allowing the guns of the ships ample time to draw a good bead on approaching planes.

The Royal Air Force, at this time, had the use of the pre-war designed Blenheim and Beaufort planes, a touch more speedy and sturdy but still extremely vulnerable, with No 22 Squadron (the forerunner of 254 Squadron) being almost decimated during some early strikes.

However, by the end of 1943, and during my time with 254 Squadron, the 'Torbeau' was in vogue, was much more effective and gave it's crews a sporting chance with it greater speed and manoeuvrability.

A most important development in the torpedo dropping technique had been established, giving the torpedo droppers a much better chance of success — and survival — by the creation of the 'Strike Wing'. Simply, two squadrons of Beaus would function as 'anti-flak' aircraft, by diving, from about fifteen hundred feet, onto the ships, and hopefully saturating their guns with cannon fire. Later, these aircraft were also fitted with 60lb rockets, producing a quite awesome hail of death and destruction. These anti-flak planes made their attack while flying in loose 'vics' of three and some several hundred feet ahead of the torpedo planes. This barrage of firepower, allowed the closely following torpedo aircraft, flying 'in line abreast' and 'on the deck' at about fifty feet, an opportunity to align on the target without too much nuisance from flak.

The Charge across the North Sea

Next to the actual attack, this was probably the most exhilarating part of the exercise. To avoid detection by the German Radar, the planes tried to creep below the effective height of that equipment and this meant getting down to about fifty feet above the sea. To fly at such low heights was outside the function of the standard height gauge of all aircraft, the Kolsman Sensitive Altimeter, which responded to changes in atmospheric pressure only very sluggishly, whereas the radio altimeter gave instant indication of change of height above the waves. Needless to say, it was a considerable strain on pilots to fly to this degree of accuracy, for the journey out of an hour or an hour and a half, where concentration could not lapse even for a couple of seconds without disaster striking.

"Good on yer, Mac, you were real beaut!"

Usually, the Strike Wing was lead by one of the Wing Commanders, whose navigator did the appropriate 'honours' by getting us to the target, so the remainder of us could sit back and enjoy the outward ride, keeping only a simple navigation chart updated. But on the way back it was rare to see another aircraft, so it was prudent to have a good awareness of position, particularly as the fickle North Sea weather could quickly 'clamp-down' causing difficulty in making an accurate 'landfall' on the friendly shores of England.

With thirty or more aircraft charging along in a kind of loose 'gaggle' just above the smooth or storm tossed waves, with the white spume blowing in gusts, the impression of speed was virtually breathtaking, to be enjoyed to the full with no responsibility to endure the hard concentration of my pilot. There was, of course, a slight but constant change of position of all aircraft relative to each other, as no attempt was made by the pilots to retain a rigid formation, and this was also intriguing to navigator "loafing in the back seat".

Service life is full of interesting quirks and homilies, and as our flying took place almost entirely over the sea, and at very low level, where the salt spray was visibly part of our environment, it became a matter of pride to Beaufighter crews to attribute the weathering and tarnishing of our RAF cap badges as resulting to our "dicing" down where few other flyers would venture. It was always good for a friendly argument and leg-pulling and, as all matters like this, great for the boosting of morale.

Not a lot of conversation took place between pilot and navigator, other than when a plane ahead deviated too much from his general position and his slipstream jogged the following plane, demanding a quick grip of the control column and rectification of position by the latter. This invariably resulted in a not too kind expletive, with the shortcomings of the errant pilot agreed, with some vehemence, by the following crew, as there was little latitude for even an instants loss of control of the plane at the height of fifty feet. Earlier in the memoirs, I have written of the occasion when a incensed pilot, peeved by the preceding aircrafts irregular course, fired a burst of cannon fire over his wing in order to 'bring him to heel'!

Our Strike Wing always had these lonely seas and sky to itself, I recall no instance of sighting any ship or object, but there was evidence of life in the form of sea birds, swooping and diving as we thundered along at sea level, no doubt fluttering their wings as we passed by, causing a rousing chorus of annoyance.

Well into the flight, this phase of—contentment, enjoyment come to mind—we were made conscious of the enemy over the horizon by the gradual awareness, and increase, of a rasping, warbling note in the headphones. This was the radar detection devices of the German Coastal forces giving warning of our approach and no doubt alerting the big guns and fighter aircraft to welcome our arrival. This sound had an eerie note, as did the air raid sirens in Britain, both of which can be easily brought to mind even with the passage of time, and our senses and bodily rhythms took on a new tempo as conflict neared.

"Getting sorted Out"

Radio silence had been maintained up to this point — how far out to sea we had been detected I never discovered — but when, suddenly, the Strike Leader broke this silence when nearing the coast, another and vital phase was about to begin. The strength and confidence of the voice of the Leader instilled the same in all and there came a determination to perform to the best of one's abilities, and the order to "form up" was a welcomed prelude to the forthcoming action.

So, from the loose gaggle, the flight swung into "attack mode", that is the anti-flak planes nipped up to about twelve hundred feet to form vics of three planes and the torpedo aircraft climbed to their dropping height of one hundred and ninety feet. The eighteen inch marine torpedo, which was fitted with a quite fragile plywood tailplane, had to be dropped under several critical parameters — steep enough to ensure that it would smoothly enter the water without breaking its back, but not too steeply, or it would plunge to the bottom of the sea. The optimum height for this aspect was about one hundred and ninety feet, which the pilot set on his radio altimeter.

"Looking for Trouble"

After coming up into attack formation, the Wing Leader, with radio silence having been broken, was free to issue orders over the VHF radio, and seldom hesitated to do so, as he was always highly experienced, and of course was leading "from the front". The responsibility for the success of the mission was quite onerous and never shirked. His call, usually quite staccato, to the pilots to "close up" in formation and "open up" the throttles, gave all a big boost.

Each such sortie was different: sometimes a known target was to be attacked, whilst at others the Wing flew along a predetermined portion of the coast, looking for any suitable target. In the former case, the Leader arranged to arrive at the coast at a suitable point and angle to allow the attack to be made, preferably on a bearing of sixty degrees to the course of the ships, which gave the torpedoes chance of a better hit.

In the latter case, a target may suddenly loom up out of indifferent weather and then the Leader had to make a quick decision as to how the attack would be carried out. In this instance, the general flying discipline, and calibre of the leader assumed even more importance in achieving good results, as rapid instructions had to given to all pilots to take up positions appropriate to carrying out the most effective attack and to minimise the probability of planes being lost in a melée of 'friendly' crossfire. The camera films, synchronised with the gun firing button, of previous Strike actions, were shown to the crews once a month, for instructional purposes, and it was horrifying to see our planes suddenly enveloped in each other's tracer fire; we could only hope that all our mates came through unscathed.

This period, immediately prior to an attack, with a large number of aircraft at all angles and in very close proximity with the pugnacious growl of those Hercules engines, together with the overpowering sense of anticipation of immediate and deadly action, completely took over the senses and the world was left behind.

"Attack, Attack, Attack"

The "moment of truth." — "This is it." — "Here we go." I suppose all aircrew had their own personal expression for this such moment, when the die is cast and the only way is forward. What heady wine to sup and how sorry one feels for those who have never experienced such a moment in life. That deep-seated instinct of aggression — perhaps brutality or male instinct for dominance, perhaps survival — sweeps all other thoughts aside and every fibre quivers with anticipation.

The glimpse of the target "stooging" along ahead, suddenly the focus of what it's all about, the enemy, to be hammered as hard as possible, but devoid of 'human' terms, being simply ships to be sunk. Not like, say, a bayonet charge when one meets the enemy on a man-to-man basis. In fact, the ships always looked quite serene, but they had learned from experience of the overwhelming firepower of a group of Beaufighters and in consequence their defensive fire, in particular from the dreaded *Sperrbrecher*—flak-ship—now more evident, indicated that they were getting more organised as time went by. Sweeping up towards our approaching aircraft, the tracer marked out a line of soaring steel that confronted us, and the battle was now fully committed, steel against steel. The tang of cordite from the cannons below my feet and the powerful vibration as thirty shells per second hurtled towards the target, did things to the senses and reached spots that were unavailable to any other sensation.

However, flying as 'anti-flak', with the headlong dive from fifteen hundred feet, evoked different sensations from the long run-in—over one thousand yards or so, just above the waves, straight and level—when on a torpedo drop. In tight formation in the former situation, the aircraft seemed to be almost cheek by jowl, as was the intention, and with the pilot concentrating on selecting and loosing his firepower to best advantage, the navigator took on a new role during this exciting power dive.

Head swivelling like watching a tennis match, he tried to anticipate the probable path of all the surrounding aircraft and shout warnings to his pilot, "left," "right", "up" "down", in order to avoid collision, which was a most serious hazard at this phase.

Nevertheless, although it distracted his attention from the oncoming fire-power, all crew members seemed to be enveloped in a whirlpool of shot and shell and smoke and fire and the sea was turned into a boiling cauldron by the impact of the cannon fire and rocket strikes. At the time of the "break-away" over the ships, the planes were travelling at very high speed, "jinking"—rapidly altering attitude and course as quickly as possible—to avoid the efforts of gunners on the ships to fire in retaliation.

The torpedo "run-in" however, was different. It took some pretty smart flying by the pilots to get into line-abreast formation, with the wings of each aircraft within a hundred feet or so of each other, all in a straight line and all this to be done at very low level. The pilots also had to in a correct position in relation to the "anti-flak" aircraft. From their low level, the optimum relationship was to view the former at about forty five degrees upward, so that when those planes attacked and hopefully "saturated" the flak, the long approach of a thousand yards would be less "flak-prone"! On the other hand, to be too close under the anti-flak planes would greatly increase the possibility of being 'clobbered' by friendly fire.

It was, however, a long and lonely one thousand yards, after the torpedo was dropped with no alternative other than to keep going over the convoy, the pilot taking whatever avoiding action was possible at sea level, with the anti-flak planes well on their way ahead and the ship's gunners having a brief respite to regain their breath and once again open up on the attackers. I felt this to be the most vulnerable time of the whole attack, perhaps because we were no longer 'face to face' with the enemy but restricted to hasty glances over the shoulder to see what was looming up behind.

Having used the element of surprise and blasted away as hard as possible at anything which presented itself as a target, it was not possible, usually, for the Wing to form up to mount a repeat performance. The strength of this form of aerial attack, or manoeuvre, lay in the concerted fire power of many aeroplanes striking together against the fierce and numerous weapons mounted on the stable and convenient decks of the ships, particularly the "Schperbrekker" which was designed specifically to respond to attacks such as ours. Low flying aircraft attacking in the way the Strike Wing did were extremely vulnerable and not doubt provided excellent "target practice" for the German gunners.

On one occasion we were out in considerable strength, some forty or so aircraft. As we swept around in the vicinity of Heliogoland, looking for a "target of opportunity", we came upon a couple of armed trawlers in the otherwise blank sea, going peacefully about whatever was their business.

It was decision time for our Leader and he decided to attack these apparently innocent seafarers. Carrying out the usual swoop and fire, and breaking away after flying over the ships, it was evident that there was not a lot of retaliation from them, which was not surprising as they were keeping their heads down at the sudden and overwhelming "blitz" that they had received. The blood of most pilots — including mine — was now well and truly up and a second bite of the cherry was irresistible, so around again the procession went until these two poor boat were just about lifted out of the water by twenty millimetre shells and rockets. Despite it being our bolden duty to show no mercy and kill whenever and wherever possible, I must confess to much squeamishness to see these hapless ships suffer so, and I recall that by the time we left, one of them had already disappeared beneath the waves.

A good standby expression for this and similar circumstances was "If you can't stand a joke you shouldn't have joined." It provided a touch of comfort on the way home that day.

One of the most remarkable aspects of our usual form of strike was the immediate transition from the quite awesome power that was unleashed, in a brief moment in time, with its attendant excitement and fury, and a few seconds later to be alone in the peaceful sky with no other aircraft or ships in sight. It was all over in almost the twinkling of an eye, followed by the instant sense of relief that one was still 'alive and kicking'.

However, this was still no time to relax, as the ships would no doubt have alerted their control station of our attack and also the aerodromes that housed the Luftwaffe fighters that situated close to the coast and our area of operations. It was always a contemplative thought, as we neared the coast on the way in, that perhaps at that moment, the Tannoy systems on these aerodromes were ringing loudly with the German equivalent of "scramble" and the Mercedes Benz engines were singing their song of power for the take-off. The thought of pursuit as we turned westerly, persisted for many miles beyond the actual reach of these very competent young German pilots in their equally efficient flying machines.

Homeward Bound

Now west was the course, with an hour or so to go. As the possibility of being jumped by the fighters was diminishing, a quite euphoric and pleasant, almost lethargic, feeling took over, probably as reaction to the stimulating events shortly before. It was a time for bit of reflection and the sense of relief that our survival persisted for most of the way home.

To be shot at is a unique experience and not the 'privilege' of all. Perhaps it does something to the soul. It is certainly memorable, like one's first burn on the kitchen stove. It penetrates deep into the mind, a hangover, perhaps, from the violent societies of more primitive times when man lived by the sword. To survive induces a sense of some inviolability, even immortality; it certainly implants a feeling of having had an experience that comes not to all and sets one apart from one's fellow men. Those who went through the war without being exposed to the fire of the enemy almost seem to mourn the loss of opportunity, so deeply ingrained is this fierce attitude in the male of the species.

There were, of course, two main areas of hazard. The basic or primary one, of the flying itself, in that long flights were made, at very low level in the variable and largely unpredictable weather conditions over the North Sea, in aircraft that performed indifferently should one engine fail, with recovery, control and return to base very unlikely, even with a very skilled and experienced pilot. Flying at fifty feet or so, any instantaneous loss of power, left virtually no time at all for regaining control,—with the ever present and waiting sea,—providing no survivable cushion of welcome.

The loss of an engine must have accounted for a large proportion of crews who "failed to return to base".

Although I, like my contemporaries, was more or less constantly mindful of the odds of survival from actual "combat", looking back, I recall no time that the dangers described above ever preoccupied my thoughts during the flights or other times,—or, in fact even intruded into my awareness. On the contrary, I seemed to enjoy an affinity with those rugged and changeable elements of sea, cloud and the wide skies, and the unique smell, vibration, sense of power, of the Beaufighter which held me in this environment, and speed swiftly on whatever course I had had the pleasure of passing to my pilot Mac.

I realised many years later that the same appreciation of closeness and comfort with the environment, at any given time and situation, was an inherent characteristic of the indigenous people in Southern Africa,—the natural elements being a fundamental part of their whole psyche—and living there I soon grew to also welcome this deep-seated mental and physical balm.

A powerful element in establishing my trust and lack of anxiety in regard to the performance of the Beaufighter, was entirely due to my confidence in Mac my pilot. He was several years older than me, had vast more "worldly experience" and the rugged individuality of the New Zealander. He had also flown more hours than the average pilot, when we crewed up, having flown, in the Middle East, that willing but inefficient aeroplane the "Hampden", a supposedly "torpedo bomber"

My faith in him was immediate from when we decided to fly together and I never had even one flicker of loss of confidence in his ability to see us through whatever fate threw at us. His calming words immediate prior to him opening the throttles to take off, making sure that I was ready and strapped in, and as the plane swept up into the night air, lifted my spirits and confidence to a point that failure of any kind was just not possible. During all our attacks, he never faltered and pressed home to the utmost our part in the efforts of the Wing, responding to any shouted warnings that I gave when danger loomed from collision with our comrades, in the melee that always occurred.

During the many long and sometimes tedious reconnaissance flights, alone without the boost of the friendly presence of one or more of our "mates", he flew almost like a robot pilot and although not a lot of conversation took place, our occasional interchanges gave me, in my isolation in the rear of the plane, all the moral support that was required. Towards the end of a long trip at night, the roar of the two Hercules engines seemed to fade away, and we seemed to be suspended in limbo, with only an odd glimpse of a star to indicate that we were still within the earths grasp.

It was a feeling of almost total disembodiment, with nothing behind us in time or place, and nothing in front of us either. It gave no cause for concern or for any deep and complex thoughts or questions as to the more esoteric aspects of life and existence, but induced a feeing of total relaxation. Those times were unique and as the circumstances can never be repeated, the reflections and emotions are to be kept and treasured for all time.

Anyway, Mac and I are on our way back to the comfort and safety of North Coates, or, if closed because of bad weather, to a diversionary aerodrome within the range of our fuel reserves, and we established some very simple and easy routines during the return flight.

Always at low height, and with no easy task in handling the not easily tamed Beaufighter, Mac was limited as to what he could do to provide for his comfort. With no "George" — automatic pilot — to relieve for a period, the plane had to be constantly hand-flown, and he was therefore locked in his seat.

A cigarette was the first requirement and I crawled through the armoured doors separating us, perched sideways on the main spar of the plane which was just behind the pilots seat, and, as I had by then stopped smoking, kind of blocked my lungs, stuck a, probably, Players Medium Cut between my lips, struck a match and puffed away, and, like some politicians of these days, referring to canabis, not inhaling, but having got a glow established, stuck it smartly in Macs mouth.

A light snack followed, that is, a small tin of orange juice and a bar of chocolate, and all was well as we "stooged" homeward.

England, or on several occasions, Scotland, was sighted with comfort and satisfaction, but the actual point of landfall always of interest. I must confess to getting a "kick" out of quickly recognising the specific point on the coast, and if it coincided with my navigational work, so much the better. Caution had to exercised, however, as the defensive coastal guns were a bit prone to let drive, and care had to taken not to get tangled up in the cables of the Balloon Barrages that protected vital parts of the coast.

And so, into the aerodrome circuit, watch out for other of our planes, and the Luftwaffe intruder fighters looking for an easy target, onto "finals", and the thump as the undercarriage hit the deck, the taxi around to dispersal point, engines off, with the usual persistent crackle as they cooled down, crawl out underneath the cockpit, transport, with our young ladies already spoken of, to the de-briefing room, tell the Intelligence Officers what we did and saw, get rid of our clobber, and then to get a repeat of our pre-flight meal in the dining room.

The success of our efforts was celebrated later, by the usual beery and vigorous party in the Mess, with many and varied delightfully crude ditties, songs and stories, but almost always there was the need to suppress, within ourselves, the loss of recent, and, with more impact, earlier friends on the Squadron. But that was the way it was and it happened to so many of us in those memorable days of our youth. Rest well, old friends.

Addendum: The following Table was calculated by the RAF in Novenber, 1942

Percentage Chance of Survival

	One Tour	Two Tours
Heavy & Medium Bombers	44	19.5
Light Bombers	25.5	6.5
Day Fighters	43	18.5
Night Fighters	39	15
Long Range Fighters	59.5	35.5
Torpedo Bombers	17.5	3.0
Heavy GR Landplane	71	50.5
Medium GR Landplane	56	31.5
Light GR Landplane	45	20
Sunderland Flying Boat	66	43.5
Catalina Flying Boat	77.5	60
Fighter Reconnaisance	31	9.5
Bomber Reconnaisance	42	17.5

Note: The very heavy loss rate for the Torpedo Bombers occurred in the early years of the war, when largely unsuitable aircraft were used for this task . By the end of 1943, the Beaufighter plane came into service, with a dramatic improvement in the survival figures. Mac and I and our contemporaries were mindful that during out time with 254 Torpedo Squadron, the possibility of completing a Tour was enhanced beyond all measure.

It Took Two to Tango in a Beaufighter

Pilots come in all shapes and sizes. Some, if not all, have odd quirks. Some are garrulous, and some are taciturn, not unlike a broad cross-section of humanity in general. It is asserted that there are two types of men, those who fly aeroplane and those who don't. Perhaps this was put about by the pilots confraternity. They do, however, comprise a rather elite force, if it is still permissible to speak in 'elitist terms'. So when we newly qualified Navigators came face to face with them, at a certain stage the facial appearance, the quirks, and even the physical appearance of these gentlemen greatly taxed our ability to sort out the 'wheat from the chaff'.

This, of course, took place at Operational Training Unit, and, after some two years or so training, it seemed a pity to jeopardise all the costs of this, not to say our bodily safety, by committing ourselves, willy nilly, to a pilot of short acquaintance and talents not obviously apparent . At first impact, our two respective groups sized each other up with hopefully disguised nonchalance. Should I plump for a 'large' fellow, with hands that seemed likely to be able to do useful work with a 'control column', hailing, it would appear from the 'high veld ' of South Africa, and probably not prone to panic, when things were not going to plan? Or perhaps a 'small' one, maybe a 'used car salesman' from Sydney, New South Wales, with lots of volatility. Small men, however, usually pick fights. Did I particularly want to pick fights with ME 109s or FW 190s?

These days, when boarding a 747 — -which will climb to heights unheard of in our day and obviously much more dangerous territory — do we expect to be able to give the Captain the 'once-over', to gauge his skills, in his 'glass cockpit? (frankly I don't see why not). But here we were, trying to pair off, my group, all from 'Blighty', confronted airmen from the most remote parts of the Empire (as it was). Did I prefer a 'Bluie' a 'Springbok' or a 'Kiwi'? What did I know of the Czechs, the Belgians, or the Poles on offer? Not a lot really. A bad choice here could result in an attack of the dreaded 'LMF' should incompatibility subsequently set in. Gentle probing to see how many hours — and on what — they were able to offer me, bearing in mind that few of us had more than 200 hours or so. Not so little when, in 1918 operations were started, and usually abruptly terminated with as little as 20 hours 'total time'.

There was little time to gauge personal habits, like capacity for alcohol, late night partygoing, stamina in pursuit of 'popsies' etc. Individuals had their own order of priority in such matters, complicating ready assessment of compatibility to jointly indulge in these essential diversions. It became readily apparent that the 'colonial' types would not be wanting in earning merit points in all of these subjects. Later experience showed that 'adventurous activity' in all these delights had little effect on some, and next morning a compass course would be flown with more than the usual precision, prompted, no doubt, by a sense of deep satisfaction of a successful outcome of the foray of the previous evening.

What impression we 'callow youths', sporting our hard-won half brevets, gave our opposite numbers is a matter of conjecture Our self-confidence to be able to navigate with skill and style was still fairly fragile. Moreover, we were still in some awe of the general run of pilots, who tended to be more hearty in manner and could do things with aeroplanes which often startled us and tended to hurl our navigation instruments on to the floor of the aircraft. At Air Observers School, the invariably forgot to say 'please' when the undercarriage on the faithful old Anson had to be wound up (one hundred and twenty turns), and of course wound down again, although it was not unknown for a pilot (and a trainee navigator) to experience 'a moment of mental aberration' and to be sharply 'brought to earth' by the unpleasant noise of rapidly turning propellers hitting the runway!

Anyway, I write about our impressions, and if any pilot is prepared to put pen to paper on the subject of 'crewing up', I promise his views will be read with objective interest, our shoulders being wide enough to take any 'ribbing' and umbrage will not be taken.

The general format, for the establishing of individual crews, had been well thought out be the senior officers concerned. There was little or no pressure, although time was important so that real training could continue, with the added incentive to 'polish' our skills, at both ends of the aircraft, as the 'real thing' was just about on us, or, in the hackneyed phrases of the fiction writers, 'our mettle was about to be tested'. At this stage I had a sneaky suspicion that we were all concerned as to the quality of our own mettle, but after the requisite number of ales in the mess, such doubts rapidly disappeared in the general festivities and the rendition of traditional Air Force songs, seemingly harping on being crushed beneath heavy aircraft engines or indulging in physical acts which I personally didn't quite comprehend, or if I did, thought highly improbable!

Suddenly the 'pairing process' was complete and all settled down to the final stage of training before joining an Operational Squadron. For all of us, that moment when our skills and personalities were joined for mutual benefit and survival (and for our greater effectiveness as members of the Royal Air Force) was indeed a 'moment of truth'.

Almost without exception, the fruits of this procedure of crewing, was the establishment of that almost indefinable quality of comradeship and bonding that occurred between each individual crew of Beaufighters and from then on the vagaries of 'Lady Luck' could be faced with hope and confidence. Who can forget that last operational 'sortie', whether it was in number, or in hours, or in time on 'ops', when the anxieties of all previous trips seem to roll up all into one, until that very sweet moment when the wheels hit the 'deck' and the feeling, almost of disbelief, that the 'tour' was over.

The unique experience of facing considerable hazards together, with a blend of skills and a sense of harmony, greatly enriched or lives and has remained with us to later life to be recalled with pride and pleasure. The Australian expression 'good mates' describes so aptly those days now so long ago but which are never very far from our daily thoughts.

First published in *Airmail*, Journal of the RAF Association, in June 1997.

The Runway

It all became rather more serious, in a different way, when posted to an Operational Squadron. Until then, the preoccupation had been to jump the hurdles of seemingly course after course of arduous training, with the dreaded stigma of being "CT'd" (Ceased Training) always lurking in the wings to make a swift and silent 'strike' should competence and motivation momentarily lapse. Up to this time, extraneous activity, what we understood to be part of Squadron life and took the form of wild parties in the Mess, where ribald songs followed extremely heavy imbibing, had been sensibly set to one side. So this bit of hedonism stretched before us quite invitingly.

Familiarity with the 'Beau' in all the aspects of it's functions and operating capabilities, had brought a reasonable level of confidence to be able to perform to the required standards, and, surprisingly, there was a deep sense of tangible relief that, at long last, no more tests, other than to cope with the real thing. This was also manifest in a sense of exhilaration, and a quiet, and exciting anticipation of what real 'ops' would be like. But we were still not quite there. A few local flights, then a few 'cross-countries' had to be completed, before 'voila', name in print on the 'Crew Availability' roster, in stark and a touch startling, black and white

For some the 'runway' had a very significant role in the 'real' operational trips. It seemed to be a focal point. It was the start and the finish, the departure and the arrival point of our personal, and deeply committed involvement in the affairs of that time, and always beckoned invitingly, when, at the end of a 'hard day', and the 'clag' was down, and position was uncertain, tired and anxious eyes were peeled for a first glimpse of it's comfort.

'Theatres of Operation'—as our American friends so called them—varied greatly according to the type of targets that the enemy offered and the capability of our aircraft to effectively take 'remedial action'. From the somewhat frigid and rugged coastlines of Northern Scotland, to the more tolerable English flatlands of East Anglia, 'sorties' ranged eastwards to the coasts across the North Sea. On the other hand, battle was fought over the sands and placid Mediterranean waters of the Middle East, and, probably more arduous and less likely to provide the basic creature comforts when aggression was in temporary abeyance for a few hours or so, the beautiful, but heavily wooded jungle islands to the North of Australia.

The 'Home Runway' consequently came in a variety of shapes and sizes, with, of course, attendant variation in local geographical features, to either aid or complicate easy access to or take off from. The wide variety included strips hacked out in the jungles of the East, in a most laborious way, and allowing with it's narrow width, little latitude for error on take off and landing, and with a very indifferent surface. In the Middle East, runways of compacted sand, hardened by a coat of oil, but with the 'shifting sands' of that area, somewhat ill defined.

In the early days after the landings in Europe, those made of steel mesh (I forget the 'trade name') but undoubtedly providing a 'rough ride'. And, of course, the more usual standard type of aerodrome set-up, consisting of three intersecting concrete or tarmac runways, orientated to prevailing wind direction, and speeds, and, at a lot of places, where three runways were impractical or unnecessary, a wide expanse of grass.

The pressures of war brought rapid development in all areas of technical knowledge, and in aviation the scene was constantly shifting, with new aircraft, and operating techniques being constantly introduced. It was open 'slather' and any idea, no matter who weird or improbable that offered aid to victory, was given due and serious consideration.

Some ideas relating to the 'Runway' were the fruit of extremely imaginative thinking. There was, for instance an idea to use icebergs, in mid Atlantic, as landing grounds for aircraft on Atlantic patrols against U-Boats. They were to be 'harvested 'in the North and towed to position and moored there. Strange, in retrospect, but, desperation is a hard taskmaster. Crews of land-based aircraft coming across an Aircraft Carrier at sea, and being very cautious of the inevitable 'friendly fire' noted with sharp interest the remarkable limitations of the 'sea-borne runway' and the demand for most specific skills at that 'interface' with the choice for pilots, when choice had to be made on take of and landing, greatly limited. But with the immense amount of shipping activity ranging over all areas, there was a serious shortfall of Aircraft Carriers to provide air cover for convoys. A somewhat hazardous and *ad hoc* method was introduced by fitting some quite small merchant ships with catapults to launch Hurricane Fighters. These ships were not large enough to permit any form of landing facility, and the returning pilot was obliged to choose between ditching his aircraft next to the ship or bailing out. A grim choice in the chill wastes of the North Atlantic and those pilots rate high in dedication and courage.

The 'Home Runway' with its 'creature comforts', was, of course, first choice, but bad weather, and delays due to 'prangs' etc, sometimes necessitated diversion to another landing ground. Many aerodromes had their own alternative runway known as a 'satellite' but these had few facilities and were merely somewhere to 'lob-in' until matters had been sorted out and it was possible to return to home. With the advent of more and larger aircraft, bigger loads, range etc, the 'gathering storm' gathered way and much of eastern England assumed the appearance of one large aerodrome with all the congestion of virtually overlapping airfield circuits. The amount of work in airfield construction had to be speeded up with the arrival of the American 8th Air Force—Boeing B17s and Liberator B24s—and huge amounts of concrete for building runways was used. The place was literally crawling with runways most of which were extended significantly in under and overshoot, to accommodate the demands of the new planes. It became apparent that special facilities had to be provided to handle returning aircraft with special problems, like difficulty in retaining control of the plane, and, in the extremely fickle weather of North West Europe, weather conditions which precluded landing at most, if not all, the 'home base' airfields. To this end three special landing aerodromes were installed—colloquially known as 'pranging dromes'—strategically placed on the east coast.

These had very long runways, supplemented with very extensive under and overshoots. In addition, they were fitted with 'FIDO' — Fog Intensive Dispersal Operation — which consisted of pipes alongside the runway, conveying fuel, with nozzles at interval, where the fuel was ignited when necessary to aid the incoming aircraft. The heat generated by the burning fuel, lifted and dispersed much of the fog and gave the crew a sporting chance of getting down in one piece. This also provided a glow through the weather, which aided location of the airfield. On many occasions it was a long shot, when the 'fickle finger' was being exceedingly fickle, but many crews owe their survival to this remarkable but simple device. The writer was on hand at one such drome when the weather conditions were almost zero and a B17 Flying Fortress of the American 8th Air Force made several desperate attempts to 'get down'. The last approach ended in catastrophe and the doomed aircraft ploughed through five or six Mosquito aircraft on the perimeter track near the main runway. All were totally destroyed in the ensuing flames.

One UK Beaufighter Station had one runway East/West, with the East end almost on the sea, and also a wide expanse of grass area to permit take off and landing North and South. With a large force of aircraft, say 40 or 50 or so, setting out on a planned 'strike' or seeking a target of opportunity, a somewhat special, and I think, spectacular procedure for takeoff evolved. This entailed, after briefing and start up, careful taxiing and positioning for take-off in alternative pairs. When airborne, low altitude and a lengthy run away from the aerodrome was made, with aircraft subsequently taking off and turning in towards the long gaggle and forming loose formation. The procedure was so organised, with precise timing, that when the whole Strike Wing swept back across the aerodrome at about 75 feet and with an Almighty roar, the formation had tightened up in more orderly fashion. For the crews, on such a 'fly-past', the sight of the aerodrome staff, out in their numbers by the Control Tower, to wave and cheer us on our way, was most exhilarating, encouraging and quite unforgettable.

This procedure, viewed in retrospect, was one of those aspects of Service leadership and moral, planned with little pomp or fuss, that enabled the aircrews to express their appreciation of the dedication of all ranks and trades who contributed, in whatever capacity, and in hard weather conditions, to put in the air such a potent Attack Force.

To experience the sight from the ground, when not taking a flying part, was also most moving, with the overpowering roar of those sturdy and reliable Hercules 1650 horsepower engines gradually becoming faint in the distance and the airfield overtaken by a solemn and tangible silence. Time seemed to stand still, until gradually the onlookers dispersed to carry out their many duties. Everyone was aware of the approximate time that the crews were due to return and a gentle wave of anticipation became apparent, a kind of ripple of hope, with the thought of the count of returning aircraft to be made and that, without doubt, no matter how many times the count was made, not all would be there to be counted. But hope always lingered and was extended until no further extension of time was feasible. Sometimes a buzz of excitement, long after this extension had lapsed, occurred, with news that someone had lobbed into another drome, condition unknown, casualty not stated. Anxiety once more took over, until the identity of the crew filtered through, with either the great sense of relief that a close colleague had made it or it was a crew perhaps not quite so well known who were the fortunate blokes.

Time passes, many things are forgotten but some aspects of those flying days frequently swing into sharp focus, the 'good' invariably and triggered by quite odd and apparently unconnected factors. Perhaps most of us have a specific kind of triggering mechanism. In my case, it seems to be thoughts of the 'runway'. Lincolnshire, in Eastern England, was, as mentioned, really one vast and congested 'runway', but now, with only few exceptions, the land is back to its farming use, with cattle grazing and wheat and other crops waving their heads in the English breezes where such intense activity once took place. One such runway, discovered not to be not quite so derelict as most, was 'our runway'. Many post-war years later, when the opportunity came to re-visit the scene of our Beaufighter activity, an experience, quite unexpected and startling occurred. It was a massive overload of 're-call'.

Little was left of the aerodrome, other than the main runway, running East and West. It was a bit 'tatty' but even in that state, looking down it's length, brought a heightening of sensibility and thoughts began to kaleidoscope with ever increasing intensity and the present time and surroundings began to take on a far-away aspect. A companions voice came through this haze, suggesting a quick dash down the runway. As the car gathered speed down this crumbling, but faithful old piece of tarmac, on the familiar heading of 090 due East towards the sea, I quickly and irresistibly slipped into a 'timewarp'.

Every take-off, every landing, with all the excitement, fear, exhilaration, and all the happenings of those flights of the past, totally overwhelmed me in such emotional power as to be almost incapacitating. Faces, names, visions of violent scenes, swam through my mind at lightning speed. The experience was totally unique, an 'out of dimension' happening and recovery to the then present time sluggish and not really welcome.

That 'Runway' was the place of so many takeoffs, with many sadly into that great and unknown void, with Flying Log Book subsequently ruled off, cryptically, 'Failed to Return'. Those who did make that 'Final Touch-Down' remember those friends with much respect.

First published in 'Tarmac', the Newsletter of the RAF Association, Perth.

APPENDIX V

The Horses of War

In December 1947 the all-embracing war effort had spent itself. The machines of war were now defunct, as were the skills of the men who had operated them, mere youths at the beginning of hostilities, now matured by their experience of combat by land, sea and air.

At this time, having opted for extension of service in the RAF and flying as a Navigator in Anson aircraft, I made a trip to several aerodromes in Northern Scotland to convey Senior Officers on an Inspection Tour. On approaching one airfield, an amazing sight emerged through the indifferent weather. The whole perimeter of this full-sized aerodrome was occupied, with little or no gaps, by a huge number of Lancaster Bombers — just sitting there!

I was struck by the poignant sight of these 'faithful' flying machines, now discarded. The human endeavour that had gone into their creation and the outstanding skill, courage and sacrifice of those who had flown in them, equals any war effort in history.

To capture that first glimpse of those discarded aircraft standing on that misty airfield in Northern Scotland perhaps demands poetry, however...

They stood, side by side, with their famed dominant and aggressive aura somewhat subdued, but not lost, as if, should the call be heard to perform the function for what they were created, they would instantly respond and their sturdy frames would once again pulse with life and personality.

An air of quietness permeated the whole area, a kind of spent feeling, as if with a sigh that marks the end of tasks performed, but performed well and although large in number, there appeared to be a common bond between them, a kind of solidarity of spirit, as in any group of like beings.

Difference in age was not easily discernible, and some bore evidence of rough passage, with markings of identity and degree of experience evident from symbols displayed. They were many in number, standing in a rough oval and occupying many acres. And they were the last of their kind, doomed to extinction, not, however like the beast in the Knacker's Yard, by a quick thrust, but by slow and painful dismemberment, the best bits as if by disembowelling, the remainder to be crushed and re-worked into an absurd parody of the prime reason for their creation.

The elements had been their home, they had been through dark nights, cold, heat, snow, sleet, lifted, tossed with great violence, even abused to a point almost beyond their capabilities.

Many had known them intimately, through the whole gamut of emotion, with fear no doubt being the most potent, but not arising from doubt as to their reliability and capability, but from the actions of others. Nevertheless, in times of unbearable stress, they had been cursed, blessed, urged onwards and upwards and thanked, subconsciously, or with vocal expression when their sturdiness brought matters to a safe conclusion.

Their profile was totally arresting, in it's broad symmetry, sweeping lines, and perfect interlocking of the different components of function. Harmony was very evident in the overall impression, the evident result of a concept conceived at a level beyond the capability of all but a few. The imagination, the skill, and the incredible physical effort to bring together the multitude of seemingly totally unrelated material and disparate techniques, to complete each of those in these ranks, was an effort almost beyond comprehension.

But the beauty of this impact of form and complimentary lines, in fact visually clothed and softened the awesome and violently lethal power contained within. There was an almost physical feeling of sheer power and energy radiating from the group, silent though it was, but if imagined to be simultaneously unleashed, would tremble the earth and the hills with a roar beyond human tolerance.

As the 20th Century ends, there exists, worldwide, only one Lancaster capable of feeling the wind under its wings and the exhilaration of those swinging curves and dives through the wild and endless sky.

Big Brother is Watching You ... Thank Goodness!

The rescue, deep in the Antarctic seas, of yachtsman Tony Bullimore, graphically illustrated the present day sophistication of warning and distress beacons, and the related Search and Rescue Procedures ability to function over great distances, all by the use of satellites.

It also recalled an incident, over fifty years ago, when ships and airmen in distress situations were also monitored, when recourse had to be made to the calls Pan, Mayday, and S.O.S., with more care and efficiency than they realised.

In mid-1945, I was flying as a Navigator/Wireless Operator in Anson aircraft on the daily return diplomatic mail service between Croydon, London and Le Bourget, Paris. (there never was a satisfactory technical explanation for the remarkable high incidence of "mag drops" at Le Bourget, necessitating an overnight stay, but not unconnected was the extremely artistic displays which were on show at the fabulous "Moulin Rouge" !)

The radio equipment in use was the MF/HF Marconi 1154/1155, which was situated behind my seat, with a rather horrible Bakelite Morse key on a ledge by my right hand.

On the trip in question a spare pilot, who wore (note well!) a uniform of deeper blue than that of the RAF, was perched on the top of the bags of mail, leaning over my shoulder, and seemed, for a pilot, more than usually interested in my navigation and radio activities.

Nothing untoward occurred on the flight, but there was a summons to report to the office of the Adjutant shortly after landing. My pilot and I were closely questioned as to whether, in mid- English Channel and in the vicinity of our 'track' we had seen or heard any sign of any aircraft or vessel in distress, as the monitoring service had picked up an S.O.S. call at the time and area of our flight.

We had not, and were puzzled and concerned that perhaps we should have been more diligent and observant, but we were fortified by the obvious dedication of the operators of the monitoring equipment, probably housed in a darkened room, and hunched, with poised and delicate fingers, over their "goniometers", with an aura of Guardian Angels of us wild and reckless airmen.

So what had really happened? The English Channel holds the secrets — and the debris — of conflict way back beyond the Spanish Armada, and the more recent addition of ships and aircraft reflects, no doubt, so many desperate S.O.S. calls for assistance, with fate holding sway over the outcome. That superb Band Leader, Glen Miller, and his Orchestra, for instance, were lost without trace in mid-channel in December, 1944, but his voice is still with we of that generation, and who can forget the magic of "In The Mood".

So what of our experience of a "positive "monitoring, which had no easy or apparent explanation? Was it a Ghostly echo from a desperate crew of an earlier day, when disaster was upon them?

Like a persistent toothache, the matter niggled on, and although we were adjudged to be "in the clear" by the powers that be, it was only much later, during a moment of insight, or even from a kind of suppressed guilt, that a rather mundane explanation offered itself.

The 1154 had a 'tune' position, providing low power radiation, and at some time on the flight, I must have left the switch in this position, possibly when taking a "drift".

Pilots are prone to fiddle, like the rest of us, and our 'spare bod' in the back, bored or vaguely dreaming of becoming a Radio Ham after demobilisation, undoubtedly could not resist getting his hand on my Morse key. I can only conclude that his knowledge of the Morse code was limited to two letters, being those of three dots and of three dashes, sent, perhaps with a heavy and inexperienced hand, but strong enough to tickle the sensitive goniometers of those Guardian Angels doing what conscientious Guardian Angels do in their lairs hidden away from our mortal eyes. It really was a most comforting incident.

Notes on items donated to an Aircraft Museum

Astro Compass

This Instrument was used in the aircraft and on the ground. It is similar to a small theodolite, and measures angles in the horizontal and vertical. When used in the course of Air Navigation it had several useful facilities:

> To take visual bearings on ground objects

> To check or steer a course on the aircrafts magnetic compass by reference to the Sun, Moon, or Stars.

> To identify the heavenly bodies, by setting the necessary information, obtained from various tables, and being aware of the approximate position of the aircraft.

On the ground, it was used to "Swing the Compass" of the aircraft, by reference to fixed ground objects, or the Sun and so determine the "deviation" of that compass. This necessitated physically turning the aircraft onto the Cardinal Points of the compass and then checking the aircraft compass The difference was then tabulated and used by the pilot to obtain the "compass course" to be steered" which differed from the course found by "plotting" done on the navigation chart.

Bendix Radio Frequency Meter

It was necessary, for the safety of the aircrews, and the efficiency of the operation being carried out, that the radio frequencies set on the radio equipment in the aircraft were very accurate, both for normal communication, and should an emergency arise. This meter, a most precise and well made instrument, was used by the ground technicians to ensure that this was achieved.

High Frequency and Very High Frequencies were used in Beaufighter aircraft. For activities such as obtaining clearance to "take-off" and " land," to obtain the barometric setting for the altimeter, a most important requirement particularly if the weather and visibility were not good, and, in some situations, to obtain a "compass course" to steer to reach the aerodrome, the pilot handled these functions.

The other crew member, known as the "Observer" or Navigator / Wireless Operator in other theatres of operation, was provide with the "H.F." radio equipment. This was capable of achieving good communication with ground stations over much longer distances. Many "Operational Sorties" consisted of Reconnaissance flights to detect the activities of the enemy, to gauge his strength and report back to base in order for the Station Commander to assess the situation and lay on a "Strike". Such duties were carried out by the Navigator, using coded messages.

Kolsman Sensitive Altimeter

Possibly the most important instrument in the aircraft, and demanding careful attention, because it indicates "height", which, in itself is grossly misleading. This is it's fundamental use, and regrettably, this instrument was, and still is, perhaps, responsibly for many accidents.

The "basic movement" is an "aneroid barometer", such as you would find in the Hall of many homes, and which suffers to be "tapped" by passers by, to see whether it goes up or goes down. The Rule of Thumb is that "up" it's going to be fine and "down" it's going to rain. What it indicates, however, and tabulated in "feet" — still used world wide — is change in the atmospheric pressure surrounding the aircraft. Unless the atmospheric pressure at the point at which the aircraft is flying is know, then there is no reference point of comparison and the indication is just that, an indication only, and insufficient to accurately determine the true height of the aircraft above the ground.

This problem is overcome, to some degree, by aircrew being advised of actual barometric pressure at aerodromes, which is then set on the altimeter to ascertain the height above the ground. Fortunately, in present times, many sophisticated instruments have largely overcome the shortcomings of the long used Kolsman Altimeter.

Aeronautical Sextant

Since mans early days the apparent movement of the Heavenly Bodies has been a source of wonderment and fascination and used to regulate agriculture and religious ceremonies. Constant attempts were made to record such movements and with the invention of the telescope and accurate clocks, more precise details have been established and refined over the years. The Astronomical Sextant is used for navigating aircraft, by utilising this fundamental framework of stars to determine it's position, with acceptable accuracy, and where no other means are available.

The instrument, basically, measures the angle above the horizon of specific stars — and the Sun and Moon. By reference to detailed Tables, which are carried in the aircraft, of the position of the stars, and being aware of the approximate position of the aircraft (to a fairly wide degree) and with the time of the observation having been, recorded, an accurate "position" can be quickly determined. In order to obtain a "datum" in a moving aircraft,from which to measure the angle of the star, it not being possible to use the horizon, as with a "Marine Sextant" used on ships, the Aircraft sextant makes use of a "bubble" of air in a small chamber which acts as a spirit level. It is necessary to "shoot" the angles of three stars to obtain "position lines". Owing to the time lapse between the three "shots" and the speed of the aircraft, these lines have to be entered on the navigation chart and adjusted for these factors.

The result is what is know as a "triangle of probability", or, in colloquial terms a "cocked -hat" In actual operation the aircraft is flown in a constant attitude and with minimum variation in speed so that the "bubble" is as stable as possible. The navigator then "sights" the star selected, by adjusting the controls of the sextant to place it in the middle of the bubble, then takes the time (GMT) and notes the angle from the scale on the sextant.

Great skill in the use of this instrument was developed by many early aviators on their record breaking flights, over the worlds oceans, in the 20s and 30s. To those who have used the sextant in later years to this, and in the early stages of training have had difficulty taking position lines that would even relate to the navigation chart in use, the vision of those early flights, in unstable aircraft and weather conditions say in mid- Atlantic, indicate the skills of those intrepid air pioneers. The Aircraft Sextant was not used by Beaufighter crews, owing to the type of operations and the unsuitability of the aircraft generally.

The modern system of aircraft navigation, by the Ground Positioning Satellites, (G.P.S.) is remarkable in it's similarity to the principle of the now obsolete "Bubble Sextant" used to "shoot the stars". The latter used the visual system of physically observing three stars, which are moving relative to the earth, but whose positions are known in relation to all positions on the globe.

The "Ground Positioning Satellite" system provides for three (or more) satellites, in known fixed orbits relative to the earth, which transmit radio signals. When these three signals are received in the aircraft, the radio receiver automatically compares the difference in time between receiving these signals, processes this data and automatically displays in the cockpit the exact position of the aircraft on latitude and longitude. Such is the magic of technology!!.

Douglas Protractor and Navigators Dividers.

Before any aircraft flight is undertaken a "Flight Plan" is prepared. Using a map, known as a Mercators Chart, and using a simple example, the starting and destination points are marked on the chart and the line connecting these points is known as the "track", which is referred to as a "heading" within the compass range of 0 to 360 degrees.

If no wind existed, then the pilot would simply set this bearing on his compass,(with some minor amendments) fly away and duly arrive at his destination. However, an aircraft is carried by any whim of the wind, however strong and from every direction, unless this is compensated for by turning the heading of the aircraft in the proper, offset direction.

This basic procedure of navigation, known as "Dead Reckoning", calculates the amount of "offset" to be applied to a compass course and involves the use of the above instruments and also what was known as a "Dalton Computer".(regrettably it has not been possible to locate one of these devices, which was the Navigators main "tools" of his trade.)

The term "computer" is somewhat of a misnomer, it had no electronics or batteries, and was a circular version of a Slide Rule, on which, in earlier days major engineering projects were calculated with skill and dexterity.

Having set course, using the wind speeds and direction provide by the weather forecasters, it was the navigators duty to constantly check on the progress of the aircraft in relation to the course to it's destination. This consisted, in basic form, to observing the ground and looking for ground features which could be identified by reference to a "topographical" map which highlighted prominent features, such as roads, railways, hills etc. Having obtained what was known as a "Fix", the deviation of the aircraft from it's intended course could then be ascertained. From this simple fact, and using the Dalton Computer, the difference between the physical location of the aircraft, and where it would have been in "still air", revealed the wind speed and direction over the portion of the flight just traversed.

This information was immediately used for the continuation of the flight, with the primary intention of keeping the aircraft on it's intended track to destination. The actual "winds" encounters on almost every flight differed, either subtly, or in some instances very significantly, from those used for the initial Flight Plan. Modern technology, for determining weather conditions, winds, cloud levels, visibility etc, over very long distances, are now sophisticated and reliable.

Air Force Issue Sunglasses (circa 1943)

A somewhat battered pair, worn through training in Canada in 1943, and then operational flying in England, mostly over the North Sea,and a short spell on the North Atlantic Aircraft Ferry Group. Also in the immediate post-war years, in quickly modified war time aircraft, such as the "Yorks" and "Lancastrians", when re-establishing the British Overseas Airways routes, to India and South Africa. In their day, regarded as an essential item in any airmans equipment, but certainly not in the same category as those now worn by the "Top-Guns". Regrettably, in 1955, or so, after many years of faithful service, suffered a severe "trauma " when accidentally sat-on in a motor vehicle in Zambia.

In those days, they were never, ever, worn on the top of the head!

Badge, R.A.F. Squadron No 254.

Bears the motto *"Fljuga vakta ok ljosta"* which is Norse, and translates, roughly, "To fly, to watch, and to strike" and embodies a raven. (Birds are so often favoured in symbols relating to aviation.)

The original Squadron, 254, was created at Prawle Point, in Devon, in England, in 1918, and was engaged in anti-submarine patrols until the end of the First World War, and worked in close harmony with the Royal Navy. It was disbanded in February, 1919.

In October, 1939, it was re-formed, moving to various R.A.F. stations, one being Bircham Newton in Norfolk. It's "modern" aircraft was the Blenheim, a fore-runner of the Beaufighter. The operational role was to escort convoys on the East Coast and protect the Fishing Fleets on the Dogger Bank, known as "Skipper Patrols" and during one such patrol, first fired it's guns in anger! Many varied, and hazardous operations were carried out around the coast and in November, 1942, the Squadron moved to North Coates, near Grimsby in Lincolnshire and re-equipped with Beaufighters.

With the increasing tempo of war, action was necessary to restrict the movement, around the North Sea and the English Channel, of enemy shipping carrying vital war material.

To this end what was known as "Strike Wings" were formed. The North Coates wing consisted of three squadrons of Beaufighters. 143 and 236 Squadrons formed the "anti-flak" component and were equipped with 20mm cannon— and later, 60 lb. rockets, and 254 Squadron carried the torpedoes, plus 4 20mm cannon. The torpedo was 18 inches in diameter, weighed about 1800 lbs. ad had a plywood tail plane to ensure that it entered the water in a stable attitude.

Each squadron flew 12 aircraft, and, together, operated as a Group, the anti-flak aircraft saturating the defensive firepower of the convoy or shipping being attacked,and inflicting as much damage as possible, with the torpedo aircraft approaching at sea level to drop the torpedoes, approximatelt 1000 yards from the target.

Many, and varied operations, involving aircraft operating solo, were performed, particularly around the time of the Invasion of Europe on "D Day" June 6th, 1944 when the German "E Boats" were very active in operations against the Allied activities to re-inforce the hard won bridge-head on the French coast.

The highs and lows of the fortunes of this Squadron are reflected in two specific situations. In February 1945, 254 and 236 Squadrons, accompanied by Spitfires as Fighter Escort, attacked shipping in the port of Den Helder on the Dutch Coast. Of the 32 Beaufighters who attacked, 254 lost four aircraft and 236 two aircraft. Many suffered severe damage. On the other side of the coin, on May 4th (the war was to end four days later) 254 and 236 together sank four U-Boats in the Skagerak.

Air Observers Brevet

The "Wings Parade", when aircrew are confirmed competent in their chosen function, and the appropriate "brevet" is pinned to the chest by a Senior Officer, is a moment treasured by all. The design of the brevets, from the early days of aviation has changed somewhat, but the general appearance clearly indicates the responsibilities of the holder, and, the "Pilots" brevet of the full, double wings, reflects his overall responsibility for the aircraft and all the crew members.

The function of "Observer" was introduced into aviation when it became apparent that the pilot needed assistance if the role of the military aircraft was to become more effective. In the First World War, aircraft were used not only in individual combat with the opposing forces aircraft, but also in support of the Army and the Navy, to observe the deployment of their troops, to advise the Heavy Artillery of the range, and the results of their fire, etc.

The Army also used captive balloons for these latter purposes and it was manned by an Observer, who because of the perilous nature of the duties, was provided with a parachute. Such care and consideration was not extended to the aircrew of aircraft, it being thought by the Senior officers that it might induce in the crews to take the easy option should the opposing aircraft appear just a bit too formidable !! Some of the more lurid portrayals of life in the front line however, invariably show the Observer "hitting the silk" with his doomed balloon disappearing in the flames above.

It is of interest to note that regardless of rank in the service, the pilot is, with few exceptions, the "Captain " of the aircraft. In the Fleet Air Arm, however, the Observer was in command in multi crewed tactical aircraft, as the prime purpose of the flight was of a "tactical" nature, and it deemed that the Observer could more readily assess these requirements.

With the arrival of larger and more complicated aircraft, the numbed in the crew rose dramatically. This brought about the aircrew grades of "Signaller" (S), "Flight Engineer" (E), "Air Gunner" (AG), and, to replace the Observer, the "Navigator" (N) . The present day "air crew trades" are many and varied, with Electronics tending to predominate.

Pilots Radio Homing Indicator

Although the true authenticity of this particular Instrument is doubtful, it closely resembles the real thing!!. With the stimulus of war, rapid improvements in the performance of aircraft by developing better instruments, lead to more aggressive performance in the air. To be able to fly and operate in bad weather, to be able to "Home" to an aerodrome, to be able to land the aircraft in poor weather conditions, and to have radio guidance when flying over long distances, all helped in this regard. This instrument, which has two needles, one on each side of the dial and moving crosswise to the centre, indicated to the pilot the heading to fly to approach the source of the transmission., usually the destination aerodrome or a another point en route. By turning the aircraft to cross the needles in the centre of the dial, the correct course would be flown.

Morse Key

The advent of reliable, instant, long distance communication, using wires, (and later, under-ocean cables), between Telegraph Stations, when Samuel Morse invented his code in 1865 ?, must have dramatic then as is the "Internet","E" Mail, and such, which are our wonders at the present time.

It is only recently that the Morse Code has been almost phased out, but those skilled in the art, as Air Force Wireless Operators, will remember that first breakthrough when, after many hours of laboriously building up their speed of sending and receiving, the procedure suddenly became totally automatic.

The development of aviation, from the early days, would not have been possible without reliable facilities for communication, and radio, particularly the morse code, met this requirement. The contact, between the aircraft and ground station, provided for many essential; services such as general weather forecasts, landing conditions at aerodromes, etc. Also, and very importantly, assistance for an aircraft to "Home" to an aerodrome when totally lost due to weather or other reasons, and in some despair for it's safety.

Simply described, the aircraft made radio contact with the ground station and then transmitted a long "dash" with the Morse key. The ground station the used it's Direction Finding" equipment to get a bearing on the aircraft requiring help, and the transmitted this in the form of a "Q.D.M" –the magnetic course required to fly to and arrive at my station — is given in degrees of the compass.

The War time flying in Europe, with bad and unpredictable weather, with many aircraft desperately seeking to reach their home base after the rigours of long missions over very hostile territory and the crew exhausted, took it's toll in losses due to crashes in England. But whilst the degree to which such losses were minimised by the use of the "Q.D.M." procedure is hard to assess, undoubtedly many aircrew owe their lives to this procedure. The knowledge that such a "homing facility" was available did much to bolster the morale of the aircrews.

Some of those who flew in the Air Force as Wireless Operators were skilled in the knowledge of radio, having qualified as "Amateur Radio Operators" prior to the start of the war and had made many friends throughout the world by using the morse code. Many were lost on operational duties, but those more fortunate have continued to practise their hobby, with great enjoyment well into later life. Many consciously regard the perpetuation of the hobby as a quiet tribute to those lost colleagues.

One always remembers the First Time: was it 599 all the way for you, too?

The interest was planted in the early thirties, when a memorable visit was made to the Shack of a well-known English Ham and aviator, and this lead to war-time qualification as a Wireless Operator, etc,

Experience in standard service equipment, such as M/F and H/F 1082/1083, R1155 and 1154, plus aircraft navigation equipment Gee and A.S.V. firmly entrenched the instinct to enjoy the personal satisfaction of operating skills and making communication, plus the inquisitive thirst to waffle to 'far away places with strange sounding names'.

It all seemed the way to go when peace took over from those hectic years, and a real prize, for having risked life and limb for King and Country, —and a bit of excitement thrown in for good measure—was that for Service qualified Wireless Operators, a full Ham Licence was obtainable without the need for a test. Whacko!!

But by this time, having plied a Dalton Computer and Astro Navigational Sextant rather more than a Morse key, the edge of my C.W. speed was blunted somewhat, and, of course, unfamiliarity with long-standing abbreviation used by Hams throughout the world had to be learned, including the less polite ones (such as — — · · · ·) the use of which in the service could have resulted in a 'fizzer' (I am unable to recall the code for 'send with the other foot').

Esconsed in a densely populated suburb of South London meant a modest antenna system, but the first sally was to obtain the 'hardware'. The Radio Society of Great Britain had by now intervened in the wholesale destruction then taking place of the massive amounts of ex-Service radio equipment which was being thrown down disused mine shafts, quarries, crushed by tractors, etc, by obtaining quantities of items suitable for Ham use, such as R1155, T1154, Class D Wavemeters, etc. But a more interesting and, to me useful type caught my attention. It was the B2 transmitter, a.k.a. a 'Suitcase Radio', which really did fit into a fairly small suitcase, and was supplied to secret and underground Agents in Europe— — those brave 'blokes and Sheilas' who parachuted into the dark and dangerous world that Europe then was.

Unfortunately, while the design and performance of the transmitter—a Crystal Oscillator plus a Power Amplifier 6V6 valve giving about twenty five watts—was efficient, the exterior design of the suitcase, perhaps the brain-child of a real bureaucrat, was a 'dead giveaway'. No doubt on the intimidating streets of Paris, the heavy hand of the Gestapo must have grasped many coat collars, uttering the German equivalent of, 'Ello, ello, ello, and what have we here, then?' Although the one I obtained had neither receiver nor power supply, they were a bargain at two pounds!

For a receiver, I had for some reason, perhaps a throwback to my early pleasure of 'tickling the old cats whisker' decided that a simple OV1 using a double triode valve, 6C8G would suffice for this purpose, but where conveniently, to obtain this precise beast. It so happened, fortuitously, that at Hendon RAF Station, from where I was 'living out', there was across the 'drome' from our activities, an American Embassy Flight flying Communication aircraft, and they had the usual extensive 'back-up' facilities common to all American bases.

The Americans in Britain were noted for their casual generosity so why not give it a go. The American airman who appeared to be 'top dog' was a Master Sergeant, unmistakeably from the South, who greeted me, the 'Limey Flyer', with great good humour. "Certainly, buddy, what would you like!" as we entered this large hangar, wherein reposed, like a Treasure Chest, a vast hoard of radio equipment of every kind, with the B.C.342 / 348, and the associated transmitter, the B610 predominating. My request for a single valve, 6C8G, seemed to the Master Sergeant unduly modest and could possibly be regarded as an insult to the American Forces.

Anyway, due to transport problems—I had no car—plus of course, the delicate business of exiting the RAF Station too fully laden, but I was exceedingly happy with my bounty of a pristine B.C.348, plus 'one off' of the required valve.

The 0.V.1, plus the power supply for this and the Suitcase Radio was quickly assembled from odds and sods bought in a back street of the West End of London, Lisle Street, where for six pence or a shilling, quality components of all types that had escaped, by routes and devices known only to the Cockney entrepreneurs, the reckless violence of the Ministry of Supply.

Lisle Street was visited with some circumspection. It was the haunt of the Ladies of the Night, who always seemed to be on double shift by day. With a modest few shillings to squander—on radio gear, that is—I would visit, perhaps on a wet Monday lunch time, with a goal fixed in my mind, of say, a 500 puff variable condenser. Approaching the several stores, and this was unkempt London at its worst, just after the war, the recessed doorways were useful lurking places for the above-mentioned ladies. As one passed by, there was invariably a hoarse whisper of "like a good time Dearie?" I found this a distraction, as in the full flush of enthusiasm for my hobby, and with a modest amount of money in the pocket, the world of desirable radio parts was my oyster. My response, perhaps a touch unkind and may have set a life long trauma of rejection was—"But I'm having the time of my life!"

As usual, the erection of any type of antenna demands much thought and usually a degree of compromise, and this was aggravated by the residential area being of relatively high density. However, as we were on the second (top floor) height would not pose any difficulty in achieving the half wave on twenty, the preferred band. A sally across the back garden and the same across the other garden to the rear of the next street, unearthed an elderly gentleman resident—he was a flautist in a symphony orchestra—who, after my request to use his chimney pot for holding up what I described as an innocuous piece of wire, beamed his approval, and even volunteered to affix the said piece of wire.

A 67 feet 'End Fed Zepp', similar to that used on the German Airforce Zeppelins during the First World War and reputedly having an immunity to carrying sparks from lightning strikes, was strung between the opposing chimneys. The feed line consisted of Open Wire feeders, made up of fourteen gauge wire, spread six inches apart by meat skewers coated in melted candle wax, a pretty standard type of practice in those days. One end of the pair went to the end of the 67 feet top, and the other merely went nowhere.

Reference to basics, indicated that some Bands would be current fed and others required voltage feed. The mnemonic, for the type of feed at the Antenna Tuning Unit — made up on plywood of and with a swinging link to adjust the load — still firmly embedded, went 'Vep and Soc', equating to:

'Feedline an even number of quarter waves long = Voltage and Parallel feed'

'Odd number of quarter waves long = Current and Series feed.'

The B2 transmitter and the O.V.1 looked lost on the six foot rack of angle iron — an old bed frame — but again this was then standard practice and left room for later expansion for, say, the popular Italian Geloso V.F.O driving high power rigs, with several 'doublers', lumpy audio transformers, etc, all bristling with 807s, 5R4GY rectifiers, and the like, the whole caboodle exuding warmth and vibrations of the pleasant kind.

My guide and mentor was 'Ted' a Marconi Marine Operator with plenty of 'sea time', evident in the sweetness of his keying fist and very tolerant of the real standards attained by we war time Wireless Operators. Like many of his radio background and talent I can only assume that Ted noted any incoming Morse signals not as anything other than plain — as in spoken words — immediately intelligible and any mental deciphering process quite unnecessarily. Ah, could but we 'sprogs' have attained such fluency and finesse in Mr Morse's art!

So, installation compete, perhaps the first real live, true, 'on the air' Q.S.O. required a guiding hand, it was, after all, a giant step into the wide net of countless radio signals pulsing around the globe unceasingly, and maybe, I thought, with appropriate trepidation, that my first fumbling Q.S.O. may break into this ordered routine and cause keys to falter and scorn be poured on my head, via, of course the aforesaid invisible media.

At that time, as I recall, V.F.O. operations had some restrictions — anyway, to construct a really stable Clapp Oscillator, demanded a fair knowledge of mechanical engineering to avoid the melodious notes which it emanated at even the approach of the hand. I did have, however, a couple of crystals down at the bottom end of the forty metre band, that would nicely double to close to the edge of twenty metres. This determined the frequency of the nervously anticipated 'Sked with Ted', with the time for the next day agreed upon.

As indicated, it was 599 all the way, a real 'ice-breaker', a great moment, and the forerunner of so many satisfying conversations with so many friends all over the world. Over fifty years down the track, with six different call-signs under my belt, having operated in six different countries on three different continents, the 'Call of the Airways' still raises the pulse a touch, as the unknown beckons, with that faint, and perhaps elusive CQ—CQ—CQ a bit like Jack London's classic story, 'The Call of the Wild' (or was it 'White Fang').

But this first contact was, however, a bit 'sneaky'.

All journeys, of whatever length, begin with a first small step, but in radio terms, this first Q.S.O. was an extremely small step. Ted's flat was two doors away and he also had found a friendly soul across his back garden who saw no objection to a long piece of wire being attached to his chimney pot. Consequently, between our two parallel identical antennas, G3ACU (Ted) and G3CYT (me) there was a space of about two wavelengths on twenty, just a touch beyond 'spitting distance'!

That's my story, how was the 'First Time' for you?

Sam Wright V.K.6 Y.N.

Sam Wright – RAF Service Record

14th May 1941	Attested (swore oath of allegiance to King George the Sixth) at Cardington, Beds, where the special hangars were built to accommodate the Airship R 101 in 1932. Service number 1433827. Rank Aircrafthand Wireless Operator. Description, 5ft 11 inches, fair, blue eyes, pale complexion. Placed on Reserve (returned to civilian life) 4th February 1942. Recommended for training as aircrew "Observer", having passed written and medical tests.
31st October 1941	"Called to the Colours" (Full-time duties in the RAF).
22nd October 1942	Promoted to Aircraftman First Class
14th February 1943	Promoted to Sergeant
14th February 1944	Promoted to Flight Sergeant
20th June 1944	Commissioned as Pilot Officer.Service number 179350
20th December 1944	Promoted to Flying Officer
20th June 1946	Promoted to Flight Lieutenant
3rd February 1948	Released from the RAF

Summary of Flying Times

	Day	Night
Dominies and Proctors	10	
Ansons	364	54
Beaufighters	314	59
Dakotas	73	26
Lancasters	15	
Liberators	13	17
Mosquito	5	
Lancastrian	30	20
York	360	60
1,184	236	
Total (Day & Night)	**1,420**	

Other aircraft flown (not recorded in Log Book): Whitley, Walrus (Flying Boat), Oxford, Beaufort.

APPENDIX XI—AERODROMES VISITED

Whilst flying with the RAF

England: Cranwell • Squires Gate • East Fortune • Turnberry • Heathfield • North Coates • Donna Nook • Strubby • Manston • Langham • Ringway • Coltishall • Docking • Blackbush • Croydon • Elmdon • Blakehill Farm • Wroughton • Hendon • Leeming • Waddington • Lyneham • Kenley • Thorney Island • Bovingdon • Horsham • Bircham Newton • Sculthorpe • Gatwick • Warton • Martlesham Heath • Hawarden • Heston • Honnington • Waterbeach • Oakington • Graveley • Hullavington Woodley • Pershore • Lympne • Abingdon • Roborough • Netheravon • Northolt • Odiham • Brize Norton • Dishforth • Syerston • Brough • Millom • Silloth • Lasham • Fairford • Halton • Kirton Lindsay • Edzell

Scotland: Dyce • Tain • Banff • Prestwick • Inverness • Arbroath • Abbotsinch • Port Ellen • Kinloss • Turnhouse • Wigtown • Turnberry.

Wales: Llanbedr • Talbenny

Canada: Mount Hope • Charlottetown • Dorval, Montreal • North Bay • Goose • Gander • Mingan

France • Le Bourget • Villay Coublay • Orly • Toussus-le Noble •

Channel Islands • Jersey

Holland • Eindhoven

Germany • Buckeberg, Hamburg, Utersen, Wahn, Gatow, Berlin.

Ireland • Aldergrove, Colinstown.

Whilst flying with British Overseas Airways

Aldermaston • Gibraltar • Lisbon • Hurn • Bournemouth • Castel Benito, Nairobi • Almaza, Cairo • Marignane, Marseilles • Wadi Seidna, Sudan • Salisbury, Rhodesia • Palmetfontein, Johannesburg • Basra • Karachi • Palam, Delhi • Dum Dum, Calcutta • Bordeaux, France • Luqa, Malta • Benina, Tunisia • Valley, Wales • Lydda, Israel.

Poetry

A Beaufighter Pilot's Prayer

Almighty and all-present power
Short is the prayer I make to Thee
I do not ask in battle hour
For any shield to cover me

The vast unalterable way
From which the stars do not depart
May not be turned aside to stay
The bullet flying to my heart

I ask no help to strike my foe
I seek no petty victory here
The enemy I hate, I know
To Thee is dear

But this I pray: be at my side
When death is drawing through the sky
Almighty God who also died
Teach me the way that I should die.

By Ernest Davey, a young Canadian pilot who flew Beaufighters with No. 404 Squadron, Royal Canadian Air Force in Scotland, and who was shot down and killed on October 2nd. 1944.

Old Airfield

I lie here still, beside the hill,
abandoned long to natures will.
My buildings down, my people gone,
my only sounds the wild birds song

But my mighty birds will rise no more,
no more I hear the Merlin's roar
And never now my bosom feels,
the pounding of their giant wheels

From the ageless hill, their voices cast
thunderous echoes of the past
And still in lonely reverie,
their great dark wings sweep down to me

Laughter, sorrow, hope and pain,
I shall never know these things again
Emotions that I came to know,
Of strange young men so long ago

Who knows as evening shadows meet,
are they with me still, a phantom fleet
And do my ghosts still stride unseen,
across my face so wide and green

And in the future, should structures tall,
bury me beyond recall
I shall still remember them,
my metal birds and long dead men

Now weeds grow high, obscure the sky,
O remember me when you pass by
For beneath this tangled leafy screen
I was your home, your friend "Silksheen"

W. Scott (ex-630 Squadron) Acknowledgements to *Action Stations* by
Bruce Barrymore Halpenny.

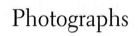
Photographs

Childhood Days – the Twenties and Thirties

43 Nottingham Rd, Spondon, home (last on left) of Sam and Mary Marshall, parents of six daughters and two boys – Emma, my Mother, being the eldest. I was born in the next house, just to the left of the picture.

Trusthorpe Holiday Camp near Mablethorpe, Lincolnshire, about 1933. My Father, Jack Wright, sporting the holiday attire of "pumps" and cricket shirt, while I, never one for the sartorial touch, seem to be wearing a motley selection of his old clothes! The "Warsaw Ghetto" look is due to my recent encounter with Rheumatic Fever. Sister Mary being skittish.

Gran and 'Gan-Gan' Marshall, my dearly loved grandparents, who raised me as their own. In my life one person stands above all others in warmth and character... and that is Sam Marshall.

The author at John O' Groats, Scotland. Almost like an RAF Blackpool crab!

The Wrights and the Marshalls in party mood (the beer and buttonholes suggest an occasion of no little importance). From left, Jack W., Tom M., Gran M., Emma W., unknown, Will Draper, (Mary M. husband), Beattie M., Mary M., Sam M., Harriet M., Author, Florrie M.

With Mum at Uncle Tom's Public House in Derby.

Mary "skittling" at Mablethorpe.

"Bringing in the Sheaves" portrayed by Grandad Sam, brother Tom and true companion 'Spot' or 'Frank'. Now that's what you CALL corn!

Helping with the crops in wartime England. Sam, Tom, Aunts Mary, Margaret, Florrie (known as 'Tol'), faithful hound and some unknowns but perhaps relatives. Strangely, no cold tea or beer evident!

Emma's 'second crop' with that good bloke Harold King, who imbued me with a love of pigeons. Betsy, Forrie and Loveice plus an unknown

The author, with freckled face, probably about ten years old and at Spondon Infants School.

CHILDHOOD DAYS – THE TWENTIES AND THIRTIES

John o' Groats Scotland, all the boys, Bill Ward, (Mary's Husband), Joe Hickling, ex-Royal Flying Corps, (Margaret's husband), Tom, Sam and Mary.

... and the girls, with Uncle Will, imbibing.

Exhibiting, with barely contained modesty, the coveted 'White Flash' denoting Air Crew Trainee. Apart from a minimum of academic ability, a not unrigorous standard of physical robustness was required, including blowing up a tube of mercury to what seemed appropriate for climbers of the Himalayas. My puny chest took a beating, but purple in face, and what seemed an eternity, the magic 60 seconds was achieved! Ladies responded to this emblem rather like moths, even from great distances!

As they go, "Johnny" Walker sporting "Goon Cap" (ear flaps drop down to prevent frost-bite), Doug Holden (the "Old Man), Ernie Tebb aka "Drifts" as he had a penchant for constant use of his Drift recorder, ??? Smith, and below, being savagely abused, Jimmy Rodgers.

Air Navigation School, Hamilton Ontario. Jimmy Rodgers centering on the "Bull" with Anstey behind with bolt up! In the rear, I appear disinterested.

A couple of blokes from the 'Class of 1875' with Andrew Rudden – my 'best mate'– and self, outside the Spondon Liberal Club. Judging by our undazed expressions, we were no doubt on the way in. What these 'old-timers' could 'put away was staggering, even to my Skipper Mac from New Zealand!

Grandad Marshall, Uncle Tom and Barbara Pemberton in a local hostelry, enjoying a real 'ploughman's lunch' before it became synthesized by upstart gourmets. Sam, Tom, Mac my pilot, and I did a 'run' to several village pubs in a pony and trap – to the severe hazard of our safety and general health!

Fully 'emblemed' but apparently in pensive mood. The 'half-wing' reflecting our Aircrew status was know by various names, some impolite, subsequently replaced, but not quite, by an 'N' instead of the 'O' but retained by us as a matter of honour of the 'old RAF days'. As NCOs we sported or 'sparks' badge on our right arm.

At the Torpedo Training School Turnberry Scotland. (from left to right) Merv Thorburn, RNZAF, pilot of Charlie Brown, who stayed on and became a Sqdn Ldr, married young 'Meg' from the nearby village, spent time on the fishing boats, earned a degree at University in Scotland but died relatively young; Harry Bennet, RNZAF pilot of 'Nick' Nicholls who later went to Burma and disappeared on a sortie over the jungle; 'Chas' – aka Charlie Brown; 'Nick', a Liverpool lad with whom I had a great friendship. He visited my family in Spondon and became a favourite of my Aunts; 'Mac' in taunting mood (perhaps I was doing something stupid rather than asking them to 'say cheese'!). On the right, an RNZAF pilot, whose name I cannot recollect, but' like all the Kiwis' 'a good bloke'.

'Pooch' – our per dog and mascot.

Merv,Mac and Charlie – somewhere on the North Coates aerodrome.

Self, Chas, Simmy (note the two fingers) and John Knight, getting familiar with long distance navigation. Keeping the 'heavenly body' at the centre of the 'bubble' proved to be difficult – even on the ground!

The mosquitoes in Canada were extremely large! Sitting at the sharp end with the pilot and flying low was just about as good as flying could get. Armchair aviation analysts say that this aircraft could have won the war almost by itself. Not bad for a plane made of plywood and glue!

Self enjoying a 'forbidden fruit' available only to expectant mothers in wartime Britain.

Enjoying a weekend in the Canadian backwoods not far from Montreal.

Attempting gymnastics with the none-too-slender Charlie Brown.

John Knight providing photographic proof that a Beaufighter navigator could, if need be, land the plane and walk away from it. Note his smile of quiet satisfaction!

Whitchurch Aerodrome, Bristol, February 1946 and a group of 'secondees' to BOAC aspiring to become civilian Navigating Officers and see the world without being shot at! Redundancy, through the advent of the GPS (Ground Positioning Satellite) was nearly fifty years in the future. Perhaps, through nostalgia, however, the professional body is still known as The Guild of Airline Pilots and Navigators. Our reversion to civilian clothes sat strangely after years in the dark blue of the RAF.

A couple of pictures from Cairo.

First, the Heliopolis Hotel – a splendour in marble; second, self on a camel (I picked the prettiest one for this picture!).

In this Lancastrian, after finding a tail wind over France, we flew straight down the Med to Lydda, Israel, solely on Astro Navigation, in eleven and a half hours, a 'beaut' trip. Later on, over the desert in the M.E. Captain Dobson – on the right – put me in the pilot's seat and tried his hand at navigating. I was drunk with power with four Merlins at my mercy and Dobbie got us there despite my inability to stay on course! He was a great guy and his tragic end in 1965 is described in the text.

Captain "Slim" Gregory, an old Imperial Airways pilot, with many, many hours in his Log Book. The contrast, in so many ways, between the pilots of those early days and the new breed of war-time service pilots with DFCs etc, was marked and of frequent amusement to the likes of we Navigators!

The Avro York – 30 tons of flying machine about to do a 'wheelie'. Note the big, single undercarriage wheels, standard on 'heavies' of those days, as against sixteen or so wheels of present-day big jets which have a maximum take-off weight close to 500 tons.

The Avro Lancastrian – not as convenient as the York from the Navigator's operating position but flying in this 'son of the Lancaster' caught the sheer exuberance of flight in an unforgettable way. If ever an aircraft had an ability to bond with its crew, it was this one!

Flying with this Squadron provided a wonderful opportunity to 'see the world' – well, at least around North West Europe – and I flew into 72 different aerodromes just in the UK. We also had a modest version of the Australian 'Flying Doctor Service' with an Anson aircraft installed with a long door on the side to allow a stretcher to be loaded. A WAAF nurse (below) of the Medical Section accompanied to tend to the injured party. I did a night flight from Hendon to Aldergrove in Northern Ireland to uplift a wing Commander who, late at night in the Mess, after a few 'tipples', fell into an open fireplace and was badly burned. We took him to the RAF Hospital at Halton for urgent treatment. With the young lady in the picture, we also flew a terminally ill airman to Inverness, for his final days at home.

THE BEAUFIGHTER

These two shots do well to capture the beauty in flight and the pugnacious appearance of the Beaufighter. Known somewhat incongruously as 'Whispering Death' by the Japanese because its arrival was preceded by the roar of twin Hercules engines and followed by the devastating effect of four twenty millimetre cannon and Browning machine guns. The ability of its sturdy airframe and "radial" engines to withstand the onslaught of "flak", both light and heavy, saved many crews from disaster.

THE BEAUFIGHTER AEROPLANE

The Cockpit of the Beaufighter, or what, in modern parlance would be described as Mac's "Work Station". Apart from the standard panel of the instruments used to simply control the flight of the plane, there were twenty seven other switches, levers and such like that demanded constant and vigilant attention. The pilot was, of course, unable to move from his seat and the Automatic Pilot "George" was never fitted to Beaufighters, so at the end of a sortie of over five hours, fatigue was very evident. But never a grumble or a growl from my "Skipper", who showed the same good humour whatever our circumstances The function of the switches are as listed below:-

1 Hydraulic Power Lever.	15 Torpedo and Bomb Selector Switch.
2 Hydraulic Emergency Selector Lever.	16 R.P. rails jettison control lever.
3 Fuel Contents Gauges (port).	17 Bomb Fusing Switches.
4 Undercarriage Position Indicators.	18 Rudder trim tab control.
5 Radio Altimeter.	19 Elevator trim tabs hand wheel.
6 Feathering Push Buttons.	20 Windscreen de-icing pump.
7 R.P. Selector Switch.	21 Hydraulic hand pump.
8 Torpedo Sight Control.	22 Elevator trim tab indicator.
9 Fire-extinguisher switches.	23 Full pressure warning lights.
10 R.P.Firing Push Buttons.	24 Electrical services switch.
11 Camera and Gun Firing Switch.	25 Fuel jettison levers.
12 Reflector Gun Sight.	26 Undercarriage selector switch.
13 Torpedo Sight Control Switch.	27 Flap control lever.
14 Wheel Brakes Lever.	

On the Lambes farm near the "Byne", close to Girvan; what a handsome couple!

Promenading at Bournemouth between trips with BOAC.

With those rugged Scots farmers, Alec and Annie Lambe in the tough rolling hills of Ayrshire, and what could be more delightful than feeding a new-born lamb with a bottle!

Alwynne Mansions, Wimbledon, with Joy and the recently arrived young lad, Nicholas John, who completed our very Happy Family.

Three generations of aviators, Jonathan, Nick and Sam Wright, of Gooseberry Hill.

Flying is a family tradition

With flying firmly in the blood of three generations, the Wright family of Gooseberry Hill is used to being asked whether or not they are related to those other famous Wrights.

Sam's association with flying began during World War II, where he was a navigator with the Royal Air Force, flying Bristol Beaufighter Torpedo Bombers.

After the war, he continued to fly as a navigating officer with British Overseas Airways Corporation.

These days, Sam relives his experiences with fellow aviators at the Beaufighter Group of WA, and is even writing his memoirs for his family.

Sam's son, Nick, was also fascinated by flying but preferred jumping out of planes rather than landing in the normal manner.

His son Jonathan, however, can't understand why anyone would want to skydive out of a perfectly good aircraft.

After having his private licence for about three years, Jonathan has taken his love for flying a step further, recently gaining his commercial pilot's licence.

Fast Forward to Y2K

My Son, Nicholas John
Age 53

Aspired to piloting but circumstances lead instead to Sky Diving, with some 700 "take-offs' in aeroplanes—but only a few conventional landings—resulting in "Free-Fall Time" of about 4 hours!

He loved the sport and Carol and I were enthusiastic on-lookers, never doubting his ability and confidence, and exhibiting more than the usual parental pride at the exploits of our son.

My Grandson,
Jonathan James Age 22

Quickly became determined to become a pilot and aimed high to obtain a Degree B.Sc.(Aviation), plus a Commercial Pilots Licence, with endorsements for Instruments, Night Flying, Aerobatics etc.

Currently flying as a "Bush Pilot" in Australias Northern Territory and servicing the Aboriginal Communities, in what is typical "Crocodile Dundee" terrain. Accumulating flying hours with the intention of joining a major airline and flying the big, heavy Jets.